Praise for *The Terror of the Unforeseen*

"Henry Giroux, a brilliant and revolutionary thinker, helps us understand why we must refuse to equate capitalism and democracy, or to normalize greed or accept individualism as the highest form of human life. In this exciting new take on social reality, Giroux describes how the neoliberalism that has for the past 40 years has been paving a path to fascism that will have a distinctively contemporary flavor, yet will be just as destructive as fascisms of the past. Filled with passion and insight, *The Terror of the Unforeseen* is a book that should be read by anyone who wants to understand and prepare for the dangers and opportunities of political struggle in the 2020s."

— Rabbi Michael Lerner, Editor of *Tikkun Magazine*
and author of *Revolutionary Love*

"Henry Giroux has, for decades, combined passion and intellect to map out the often terrifying directions of US politics and economics, while recognizing, as too few on the left have, that culture matters. Refusing to give in to despair, *The Terror of the Unforeseen* argues that education is the necessary cornerstone of any democratic political struggle. It demonstrates, once again, why Giroux is one of the most important public intellectuals in the United States."

— Lawrence Grossberg, Morris Davis Distinguished Professor
at UNC Chapel Hill

"Henry Giroux's *The Terror of the Unforeseen* provides an urgent warning in response to Donald Trump's collapsing of language, showing us an alternative path through his own thoughtful, compassionate, sincere, and sophisticated writing."

—Nick Pemberton

THE TERROR OF

THE UNFORESEEN

THE TERROR OF
THE UNFORESEEN

HENRY A. GIROUX

LARB
PROVOCATIONS

This is a LARB Provocations publication
Published by The Los Angeles Review of Books
6671 Sunset Blvd., Suite 1521, Los Angeles, CA 90028
www.larbbooks.org

Cover Artwork: Lanpinjarvi Finland by Isaac Cordal, copyright © Isaac Cordal.
Courtesy of Isaac Cordal.

ISBN 978-1-940660-49-3

Library of Congress Control Number: 2018965700

Contents

For Rania

For Tony Penna, Donaldo Macedo, Jasmin Habib,
Ray Seliwoniuk, friends to the end

Introduction

Julian Casablancas

When I speak about politics, I'm not speaking as a musician; I'm speaking as a citizen of a country imperiled. And because Henry so kindly and humbly handed me the microphone.

Since the dawn of modern civilization the influence of wealth on power has been a relentless, often brutal, force. It might shape-shift through the eras, but the phenomenon has regenerated itself countless times. Whether it manifests through sheer military might or elaborate fraud and subterfuge, it is ever-present, ever-toxic, and ultra-persistent.

The wealthy don't need to hire armies to maintain their oppressive schemes anymore — they bribe politicians and control media elements instead. There is no system of oversight by independent bodies that can be trusted to maintain public welfare or truth as their priority. The internet is now the world's largest subduction zone of myth. Weaponized media is the new propaganda, essentially an evolution of the medieval model of affluence and oppression.

The elusiveness of truth is a central problem facing democracy as we now know it. That's why reading and celebrating people like Henry Giroux, who have dedicated themselves to uncovering and teaching the truth, is so important.

In this moving and passionate book, Henry revives a spirit we can find in the great abolitionist Fredrick Douglass's words: "It is not the light that is needed, but fire; it is not the gentle shower, but thunder. We need the storm, the whirlwind, and the earthquake. The feeling of the nation must be quickened; the conscience of the nation must be roused; the propriety of the nation must be startled; the hypocrisy of the nation must be exposed." Henry eloquently describes an economic system that has produced massive inequities in wealth and power, undermining the very notion of justice, equality, and democracy itself.

I wish to offer a rallying cry for the separation of wealth and state, while lovingly confining capitalism to the private sector, as opposed to having a for-profit government, and various other for-profit political vehicles. Of course, not all business activity is bad. But as many folks are finally beginning to realize, the corporate world's indifferent attitude to the suffering it creates — not to mention their control over policy — will likely end up trashing earth. The divisive jargon and disinformation in support of neoliberal ideals is all political distraction, a basic con laid out by billionaires for one dumb reason: so that they can pay no taxes.

The word for this clean-cut attitude of modern pillaging is neoliberalism. This savage word is one that Henry uses a whole lot. It sounds so sophisticated, civilized, and reasonable: the "free market" is to be left alone to do its thing. Sounds positive, right?

But the fatal flaw of unchecked free markets and privatization is that the private sector doesn't care if people die. The private sector doesn't care if people suffer, or even if they are themselves the cause of the suffering.

Capitalism can work (the night is young!), but it must be more in balance with other important human values. Values like truth. Values like freedom while respecting the freedom of others. The value of human happiness over harming people to make a buck.

In an ideal civilized world, companies and people would be incentivized to not hurt people. Currently, it's the other way around. Instead of using research to stop deadly behavior we use it to minimize costs. To evolve past medieval cultural values, we have to require that business succeeds without causing horrific suffering.

Our system motivates and rewards this behavior. It perpetuates greed as our only clear value. Corporations will never change the system and relinquish their power; it is the system that must change. That's why, for the good of everyone, we need to lovingly return real power to the people.

Henry Giroux's work, *The Terror of the Unforeseen*, is perhaps his most painfully relevant work yet, is a brilliant condemnation of the most oppressive force of this modern era: propaganda. It is a clarion call for citizens who seek truth in the face of disinformation and oppression.

Julian Casablancas
2019

THE TERROR OF
THE UNFORESEEN

I. THE UNFORESEEN IN THE ERA OF FEAR

Chapter 1

The Ghost of Fascism in the Age of Trump

The murdered are [now] cheated out of the single remaining
thing that our powerlessness can offer them: remembrance.
— Theodor Adorno

IN THE AGE OF TRUMP, history neither informs the present nor haunts it with repressed memories of the past. It simply disappears. This is especially troubling when the "toxic passions"[1] of the fascist past seem to re-emerge in an unceasing stream of racism, demonizing insults, lies, and militarized rhetoric, serving as emotional appeals that are endlessly circulated and reproduced at the highest levels of government and the media. Power, culture, politics, finance, and everyday life have merged in unprecedented ways and pose a threat to democracies all over the world. In the current historical moment, the new mix of old media and new digitally driven systems of production and consumption produce, shape, and sustain desires and modes of agency with extraordinary power and influence. Take, for instance, robot-generated lies and misrepresentations, the endless charges of fake news aimed at traditional media sources critical of the White House, the growing debasement of evidence and facts in a post-truth world, the power of the digital media in spreading "viral" hoaxes, toxic partisan politics, and misinformation, and the utilization of all of these via Facebook "to erode the informational underpinnings of democracy."[2]

The informal educational apparatuses — particularly the corporate controlled media — increasingly reinforce what might be called "The Trump Show," wittingly and unwittingly, in spite of their growing criticism of Trump's lies and reckless policies. Obsessed with Trump's daily barrage of tweets, insults, and spectacularized diversions, the mainstream media have become complicit in giving Trump unprecedented power to shape the daily working of the established media.[3] Mike Allen writes in *Axios* that "Trump and the media, for all of his attacks and despite the cultural chasm between them, just can't quit each other … Cable news is setting records, books are hot again, newspapers are racking up the digital subscriptions and an op-ed is a hot gossip topic — all because of the national obsession with … Trump fever."[4] Tom Engelhardt extends this argument and calls Trump "a perpetual motion machine of breaking headlines." He writes:

> As a start, it's indisputable that no one has ever gotten the day-after-day media coverage he has. Not another president, general, politician, movie star, not even O.J. after the car chase. He's Da Man! Since that escalator ride, he's been in the news (and in all our faces)in a way once unimaginable. Cable news talking heads and talk-show hosts can't stop gabbling about him. It's the sort of 24/7 attention that normally accompanies terrorist attacks in the United States or Europe, presidential assassinations, or major hurricanes. But with him, we're talking about more or less every hour of every day for almost two-and-a-half years without a break. It's been no different on newspaper front pages. No one's ever stormed the headlines more regularly … There, he has, if anything, an even more obsessional audience of tens of millions for his daily tweets, which instantly become "The News" and then, of course, the fodder for those yakking cableheads and talk-show hosts.[5]

Such media coverage is particularly dire in light of the growing pedagogical importance of the new media and the power they now have on the political imagination of countless Americans. And it is particularly true of the conservative media empire of Rupert Murdoch, along with Clear Channel, which dominates the radio airwaves with its ownership of over 1250 stations, and Sinclair Media Group, which owns the largest number of TV stations in America, and which all trade in outrage, hate, scorn, humiliation, and bullying.[6] Right-wing hosts such as Rush

Limbaugh and Sean Hannity have audiences in the millions, shaping much of what America learns, and, it would appear, the entirety of what Trump watches and hears. Moreover, for media giants such as Fox News, the line between its conservative opinion makers and its news operation has collapsed. Referring to Justice Brett M. Kavanaugh's interview on the channel, James Poniewozik, the chief television critic for *The New York Times*, remarked that Fox's "news operation is no less part of the White House messaging structure than Judge Jeanine."[7] These outlets have played a dangerous role channeling populist anger, and David Bell is right that the educational force of this media machine poses a threat to the United States.[8] The first casualty of this re-education of America has been truth, the second moral responsibility, and the third the last vestiges of justice. The result is a massive increase in human misery and suffering worldwide.

More than a dystopian dismissal of the truth, this is a normalization of deceit, a challenge to thinking itself, and a repudiation of the educational conditions that make an informed citizenry possible. Truth is confused with opinions, and lies have become normalized at the highest level of government. Trump's mendacity, bolstered by Fox News and other media, is used not only to discredit scientific reason and traditional sources of truth, it also blurs the relationship between fact and fiction, making it difficult for the public to make informed judgments. Presidential tweets now flood the public realm, which make outlandish allegations about voter fraud, slanderous assertions regarding immigrants and crime, and even such whoppers as claiming "unsung success" for the disastrous government response to Puerto Rico in the aftermath of Hurricane Maria, in which 3,000 people died, and where rebuilding was barely addressed.[9] Trump's penchant for cruelty is particularly evident in his refusal to provide Puerto Rico with much needed aid. As of 2019, he has "threatened to kill any bill that includes substantial new assistance to Puerto Rico that Democrats are demanding."[10] Under the Trump administration, moral responsibility morphs into legal irresponsibility as undocumented workers come under attack, thousands of Vietnamese who have lived in the U.S. are threatened with deportation, and policies are implemented that overturn financial regulations designed to prevent another economic recession. In Trump's worldview, justice is measured by one's loyalty to the administration rather than to the rule of law. How else to explain Trump's firing of James Comey, his criticisms of the intelligence agencies, his critique of his own Attorney General for recusing himself from the Russian investigation, and his administration's endless attacks on the Mueller investigation? Not only has Trump violated the rule that Presidents refrain from involvement in individual criminal investigations, he has threatened to shut down a Justice Department investigation by top law enforcement agencies that involve him, his family, and a number of his closest advisors.[11]

Trump insists that the Department of Justice be used as a political tool to punish his enemies and reward his friends. For example, he put pressure on the former Attorney General Jeff Sessions to wage a criminal investigation against *The New York Times* for running an anonymous op-ed that called into question Trump's ability to govern, if not his sanity. In the op-ed, an alleged senior official in the administration stated that Trump was amoral and erratic in his decision-making, using "misguided principles," and was simply unfit to be president.[12] Trump condemned the article "as an act of treason." Trump's unapologetic embrace of lawlessness and his blind spot for constitutional principles border on the pathological. He has argued that protesters should be thrown in jail, immigrants seeking asylum should be denied due process, and people who burn the flag should lose their citizenship. Emulating the rhetoric of gang bosses, he has stated that individuals who cooperate with federal prosecutors in criminal investigations are disloyal and that such cooperation or "flipping … almost ought to be outlawed."[13]

Trump shamelessly relativizes the meaning and implementation of "law and order" depending on whether the perpetrator of the alleged crime is a friend or an enemy. "Illegals" or anyone in his target audience of "criminals" he insists should be roughed up by the police, but friends such as Rob Porter, a former White House senior aide charged with abuse by both of his ex-wives, should have criminal charges dismissed. He criticized Jeff Sessions and the Justice Department for bringing charges against two popular Republican Congressmen, Chris Collins (NY) and Duncan Hunter (CA), suggesting the charges against them be dropped because they are loyal to him and that their "two easy wins [in the November 2018 elections are] now in doubt because there is not enough time."[14] Collins was charged with a series of crimes including insider trading and multiple counts of securities fraud while "Hunter has been charged with wire fraud, false campaign reporting, and using hundreds of thousands in campaign contributions for his own personal 'slush fund' to cover vacations and personal medical expenses."[15]

As Chris Hayes observes, law and order for Trump has little to do with justice or the rule of law:

> If all that matters when it comes to "law and order" is who is a friend and who is an enemy, and if friends are white and enemies are black or Latino or in the wrong party, then the rhetoric around crime and punishment stops being about justice and is merely about power and corruption. And this is what "law and order" means: the preservation of a certain social order, not the rule of law.[16]

The United States is one of the wealthiest countries in the world with a GDP per capita of $62,152, and yet its current policies relating to inequality and extreme poverty will make matters worse.[17] As Professor Philip Alston, the United Nations Special Rapporteur on extreme poverty and human rights, has reported, Trump's tax approach "stakes out America's bid to become the most unequal society in the world and will greatly increase the already high levels of wealth and income inequality between the richest one percent and the poorest 50 percent of Americans."[18] Trump's health care reforms, particularly the elimination of the individual mandate, which requires nearly all Americans to get coverage or be strapped with a penalty, threatens to leave close to nine million people without health insurance in 2019.[19]

Americans increasingly find themselves in a society in which those in commanding positions of power and influence, rather than refusing to cooperate with evil, exhibit a tacit approval of the emerging authoritarian pathologies and acute social problems undermining democratic institutions and rules of law. Many politicians at all levels of power remain silent and therefore complicit in the face of such assaults on American democracy. Ideological extremism and a stark indifference to the lies and ruthless policies of the Trump administration have turned the Republican Party into a party of collaborators, not unlike the Vichy government that collaborated with the Nazis in the 1940s.[20] Both groups were more than ready to buy into the script of ultra-nationalism, cultivate toxic masculinity, demonize racial and ethnic others, support unchecked militarism and fantasies of empire, and sanction state violence at home and abroad. The noble history of a World War II resistance that bore witness to human suffering and mounted the courage to face "the unspeakable" while being "committed... to the unimaginable" casts a dark shadow today over a

Republican Party and other politicians who look away in the face of an emerging fascism at all levels of government.[21]

Former conservative commentator Charles Sykes is right in arguing that members of the current Republican Party are "collaborators and enablers" and, as such, are Vichy Republicans who are willingly engaged in a Faustian bargain with an incipient authoritarianism. Corrupted by power and all too willing to overlook corruption, stupidity and the growing savagery of the Trump administration, Republicans have been disposed to surrender to Trump's authoritarian ideology, economic fundamentalism, support for religious orthodoxy, and increasingly cruel and mean-spirited policies, which has "meant accepting the unacceptable [reasoning] it would be worth it if they got conservative judges, tax cuts, and the repeal of Obamacare."[22] Alarmingly, they have ignored the criticisms of Trump by high-profile members of their own party. For instance, former Senator Bob Corker, the chair of the Senate foreign relations committee, accused Trump of "debasing the nation," "treating his office like a reality show," and warned "Trump may be setting the US on the path to World War III."

This is not to propose that the Republicans who support Trump, or the media commentators who defend his callous policies and assaults on the truth, or the intellectuals who turn the other way and either apologize for Trump or remain silent, are simply updated Nazis.[23] Nevertheless, it is meant to suggest a real and present danger. People of power have turned their backs on the cautionary histories of the fascist and Nazi regimes and, in doing so, willingly embrace a number of authoritarian messages and tropes: the cult of the leader, the discourse of the savior, white nationalism, a narrative of decline, unchecked casino capitalism, systemic racism, silence in the face of a growing police state, the encouragement of state endorsed violence, the hollowing out of democracy by corporate power, a grotesque celebration of greed, a massive growth in the inequality of wealth, power, and resources, a brutal politics of disposability, an expanding culture of cruelty, and a disdain for public virtues, all wrapped up in an authoritarian populism. These tropes are both the cause and effect of a growing culture of social and historical amnesia that normalizes fascism and mobilizes language into an instrument of violence. As the renowned British historian Richard J. Evans observes:

Words that in a normal, civilized society had a negative connotation acquired the opposite sense under Nazism . . . so that "fanatical," "brutal," "ruthless," "uncompromising," "hard," all became words of praise instead of disapproval . . . In the hands of the Nazi propaganda apparatus, the German language became strident, aggressive, and militaristic. Commonplace matters were described in terms more suited to the battlefield. The language itself began to be mobilized for war.[24]

Even disposability is no longer the discourse of marginalized extremists. It now exists at the highest levels of government. Examples of such reckless rhetoric include: Trump's immigration policy teeming with threats of a wall to keep out Mexican "criminals" and "drug dealers"; his Muslim ban and efforts to curb newcomers from "shithole" countries; his zero tolerance policy towards undocumented workers, which separated children from their parents and then incarcerated the children — some as young as five years old; and his revoking of the temporary protected status of hundreds of thousands of people from Honduras and San Salvador, among other countries, which furthered such racist and exclusionary agendas.

Fantasies of absolute control, racial cleansing, and class warfare are at the heart of an American imagination that has turned lethal. This is a dystopian imagination marked by incendiary words, cleansed of any critical ideas, and devoid of any substantive meaning. Even domestic populations, such as youth subject to mass shootings in their schools, fare poorly in Trump's worldview. In the wake of the school shooting massacre in Parkland, Florida, Trump and Betsy DeVos, the Secretary of Education, have called for the arming of teachers as opposed to restricting gun access or providing support services for students in the face of such carnage.

Ignorance now rules America. Not the simple, if somewhat innocent ignorance that comes from an absence of knowledge, but a malicious ignorance forged in the arrogance of refusing to think hard about an issue. James Baldwin was certainly right in issuing the stern warning in *No Name in the Street* that "Ignorance, allied with power, is the most ferocious enemy justice can have." Trump's ignorance lights up the Twitter landscape almost every day. He denies climate change along with dangers that it poses to humanity, shuts down the government because he cannot get the funds for his wall — a grotesque symbol of nativism — and heaps disdain on the heads of his intelligence agencies because they provide proof of the lies and misinformation that shapes his love affair with tyrants. This kind of power-drunk ignorance is comparable to a bomb with a fuse that is about to explode in a crowded shopping center. This dangerous type of ignorance fuses with a reckless use of state power that holds both human life and the planet hostage.

There is more at stake here than the production of a toxic form of illiteracy the shrinking political horizons. What we are witnessing is a closing of the political. That is, the very conditions necessary for enabling people to make informed decisions are under siege as schools are defunded, journalism becomes more corporatized, and reality TV becomes the model for mass entertainment. Voting remains one of the few sites where people can actively participate in politics, but even here, turnout has remained at historic lows. Under such circumstances, there is a full-scale attack on thoughtful reasoning, collective resistance, and the radical imagination. The unprecedented attacks on the mainstream media and the practice of independent journalism bear witness to these changes. Steven Levitsky and Daniel Ziblatt are right in arguing that Trump's threat to use "libel laws," his labeling of critical news outlets as "fake news," and his notion of the media as the "enemy of the American people" — another phrase linked to authoritarian regimes — are key warning signs of a fascist politics.[25] Trump has legitimated the inexcusable, and defended the indefensible.

Of course, Trump is only a symptom of the economic, political, and ideological rot at the heart of casino capitalism — its social and political pathologies have been festering in the United States with great intensity since the late 1970s, when, as Ronald Reagan made clear, government was the problem and the social contract was an enemy of freedom. Both political parties decided that matters of community, the public good, the general welfare, and democracy itself were a threat to the fundamental beliefs of the financial elite and its institutions. Government, framed as the enemy of freedom and purged theoretically of any responsibility for a range of basic social needs, was replaced by an ideology of individual responsibility, where compassion gave way to self-interest, manufacturing was replaced by the toxic power of financialization, and a rampaging inequality left the bottom half of the US population without jobs, dreams, or a future of meaningful work. Donald Trump is a symbol of the pillaging of the democratic state by a corporate, financial, and military oligarchy. As Chris Hedges rightly notes:

> The destruction of democratic institutions, places where the citizen has agency and a voice, is far graver than the ascendancy to the White Hose of the demagogue Trump. A creeping corporate coup d'état has destroyed our two-party system. It destroyed labor unions. It destroyed public education. It destroyed the judiciary. It destroyed the press. It destroyed academia. It destroyed consumer and environmental protection. It destroyed our industrial base. It destroyed communities and cities. And it destroyed the lives of tens of millions of Americans no longer able to find work that provides a living wage, cursed to live in chronic poverty or locked in cages in our monstrous system of mass incarceration.[26]

Trump added a new swagger and unapologetic posture to this concoction, embodying a form of populist authoritarianism that not only rejects egalitarian notions of citizenship but also embraces a fear of, if not disdain for, democracy that is at the heart of any fascist regime. How else to explain a sitting president announcing to a crowd during a speech in a Cincinnati suburb that Democratic Party congressional members who refused to clap for parts of his State of the Union Address were "un-American" and "treasonous"?[27] This charge was even more disturbing given that in the speech he repeatedly invoked bipartisanship and the idea of national unity.[28] Words carry power and enable certain actions; they also establish the grounds for legitimating repressive policies and practices. Such threats are not a joking matter and cannot be dismissed as merely a slip of the tongue. Treason is punishable by death, and when the refusal to offer up sycophantic praise is declared treason, the plague of fascism is not far away. The call for political unity also takes a dark turn when coupled with his use of hateful rhetoric to connect inner cities with a culture of criminality, undocumented immigrants with savage crimes, and Muslims with terrorists. Trump's rhetoric on criminality resonates with a fascist politics in which law and order has little to do with addressing real injustices and a great deal to do with defining as lawless those groups defined as other, excess, threatening, or disposable.[29]

In Trump's world, the authoritarian mind set has been resurrected in a new key. As the journalist Matt Taibbi has pointed out, he has amal-

gamated the mania and violence of pro wrestling with the harsh, survival-of-the-fittest ethos of reality TV.[30] He successfully combines the
currency of fake reality with an entertainment culture that thrives on
extreme violence and cruelty, an approach to politics that echoes the
merging of the spectacle and ethical abandonment of past fascist regimes, all with the glossiness of TV. Naomi Klein rightly argues that
Trump "approaches everything as a spectacle" and edits "reality to fit
his narrative,"[31] and as his obsession with ratings suggests, he does so
with an obsessive eye on his marks.

Trump's infantile production of Twitter storms transforms politics into
spectacularized theater: verbal grenades that explode in an array of
racial panics, fear mongering, and hateful speech. As the bully-in-chief,
he militarizes speech while producing a culture meant to embrace his
brand of authoritarianism. Consider for example, the "fire and fury"
rhetoric and school yard taunts President Trump directed at North
Korean leader Kim Jong-un — and Trump's tune would change over
time. An over the top gesture even for Trump who more often than not
uses his pulpit to praise authoritarian leaders such as Vladimir Putin,
Jair Bolsonaro, and Rodrigo Duterte. His speeches and policies pit
white working and middle class males against people of color, men
against women, and the economically insecure whites against economically insecure ethnic and immigrant groups — a politics of diversion that is meant to gloss over his massive assault on the planet
and his policies, such as his tax bill. For example, Trump's alleged affair
with porn star Stormy Daniels initially garnered far more headlines
than his dismantling of environment protections that benefit the fossil
fuel plunderers who are a politically strategic and part of the corporate
empire.

Economic pillage has reached new and extreme levels. For instance,
workers' wages have remained largely stagnant for the last 20 years,
yet the pay gap between the top CEOs and American workers is at
startling levels. According to Fortune Magazine, "the average CEO of a
large US company makes 271 times the wages of the average worker."[32]
While the opioid crisis had claimed over 200,000 lives, *The Washington Post* reports that some members of Congress "allied with the nation's major drug distributors, prevailed upon the DEA and the Justice
Department to agree to a more industry-friendly law, undermining
efforts to stanch the flow of pain pills, according to an investigation
by *The Washington Post* and "60 Minutes." The DEA had opposed the

effort for years."[33] Trump legitimates ignorance of the processes that, as Jim Sleeper puts it, transform:

> citizen sovereignty into the mirage of consumer sovereignty by groping us, titillating us, goosing us, insulting us, scaring us, indebting us, monitoring us, stressing us; and, after we're too ill to bear our sicknesses or their cures, presenting us with a rapacious marketer-in-chief who says he can liberate us because his own power proves that "free markets make free men."[34]

According to Roger Cohen, "Trump has lowered expectations. He has inured people to the thread of violence and meanness lurking in almost every utterance; or worse, he has started to make them relish it."[35] Cohen does not go far enough. Like most authoritarians, Trump demands loyalty and team membership from all those under his power, and he hates those elements of a democracy, such as the courts and the critical media, that dare to challenge him. Echoes of the past come to life in his call for giant military parades,[36] in White House press secretary Sarah Sanders calling people who disagree with his policies "un-American,"[37] and in his Department of Justice threatening to arrest and charge mayors with a federal crime who do not implement his anti-immigration policies and racist assaults on immigrants.[38] His minions and collaborators, like Devin Nunes, attack law enforcement agencies including the Justice Department, FBI, and individuals such as Special Counsel Mueller for attempting to enforce the law.[39] What can be learned from past periods of tyranny is that the embrace of lawlessness is often followed by a climate of terror and repression that is the essence of fascism.

Trump's call for blind loyalty reflects more than vanity and insecurity. Trump lives, as Masha Gessen observes, "surrounded by enemies, shadowed by danger, forever perched on the precipice."[40] He has in not too subtle ways also convinced a wide range of radical extremists, from the Ku Klux Klan and neo-Nazis to the racist and fascist alt-right movement, that he shares their hatred of people of color, immigrants, and Jews. Imaginary horrors inhabit this dystopian world and frighteningly resemble shades of a terrifying past of genocide, concentration camps, and world war. As Jeffrey St. Clair puts it, "Trump projects the image of president as gravedigger," offering up to fearful, angry, scared, and resentful whites "sacrificial killing[s] on their behalf. Mass arrests. Torture. Deportation of the sick and helpless. He vows to turn entire nations into glowing morgues. All for them. And they eat it up, savoring the bitterness."[41]

State of Disunion

Nowhere is this dystopian vision more succinctly contained than in Trump's first State of the Union Address and the response it garnered.[42] Billed by the White House as a speech that would be "unifying" and marked by a tone of "bipartisanship," it was in actuality the opposite. Steeped in divisiveness, fear, racism, war mongering, nativism, and immigrant bashing, it once again displayed Trump's contempt for democracy. Claiming "all Americans deserve accountability and respect," he spent ample airtime equating undocumented immigrants with the criminal gang MS-13, regardless of the fact that undocumented immigrants commit fewer crimes than American citizens do. As Juan Cole points out, "Americans murdered 17,250 other Americans in 2016. Almost none of the perpetrators was an undocumented worker, contrary to the impression Trump gave."[43] According to Cole, "Where the race of the perpetrator was known in 2016, about 30 percent were white and 36 percent were black; less than two percent were known to be of another ethnicity. However, Trump foregrounded murders by immigrants. Homicide tracks pretty closely with poverty, not with race."[44] For Trump, as with most demagogues, fear is the most valued currency of politics. Moreover, he delivered it in spades, suggesting that the visa lottery system and "chain migration" — in which individuals can migrate through the sponsorship of their family — pose a threat to America and "present risks we can just no longer afford." He suggested even DREAMERS were part of a culture of criminality and in a not too subtle expression of derision stated "Americans are dreamers too." White nationalists such as Richard Spencer and David Duke cheered Trump's remark. This was one of many gestures well-suited to his white nationalist base.

Trump proudly declared that he was not going to close Guantánamo and once again argued "terrorists should be treated like terrorists." The ruthless policy of "extraordinary rendition" and torture, rather than being seen as war crimes, fan the paranoia, nihilist passions, and apocalyptic populism that feed his base. Pointing to menacing enemies all around the world, Trump argued for expanding the nuclear arsenal and the military budget. He also called on "the Congress to empower every Cabinet secretary with the authority to reward good workers — and to remove federal employees who undermine the public trust or fail the American people" — in other words, to rid the federal workforce of those who disagree with him, allowing him to fill civil service jobs with friends, families, cronies, and sycophants.

His insistence on "loyalty" instills fear in those he appoints to govern-ment positions if they dare to hold power accountable. This is what happens when democracies turn into fascist states. As Jacob Levy points out:

> [Trump's call] on Congress to allow Cabinet officials ... to fire civil servants on grounds of political disagreement, ending the century-old rule of a professional and apolitical civil ser-vice that stays on as political appointees come and go. This is of a piece with the months-long rhetorical assault on the so-called "deep state" by Trump and the Trumpist media. Maybe there will be no such legislation. But Trump saying it matters. House Speaker Paul Ryan echoing the call for a "purge" at the FBI matters. Fox News's constant public dele-gitimation of the civil service matters. It matters in particular for the Russia investigation, of course. Trump means to push out anyone who isn't on "his team" in a way that the FBI and the Department of Justice are really not supposed to be, and that process is underway in front of our eyes. But it also mat-ters more broadly for the character of the American state and bureaucracy. By discouraging professionals and encourag-ing politicization, Trump is already changing the civil service by his speech.[45]

None of this is entirely unexpected. As Michael Tomasky puts it, "Hon-estly, who couldn't have imagined any of this? To anyone who had the right read on Trump's personality — the vanity, the insecurity, the contempt for knowledge, the addiction to chaos — nothing that's hap-pened has been surprising in the least."[46] Nevertheless, Trump is worse than almost anyone imagined: he is not only the enemy of democracy, he is symptomatic of the powerful political, economic, and cultural forces shaping this new American fascism.

Roger Cohen, writing for *The New York Times*, argues that Trump has so degraded and soiled public discourse that people have become numb and exhausted. How else to explain the sycophantic posturing of the mainstream press and much of the American public in the face of Trump's racist State of the Union Address? As Cohen observes:

> Many commentators swooned. It was enough that Trump did not go on walkabout. For NBC's Savannah Guthrie, "It was optimistic; it was bright; it was conciliatory." Frank Luntz, a respected Republican pollster, thought that only one word qualified: "Wow." He tweeted that the speech was a "brilliant mix of numbers and stories, humility and aggressiveness, traditional conservatism and political populism." Jake Tapper of CNN discerned "beautiful prose." Even the Washington Post saw "A Call for Bipartisanship" (its initial Page One headline) lurking somewhere. Three in four American viewers approved of the speech, according to a CBS News poll.[47]

There are some critics who claim that Trump is simply a weak president whose ineptness is being countered by "a robust democratic culture and set of institutions" and not much more than a passing moment in history.[48] Others, such as Wendy Brown and Nancy Fraser, view him as an authoritarian expression of right-wing populism and an outgrowth of neoliberal politics and policies,[49] while historians such as Timothy Snyder and Robert O. Paxton analyze him in terms that echo some elements of a fascist past. Some conservatives such as David Frum view him as a mix between a modern day, self-obsessed, emotionally needy narcissist and demagogue whose assault on democracy needs to be taken seriously and asserts that whether or not he is a fascist is not as important as what he plans to do with his power. For Frum, there is a real danger that people will retreat into their private worlds, become cynical, and enable our collective slide into a form of tyranny that would then become difficult to defeat.[50]

Corey Robin argues that we overstep a theoretical boundary when comparing Trump directly to Hitler. According to Robin, in comparing Trump to Hitler or the policies of the Third Reich, we not only exaggerate the threat that Trump poses to the values and institutions of democracy but overestimate the growing threat of authoritarianism in the United States. For Robin, Trump has failed to institute many of his policies, and thus is just a weak politician with little actual power. He contends that George W. Bush's policy decisions were far worse than anything we have seen in Trump's emerging administration and concludes that while Trump talks like an authoritarian, he never really gets what he wants. Jacob Levy sums up Robin's argument, "A year later, we're still in NAFTA and NATO, there haven't been mass deportations, Hillary Clinton hasn't been thrown in jail, the separation of powers is intact, and so on. Just ignore his words."[51]

But words matter. They matter because they not only provide the ideological and affective scaffolding for policies but also because they function as pedagogical tools to define social relations, mobilize desires, create modes of identification, and shape one's relationship to others and the larger world. Thus, Trump's racist language has enabled the rise and increasing normalization of the alt-right, neo-Nazis, and a surge of white nationalism. His rhetorical attacks on the critical press, journalists, and others who criticize him send a chill through American society and undermine the foundations of dissent. His verbal attacks on undocumented immigrants and Muslims enable and encourage the proliferation of hate crimes. His impetuous insults aimed at allies work to undo the liberal international order. His praise for the uber-rich and corporate elite breathes new life into a criminogenic casino capitalism.[52] As Hannah Arendt has argued, language is a form of action, and that action is often pedagogical. Trump's discourse makes clear that education is at the heart of politics; it carries the weight of weapons forged in the realm of the symbolic and pedagogical, and changes how people see things, how they invest in themselves and others.

As Jeffrey C. Isaac notes, whether Trump is a direct replica of the Nazi regime has little relevance; more important is the threat he poses to the DACA children and their families, to poor, undocumented immigrants, and a range of others.[53] The oppressive and regressive policies already put into place by the Trump administration — the expansion of the military-industrial complex, the elimination of Obamacare's individual mandate, the US recognition of Jerusalem as Israel's capital, and a range of deregulations that will impact negatively on the environment for years to come — will have long-term effects on United States and the world. As Richard J. Evans has noted, "Violence indeed was at the heart of the Nazi enterprise," and "Every democracy that perishes dies in a different way, because every democracy is situated in specific historical circumstances."[54] Our circumstances include the threat of a nuclear war, the disappearance of health care for the most vulnerable, the attack on free speech and the media, the rise of the punishing state and the increasing criminalization of social problems, the destruction of the environment, and other forms of violence.

American society has entered a dangerous stage in its history. After 40 years of neoliberalism and many more of systemic racism, many Americans lack a critical language to understand the growing rootlessness, gutted wages, lost pensions, collapsing identities, feelings of disposability, the loss of meaningful work, the demise of shared responsibilities, an epidemic of loneliness, and a culture of violence, cruelty, and greed. Since 9/11, Americans have been bombarded by a culture of fear that, in dampening their willingness to be critical agents, ultimately depoliticizes them. Shared fears rather than shared responsibilities undermine the basic foundations of the social ties necessary in a substantive democracy. Everyone is now a suspect or a consumer but hardly a critically engaged citizen. The ravages of debt, poverty, and the daily struggle to survive — problems made worse by Trump's tax and health policies — depoliticize some, too. Trump's aim to eviscerate public institutions, from education to the media, have made it all the more difficult for many people to become informed citizens and recognize how the "crystalized elements" of totalitarianism have shaped an American-style fascism,[55] which is not a relic of the past or an idea, but our emerging reality.

Trump is not in possession of storm troopers and concentration camps, or concocting plans for genocidal acts, at least not at the moment. But as Hannah Arendt, Sheldon Wolin, and others theorists of authoritarianism have taught us, totalitarian regimes come in many forms and their elements can come together in different configurations. Under Trump, democracy has become the enemy of power, politics, and finance. More importantly, since Trumpism will not simply fade away in the end, the comparison between the current historical moment and fascism is much needed. Adam Gopnik agrees:

> Needless to say, the degradation of public discourse, the acceleration of grotesque lying, the legitimization of hatred and name-calling, are hard to imagine vanishing like the winter snows that Trump thinks climate change is supposed to prevent. The belief that somehow all these things will some-

how just go away in a few years' time does seem not merely unduly optimistic but crazily so. In any case, the trouble isn't just what the Trumpists may yet do; it is what they are doing now. American history has already been altered by their actions — institutions emptied out, historical continuities destroyed, traditions of decency savaged — in ways that will not be easy to rehabilitate.[56]

There is nothing new about the possibility of authoritarianism in a particularly distinctive guise coming to America. Nor is there a shortage of works illuminating the horrors of fascism. Fiction writers from George Orwell, Sinclair Lewis, and Aldous Huxley to Margaret Atwood, Philip Dick, and Philip Roth have sounded the alarm in often brilliant and insightful terms. Politicians such as Henry Wallace wrote about American fascism, as did a range of theorists such as Umberto Eco, Hannah Arendt, and Robert O. Paxton, who tried to understand its emergence, attractions, and effects. What they all had in common is an awareness of the changing nature of tyranny and how it could happen under a diverse set of historical, economic, and social circumstances. They also seem to share Philip Roth's insistence that we all have an obligation to recognize "the terror of the unforeseen" that hides in the shadows of censorship, makes power invisible, and gains in strength in the absence of historical memory.[57] A warning indeed.

Trump represents a distinctive and dangerous form of American-bred authoritarianism, but at the same time, he is the outcome of a past that needs to be remembered, analyzed, and engaged for the lessons it can teach us about the present. Not only has Trump "normalized the unspeakable" and in some cases the unthinkable, he has also forced us to ask questions we have never asked before about capitalism, power, politics, and, yes, courage itself.[58] In part, this means recovering a language for politics, civic life, the public good, citizenship, and justice that has real substance. This cannot happen without a revolution in consciousness — one that makes education central to politics. One element central to developing a critical consciousness is to confront the horrors of capitalism and its transformation into a form of fascism under Trump. At the very least, this would involve developing a formative and sustainable anti-capitalist movement.

Moreover, as Fred Jameson has suggested, such a revolution cannot take place by limiting our choices to a fixation on the "impossible present."[59] Nor can it take place by limiting ourselves to a language of critique and a narrow focus on individual issues. What is needed is also a language of possibility and a comprehensive politics for the future that does not imitate the present.

And by "the present," I do not just mean Trump. Neoliberalism has sanctioned a hyper-individualism, the destruction of the welfare state, the privatization of everything, and massive inequalities in wealth and power. It has become difficult, given the neoliberal order's power to control not only markets and economics but all of social life, to imagine any other kind of economic system or society. Margaret Thatcher's claim that "there is no alternative" has been normalized. Neoliberalism has colonized memory, undercutting the capacity to remember or envision a world radically different from the present. Naomi Klein is right in arguing that what is missing from too many social movements in the United States is an inability to get beyond saying no.[60]

William Faulkner once remarked, "The past is never dead. It's not even past." Trump is living proof that we are living with the ghosts of a dark past, and not only can it return, "it's not even past." The ghosts of fascism should terrify us, but most importantly, they should educate us and imbue us with a spirit of civic justice and collective courage in the fight for a substantive and inclusive democracy. The stakes are too high to remain complacent, cynical, or simply outraged. A crisis of memory, history, agency, and justice has mushroomed and opened up the abyss of a fascist nightmare. Now is the time to talk back, embrace the radical imagination in private and public, and work until radical democracy becomes a reality. There is no other choice.

Chapter 2

Beyond the Language of Hate
in Dark Times

*I imagine one of the reasons people cling to their hates so
stubbornly is because they sense, once hate is gone,
they will be forced to deal with pain.*
— James Baldwin

GEORGE ORWELL WARNS US in his dystopian novel *1984* that authoritarianism begins with language: "newspeak," a language twisted in order to deceive, seduce, and undermine, becomes fundamental to the operations of a Ministry of Truth whose aim is to root out and abolish language that functions in the service of reason and critical thought. Reason and compassion give way to a rhetoric of rancid bigotry, which works to inform policy and inflict humiliation, misery, and suffering on diverse groups who are viewed as degenerate and repugnant.

Trump's racism surfaced with great fanfare in his assertion, when launching his presidential campaign, that "when Mexico sends its people, they're not sending the best. They're sending people that have lots of problems, and they're bringing those problems. They're bringing drugs, they're bringing crime. They're rapists and some, I assume, are good people ..."[61] Trump's shameless appeal to white racism was also evident when he repeatedly claimed that the inner cities are composed mostly of African-Americans and that black culture is synonymous with the culture of crime.[62] In 2017, Trump allegedly said that people who came to the US from Haiti "all have AIDS." Another example of such a language was on full display when Donald Trump made headlines at the beginning of 2018 saying that the United States shouldn't accept people from "shithole countries" like Haiti, El Salvador, and various African nations.[63]

Trump's attack on immigrants has drawn sharp rebukes from a number of critics who state that his language is racist, dehumanizes people, and reproduces a form of symbolic violence. In spite of these criticisms, Trump is unapologetic about such comments, wearing them as a badge of honor. For instance, he recalled his 2015 comments about Mexicans being "rapists" in a speech he gave to the National Federation of Independent Business in June 2018 and doubled down on the comments with a statement reeking with derision: "Remember I made that speech and I was badly criticized? 'Oh, it's so terrible what he said.' Turned out I was 100 percent right. That's why I got elected."[64]

In addition, Trump's racist ideology and bow to white supremacist beliefs have been on full display in many of his policies, including legislation designed to ban Muslims entering the country and his assertion that many of them hate the US. His racist messaging was also visible with his call for a US judge overseeing the Trump University lawsuit to recuse himself because of his Mexican heritage. In some of his more notorious racist comments, he has referred to immigrants as "animals"[65] and has attacked "well-known African-Americans as having 'low IQs' or being of low intelligence."[66] Some of the most prominent African-Americans whose intelligence was mocked by Trump include NBA great LeBron James, CNN Anchor Don Lemon, and Rep. Maxine Waters (D-CA). This is a view long supported by white nationalists and may explain why, during the 2016 presidential campaign, Trump refused to denounce the endorsement of David Duke, an American white supremacist, Holocaust denier, and former head Grand Wizard of the Klu Klux Klan.

Trump has a long history of demeaning African-Americans and in one notorious incident stated with no evidence that President Obama was a terrible student and that he should never have been accepted by both Columbia University and Harvard Law School.[67] Given his support for white nationalism and his coded call to "Make America Great

Again," Trump's overtly racist remarks echo the white supremacy of fascist dictators in the 1930s. Behind Trump's politics of incivility, his use of vulgarity, and his disparagement of the poor and non-whites lies the terrifying discourse of ethnic cleansing and the politics of disposability.[68]

In this case, more underlies the language of white nationalism and racial resentment. There is also a discourse that annihilates social codes and restrained political behavior and undermines the rule of law. This is a police state vocabulary that considers some individuals and groups not only as faceless and voiceless, but as excess, redundant, and subject to expulsion. It also informs policies marked by malignant cruelty, legitimates forms of state violence, and mirrors a shift in popular opinion. The United States has a long history of racist language leading to cruel and harmful practices and, in some cases, violence aimed at groups targeted by such language. It was not too long ago that politicians, pundits, and sociologists "labeled black and Latino youth as 'super-predators' to justify prison expansion, vastly increased sentencing, and overly aggressive law enforcement that has devastated communities of color."[69] The Trump administration with its legitimation of racist and demeaning rhetoric has emboldened the rise of white supremacists, the alt-right, and neo-Nazis along with a growing popular support and tolerance for such groups — matched by an uptick in violence against blacks, Muslims, Jews, Latinos, transgendered people, and others who are the object of state-approved bigotry and hatred.

While there is no denying that Trump's legitimation of white nationalists and neo-Nazis constitutes a growing threat to democracy, the real danger lies deeper in the growing power of state sanctioned violence of the police, the criminal justice system, schools modeled after prisons, gun violence, and a carceral system that imprisons mostly poor people of color. This is the fast/hard violence that is expanding under the Trump administration, one that has a long legacy in the United States and is not unique to the emergence of the Trump presidency.

As authoritarianism gains in strength, the formative cultures that give rise to dissent become more embattled along with the public spaces and institutions that make conscious critical thought possible. Words that speak to the truth, reveal injustices, and provide informed critical analysis begin to disappear, making it all the more difficult, if not dangerous, to hold dominant power accountable. The Ministry of Truth functions in Orwell's *1984* as the Ministry of Lies. History is being re-written both to eliminate dangerous memories and to align the past with narratives that reinforce anti-democratic ideologies and social relations. Terror becomes the essence of politics bolstered by the den-igration and erasure of any viable notion of morality and personal and social responsibility. Notions of virtue honor, respect, and compassion are policed, and those who advocate for them are punished.

Guided by Arendt's insight into the dynamics of totalitarianism, edu-cation both within and outside of institutionalized schooling becomes a tool not only to instill authoritarian convictions but to destroy the ability of the populace to form any convictions that are on the side of justice, freedom, and thoughtfulness. I think it is fair to argue that Orwell's nightmare vision of the future is no longer fiction. Under the regime of Donald Trump, the Ministry of Truth has become the Ministry of Fake News, and the language of "Newspeak" has multiple platforms, morphing into a giant disimagination machinery of propaganda, igno-rance, hypocrisy, and fear. Trump's language and politics have a high threshold for disappearance and zones of terminal exclusion and, as a form of pedagogical regulation, works hard to eliminate expressions of discontent, resistance, and popular democratic struggles.

With the advent of Trump's presidency, language is undergoing a shift in the United States: it now treats dissent, critical media, and scientific evidence as a species of "fake news."[70] The administration also views the critical media as the "enemy of the American people." In fact, the Trump administration has repeated this view of the media so often that "almost a third of Americans believe it" and "favor government restrictions on the press."[71] Language has become unmoored from critical reason and informed debate – the weight of scientific evidence and is now being reconfigured within new relations of power tied to pageantry, political theater, and a deep-seated anti-intellectualism. Language is shaped increasingly by the widespread banality of celeb-rity culture, the celebration of ignorance over intelligence, a culture of rancid consumerism, and a corporate controlled media that revels in commodification, spectacles of violence, the spirit of unchecked indi-vidual interest, and a survival-of-the-fittest ethos.

Under such circumstances, language is emptied of substantive mean-ing and functions increasingly to lull large swaths of the American pub-lic into acquiescence, if not a willingness to accommodate and support a rancid populism and galloping authoritarianism. One consequence is that matters of moral and political responsibility disappear, injustices proliferate, and language functions as a tool of state repression. The Ministry of Fake News works incessantly to set limits on what is thinkable, claiming that reason, standards of evidence, consistency, and logic no longer serve the truth because the latter are crooked ideological devices used by enemies of the state. "Thought crimes" are now labeled as "fake news." This president views the notion of truth as a corrupt tool used by the critical media to question his dismissal of legal checks on his power, particularly his attacks on judges, courts, and any other governing institutions that will not promise him complete and unchecked loyalty. For Trump, intimidation takes the place of unquestioned loyalty when he does not get his way, revealing a view of the presidency that is more about winning than about governing. One consequence is a myriad of practices in which Trump gleefully humiliates and punishes his critics, willfully engages in shameful acts of self-promotion, and unapologetically enriches his financial coffers.[72]

David Axelrod, a former senior advisor to President Obama is right in stating: "And while every president is irritated by the limitations of democracy on them, they all grudgingly accept it. [Trump] has not. He has waged a war on the institutions of democracy from the beginning, and I think in a very corrosive way."[73] The New York Times writer Peter Baker adds to this charge by arguing that Trump — buoyed by an infatuation with absolute power and an admiration for authoritarians — uses language and the power of the presidency as a potent weapon in his attack on the First Amendment, the courts, and responsible governing.[74] For example, Trump's admiration for a number of dictators is well known. What is often underplayed is his inclination to mimic their language and policies. For instance, Trump's call for "law and order," his encouraging police officers to be more violent with "thugs," and his adoration of all things militaristic echo the ideology and language of a number of dictators Trump adulates.[75]

Trump makes no apologies for ramping up the police state, imposing racist inspired travel injunctions, banning transgender people from serving in the military, and initiating tax reforms that further balloon the obscene wealth gap in the United States. All the while, he uses his Twitter feed to entertain his right-wing, white supremacist, and religious fundamentalist base at home with a steady stream of authoritarian comments while showering affection and further legitimation on a range of despots abroad, the most recent being the self-confessed killer, Rodrigo Duterte, President of the Philippines. According to Felipe Villamor of *The Washington Post*, "Mr. Duterte has led a campaign against drug abuse in which he has encouraged the police and others to kill people they suspect of using or selling drugs."[76] Powerful authoritarian leaders such as Russia's Vladimir Putin and China's Xi Jinping appear to elicit an especially strong and fawning attraction for Trump who exhibits little interests in their massive human rights violations. Trump's high regard for white supremacy and petty authoritarianism became clear on the domestic front when he pardoned former Arizona Sheriff Joseph Arpaio, a monstrous racist who waged a war against undocumented immigrants, Latino residents, and individuals who did not speak English. He also housed detainees in an outdoor prison, which he called his personal "concentration camp." As Marjorie Cohn observes, Arpaio engaged in a series of sadistic practices in his outdoor jail in Phoenix that included forcing prisoners "to wear striped uniforms and pink underwear," "work on chain gangs," and be subjected to blistering Arizona heat so severe that their "shoes would melt."[77] In this instance, Trump not only legitimates the practices of an undeniable racist, he is also offering expressed support for both a culture of violence and state legitimated oppression. Furthermore, Trump's fascist proclivities also become evident in both his cozying up with dictators such as Putin and Kim Jong-un as well as his use of presidential power to pardon what amounts to a parade of cons, grifters, crooks, and ideological extremists.

At the same time, it would be irresponsible to suggest that the current expression of authoritarianism in US politics began with Trump or that the context for his rise to power represents a distinctive moment in American history. The United States was born out of acts of genocide, nativism, and the ongoing violence of white supremacy.[78] Moreover, the United States has a long history of demagogues extending from Huey Long and Joe McCarthy to George Wallace and Newt Gingrich. Authoritarianism runs deep in American history, and Trump is simply the endpoint of these antidemocratic practices.[79] Empire has long had roots in diverse forms of domestic state violence while state terrorism amounted to the official memory of authoritarianism, "reaching into the smallest crevices of everyday life."[80]

The rise of casino capitalism, a savage culture of cruelty, and a winner-take-all ethos have made the United States a mean-spirited and iniquitous nation that has turned its back on the poor, underserved, and those considered racially and ethnically disposable. Powerful digital and traditional pedagogical apparatuses of the 21st century have turned people into consumers and citizenship into a neoliberal obsession with self-interest and an empty notion of freedom. Moreover, they have also created a society in which civic literacy has taken a direct hit while the formative culture necessary for creating informed and engaged citizens has withered into a grotesque economic and pedagogical apparatus at odds with democratic values and social relations. Shock, speed, spectacles, idiocy, and a culture of sensationalism undercut the discourse of civic literacy, thoughtfulness, and reason.

The ecosystem of visual and print representations has taken on an unprecedented influence given the merging of power and culture as a dominant political and pedagogical force. This cultural apparatus has become so powerful, in fact, that it is difficult to dispute the central role it played in the election of Donald Trump to the presidency. Analyzing the forces behind the election of Trump, Steven Levitsky and Daniel Ziblatt provide a cogent commentary on the political and pedagogical power of an old and updated media landscape. They write:

> Undoubtedly, Trump's celebrity status played a role. But equally important was the changed media landscape. Trump had the sympathy or support of right-wing media personalities such as Sean Hannity, Ann Coulter, Mark Levin, and Michael Savage as well as the increasingly influential Breitbart News. He also found new ways to use old media as a substitute for party endorsements and traditional campaign spending. By one estimate, the Twitter accounts of MSNBC, CNN, CBS, and NBC — four outlets that no one could accuse of pro-Trump leanings — mentioned Trump twice as often as Hillary Clinton. According to another study, Trump enjoyed up to $2 billion in free media coverage during the primary season. Trump didn't need traditional Republican power brokers. The gatekeepers of the invisible primary weren't merely invisible; by 2016, they were gone entirely.[81]

What is essential to remember here, as Ruth Ben-Ghiat notes, is that fascism starts with words and Trump's use of language and his manipulative use of the media as political theater echo earlier periods of propaganda, censorship, and repression. Commenting on the Trump administration's barring the Centers for Disease Control from using certain words, Ben-Ghiat writes:

> The strongman knows that it starts with words ... That's why those who study authoritarian regimes or have had the misfortune to live under one may find something deeply familiar about the Trump administration's decision to bar officials at the Centers for Disease Control (CDC) from using certain words ("vulnerable," "entitlement," "diversity," "transgender," "fetus," "evidence-based," and "science-based"). The administration's refusal to give any rationale for the order, and the pressure it places on CDC employees, have a political meaning that transcends its specific content and context ... The decision as a whole links to a larger history of how language is used as a tool of state repression. Authoritarians have always used language policies to bring state power and their cults of personality to bear on everyday life. Such policies affect not merely what we can say and write at work and in public but also [attempt] to change the way we think about ourselves and about others. The weaker our sentiments of solidarity and humanity become — or the stronger our impulse to compromise them under pressure — the easier it is for authoritarians to find partners to carry out their repressive policies.[82]

Under fascist regimes, the language of brutality and culture of cruelty were normalized through the proliferation of the strident metaphors of war, battle, expulsion, racial purity, and demonization. As leading scholars on modern Germany, such as Richard J. Evans and Victor Klemperer, have made clear, dictators such as Hitler did more than corrupt the language of a civilized society — they also banned words. Soon afterwards, they banned books and the critical intellectuals who wrote them. They then imprisoned those individuals who challenged Nazi ideology and the state's systemic violations of civil rights. The endpoint was an all-embracing discourse of disposability, the emergence of concentration camps, and genocide fueled by a politics of racial purity and social cleansing. Echoes of the formative stages of fascism are with us once again and provide just one of the historical signposts of an American-style neo-fascism that appears to be engulfing the United States after simmering in the dark for years.

Under such circumstances, it is crucial for anyone concerned about the dangers of fascism to chart how the texture of life changes when an autocratic demagogue is in charge of the government. That is, it is crucial to interrogate as the first line of resistance how this level of systemic linguistic derangement and corruption shapes everyday life. It is necessary to begin with language because it is the starting point for tyrants to promote their ideologies, hatred, and systemic politics of disposability and erasure. Trump is not unlike many of the dictators he admires. What they all share as strongmen is the use of language in the service of violence and repression as well as a fear of language as a channel for identity, critique, solidarity, and collective struggle. None of them believes that the truth is essential to a responsible mode of governance, and all of them support the notion that lying on the side of power is fundamental to the process of governing, however undemocratic such a political dynamic may be.

Lying has a long legacy in American politics and is a hallmark of authoritarian regimes. Victor Klemperer in his classic book, *The Language of the Third Reich*, reminds us that Hitler had a "deep fear of the thinking man and [a] hatred of the intellect" and that his "*Mein Kampf* preaches not only that the masses are stupid, but also that they need to be kept that way and intimidated into not thinking."[83] Trump displays a deep contempt for critical thinking and has boasted about how he loves the uneducated. Not only have mainstream sources such as *The Washington Post* and *The New York Times* published endless examples of Trump's lies, they have noted that, even in the aftermath of such exposure, he continues to be completely indifferent to being exposed as a serial liar.[84]

In fact, there is something delusional if not pathological about Trump's indifference to his propensity to lie endlessly even when he is constantly outed publicly for doing so. For instance, in a 30-minute interview with *The New York Times* on December 28, 2017, *The Washington Post* reported that Trump made "false, misleading, or dubious claims … at a rate of one every 75 seconds."[85] Daniel Dale, a writer for *The Toronto Star* who documents Trump's lies, claims that in the first week of August 2018, he made "132 false claims … 19 per day, almost five times his average. That shatters his previous record of 103 false claims in a week, which he set in June."[86] According to *The Washington Post Fact Checker*, Trump "has surpassed 10,000 false or misleading claims since his inauguration on Jan. 20, 2017," further stating: "It's an incredible feat of serial mendacity.

Trump's language attempts to infantilize, seduce, and depoliticize the public through a stream of tweets, interviews, and public pronouncements that disregard facts and the truth. This is about more than Trump's well-publicized desire to blur the lines between fact and fiction. His more serious aim is to derail the architectural foundations of truth and evidence in order to construct a false reality and alternative political universe in which there are only competing fictions and the emotional appeal of shock theater. Within this ongoing tsunami of lies and misrepresentation, the distinction between fiction and reality collapses as does the ethical foundation for recognizing criminal behavior, corruption, and systemic violence. State legitimized deceit both normalizes intolerance and ignorance and undermines the foundation and formative culture necessary to create critical and informed subjects and collective agents.

I think the artist Sable Elyse Smith is right in arguing that ignorance is more than the absence of knowledge or the refusal to know — it is also a form of violence that is woven into the fabric of everyday life by massive disimagination machines, and its ultimate goal is to enable us to not only consume pain and to propagate it but to relish in it as a form of entertainment and emotional uplift.[87] Ignorance is also the enemy of memory and a weapon in the politics of disappearance and the violence of organized forgetting. It is also about the erasure of what Brad Evans calls "the raw realities of suffering" and the undermining of a politics that is, in part, about the battle for memory.[88]

Trump, within a very short time, has legitimated and reinforced a culture of social abandonment, erasure, and terminal exclusion. Justice in this discourse is disposable along with the institutions that make it possible. What is distinctive about Trump is that he defines himself through the tenets of a predatory and cruel form of gangster capitalism while using its power to fill government positions with deadbeats and at the same time produce death-dealing policies. Of course, he is just the overt and unapologetic symbol of a wild capitalism and dark pessimism that have been decades in the making. He is the theatrical, self-absorbed monster that embodies and emboldens a history of savagery, greed, and extreme inequality that has reached its endpoint — a poisonous form of American authoritarianism that must be stopped before it is too late.[89] Trump's actions make clear that democracy is tenuous and has to be viewed as a site of ongoing contestation, one that demands a new understanding of politics, language, and collective struggle.

However, the language of fascism does more that normalize falsehoods and ignorance. It also promotes a larger culture of short-term attention spans, immediacy, and sensationalism. At the same time, it makes fear and anxiety the normalized currency of exchange and communication. Destabilized perceptions in Trump's world are coupled with the force of an inane celebrity culture and the war against all ethos of reality TV. In this environment, the notion of credibility is attacked, and vulgarity and crassness now become a substitute for civic courage and measured arguments. Masha Gessen rightly asserts that Trump's lies are different from ordinary lies and are more like "power lies." In this case, these are lies designed less "to convince the audience of something than to demonstrate the power of the speaker."[90]

Trump's prodigious tweets are not just about the pathology of endless fabrications — they also function to reinforce a pedagogy of infantilism designed to animate his base in a glut of hate while reinforcing a culture of war, fear, divisiveness, and ignorance in ways that often disempower his critics. How else to explain Trump's desire to attract scorn from his critics and praise from his base through a never-ending production of tweets and electronic shocks that transform politics into a pathology marked by an infantilism one associates with a petulant child. Peter Baker and Michael Tackett sum up a number of bizarre and reckless tweets that Trump produced early in his presidency. They write:

> President Trump again raised the prospect of nuclear war with North Korea, boasting in strikingly playground terms on Tuesday night that he commands a "much bigger" and "more powerful" arsenal of devastating weapons than the outlier government in Asia. "Will someone from his depleted and food starved regime please inform [North Korean Leader Kim Jong-un] that I too have a Nuclear Button, but it is a much bigger & more powerful one than his, and my Button works!" It came on a day when Mr. Trump, back in Washington from his Florida holiday break, effectively opened his new year with a barrage of provocative tweets on a host of issues.

> He called for an aide to Hillary Clinton to be thrown in jail,
> threatened to cut off aid to Pakistan and the Palestinians,
> assailed Democrats over immigration, claimed credit for
> the fact that no one died in a jet plane crash last year and
> announced that he would announce his own award next
> Monday for the most dishonest and corrupt news media.[91]

Trump appropriates crassness as a weapon. In a throwback to the language of fascism, he has repeatedly positioned himself as the only one who can save the masses, reproducing the tired script of the model of the savior endemic to authoritarianism. In 2016 at the Republican National Convention, Trump stated, without irony, that he alone would save a nation in crisis, captured in his insistence that "I am your voice, I alone can fix it. I will restore law and order." Trump's latter emphasis on restoring the authoritarian value of law and order has overtones of creating a new racial regime of governance, one that mimics what the historian Cedric J. Robinson once called the "rewhitening of America."[92]

Moreover, such racially charged language points to the growing presence of a police state in the United States and its endpoint in a fascist state where large segments of the population are rendered disposable, incarcerated, or left to fend on their own in the midst of massive degrees of inequality. There is more at work here than an oversized, if not delusional, ego. Trump's authoritarianism and nativist desires are also fueled by elements of narcissism, braggadocio, and misdirected rage. There is also a language that undermines the bonds of solidarity, abolishes institutions meant to protect the vulnerable, and wages a full-fledged assault on the environment.[93] Trump is truly the embodiment of what Robert J. Lifton has called in another context a "death-dealing age."[94]

In addition, Trump's ceaseless use of superlatives models a language that encloses itself in a circle of certainty while taking on religious overtones. Not only do such words pollute the space of credibility, they also wage war on historical memory, humility, and the belief that alternative worlds are possible. The threat such language poses for the future is telling and correlates with Trump's ongoing attempts to make "the past a burden that must be shed in order that a new kind of life can come into being."[95] For Trump and his followers, there is a recognizable threat and danger to their power in the political and moral imperative to learn from the past so as to not repeat or update the dark authoritarianism of the 1930s. Trump is the master of manufactured illiteracy and his obsessive tweeting and public relations machine aggressively engages in a boundless spectacle of self-promotion and distractions — both of which are designed to whitewash any version of the past that might expose the close alignment between Trump's language and policies and the dark elements of a fascist history.

Trump revels in an unchecked mode of self-congratulation bolstered by a grandiose, though limited, vocabulary filled with words like "historic," "best," "the greatest," "tremendous," and "beautiful." As Wesley Pruden observes, "Nothing is ever merely 'good' or 'fortunate.' … Everything is 'fantastic' or 'terrific,' and every man or woman he appoints to a government position, even if just two shades above mediocre, is 'tremendous.' The Donald never met a superlative he didn't like, himself as the ultimate superlative most of all."[96] Trump's relentless exaggerations suggest more than hyperbole or the self-indulgent use of language. This is true even when he claims he "knows more about ISIS than the generals," "knows more about renewables than any human being on Earth," or that nobody "knows the US system of government better than he does."[97] There is also a resonance with the rhetoric of fascism. As the historian Richard J. Evans writes:

> The German language became a language of superlatives so that everything the regime did became the best and the greatest, its achievements unprecedented, unique, historic, and incomparable … The language used about Hitler, Klemperer noted, was shot through and through with religious metaphors; people "believed in him," he was the redeemer, the savior, the instrument of Providence, his spirit lived in and through the German nation … Nazi institutions domesticated themselves [through the use of a language] that became an unthinking part of everyday life.[98]

Under the Trump regime, memories inconvenient to authoritarian rule are now demolished in the domesticated language of superlatives so that the future can be shaped so as to become indifferent to the crimes of the past. Trump's war on historical memory sets the stage for what O'Gorman calls a "revival of intolerance and, in some cases, literally of fascism" along with "the direct affirmation of Nazi ideology recast in versions of white supremacy."[99] Trump's unending daily tweets, his recklessness, his adolescent disdain for a measured response, his unfaltering anti-intellectualism, and his utter lack of historical knowledge are well known. For instance, he has talked about the Civil War as if historians have not asked why it took place, while at the same time ignoring the role of slavery in its birth.[100] During a Black History Month event, he talked about the great abolitionist and former slave Frederick Douglass as if he were still alive.[101] Trump's ignorance of the past finds it counterpart in his celebration of a history that has enshrined racism, tweeted neo-Nazi messages, and embraced the "blood and soil" of white supremacy.

How else to explain the legacy of white racism and fascism historically inscribed in his signature slogan "Make America Great Again" and his use of the anti-Semitic phrase "America First," long associated with Nazi sympathizers during World War II?[102] How else to explain his support for bringing white supremacists such as Steve Bannon (now resigned), and Jeff Sessions (also resigned), both with a long history of racist comments and actions, into the highest levels of governmental power? Or his retweeting of an anti-Islamic video originally posted by Britain First, a far-right extremist group — an action that was condemned by British Prime Minister, Theresa May?[103]

It gets worse: Trump created a false equivalence between white supremacist neo-Nazi demonstrators and those who opposed them in Charlottesville, Virginia. In doing so, he argued that there were "very fine people on both sides" as if fine people march with protesters carrying Nazi flags, chanting hateful slogans, and shouting: "We will not be replaced by Jews." Trump appears to be unable to differentiate "between people who think like Nazis and people who try to stop them from spewing their hate."[104] Speaking to a group of students at the University of Illinois in September 2018, former President Obama called out Trump for his failure to condemn the violence led by white nationalists and neo-Nazis in Charlottesville, Virginia in 2017. As Obama put it: "We're supposed to stand up to bullies. Not follow them. We're supposed to stand up to discrimination, and we're sure as heck supposed to stand up clearly and unequivocally to Nazi sympathizers. How hard can that be? Saying that Nazis are bad?"[105]

Trump has stated without shame that he is a nationalist. For example, in one of his rallies, he urged his base to use the word nationalism stating, "You know…we're not supposed to use that word. You know what I am? I am a nationalist, Okay? I am a nationalist. Nationalist.

Nothing wrong. Use that word. Use that word." Not only does Trump's embrace of the term stoke racial fears, it ingratiates him with elements of the hard right, particularly white nationalists. After Trump's strong appropriation of the term at an October 2018 rally, Steve Bannon in an interview with Josh Robin indicated, "he was very very pleased Trump used the word 'nationalist.'"[106] Trump has drawn praise from a number of white supremacists including David Duke, the former head of the Ku Klux Klan, the Proud Boys—a vile contemporary version of the Nazi Brown Shirts-and more recently by the alleged New Zealand shooter who in his Christchurch manifesto praised Trump as "a symbol of renewed white identity and common purpose."[107] Trump's use of the term is neither innocent nor a clueless faux pas. In the face of a wave of anti-immigration movements across the globe, it has become code for a thinly veiled racism and signifier for racial hatred.

Trump's lengthy history of racist comments and sympathy for white nationalism and white supremacy offers a clear explanation for his unbroken use of racist language about Mexican immigrants, Muslims, Syrian refugees, and Haitians. It also points to Trump's use of language as part of a larger political and pedagogical project to "mobilize hatred," legitimate the discourse of intimidation, and encourage the American public "to unlearn feelings of care and empathy that lead us to help and feel solidarity with others," as Ruth Ben-Ghiat writes.[108]

Trump's nativism and ignorance work well in the United States because they not only cater to what the American historian Brian Klass refers to as "the tens of millions of Americans who have authoritarian or fascist leanings," they also enable what he calls Trump's attempt at "mainstreaming fascism."[109] He writes:

> Like other despots throughout history, Trump scapegoats minorities and demonizes politically unpopular groups. Trump is racist. He uses his own racism in the service of a divide-and-rule strategy, which is one way that unpopular leaders and dictators maintain power. If you aren't delivering for the people and you're not doing what you said you were going to do, then you need to blame somebody else. Trump has a lot of people to blame.[110]

Trump's language, especially his endorsement of torture and contempt for international norms, normalizes the unthinkable and points to a return to a past that evokes what Ariel Dorfman has called "memories of terror ... parades of hate and aggression by the Ku Klux Klan in the United States and Adolf Hitler's Freikorps in Germany ... executions, torture, imprisonment, persecution, exile, and, yes, book burnings, too."[111] Dorfman also sees in the Trump era echoes of policies carried out under the dictator Pinochet in Chile. According to Dorfman:

> Indeed, many of the policies instituted and attitudes displayed in post-coup Chile would prove models for the Trump era: extreme nationalism, an absolute reverence for law and order, the savage deregulation of business and industry, callousness regarding worker safety, the opening of state lands to unfettered resource extraction and exploitation, the proliferation of charter schools, and the militarization of society. To all this must be added one more crucial trait: a raging anti-intellectualism and hatred of "elites" that, in the case of Chile in 1973, led to the burning of books like ours.[112]

The language of fascism revels in forms of theater that mobilize fear, intolerance, and violence and legitimates authoritarian impulses and further expands the power of the punishing state. Sasha Abramsky makes this point clear in his analysis of Trump's endorsement of torture, his offering of cathartic violence to his audiences, his declaring "entire races and religions to be the enemy," and his "interweaving of a host of fears — of immigrants, of Muslims, of domestic crime and criminals, of changing cultural mores, of refugees, of disease — and a host of deeply authoritarian impulses."[113] Abramsky is on target in claiming that Trump's words amount to more than empty slogans. Instead, his language comes "with consequences, and they legitimize bigotries and hatreds long harbored by many but, for the most part, kept under wraps by the broader society. They give the imprimatur of a major political party to criminal violence."[114] Surely, the increase in hate crimes during Trump's first year of his presidency testifies to the truth of Abramsky's argument.

The history of fascism teaches us that language can operate in the service of violence, desperation, and the troubling landscapes of hatred; moreover, it carries the potential for inhabiting the darkest moments of history. By undermining the concepts of truth and credibility, fascist-oriented language disables the ideological and political vocabularies necessary for a diverse society to embrace shared hopes, responsibilities, and democratic values. Trump's language — like that of older fascist regimes — mutilates contemporary politics, empathy, and serious moral and political criticism, and makes it more difficult to criticize dominant relations of power. Trump's language not only produces a litany of falsehoods, fears, and poisonous attacks on those deemed disposable, it also works hard to prevent people from having an internal dialogue with themselves and others, reducing self-reflection and the ability to question or judge to a scorned and discredited practice.

Trump's fascistic language also fuels the rhetoric of war, a toxic masculinity, white supremacy, anti-intellectualism, and racism. Pathological "levels of hubris, demagoguery, and megalomania" are all present in his discourse, suggesting that the Trump administration marks a destructive moment in American history.[115] What was once an anxious discourse about what Harvey Kaye calls the "possible triumph in America of a fascist-tinged authoritarian regime over liberal democracy" is no longer a matter of speculation but a dark reality.[116] Trump's assault on the truth uses language to discredit the media while labeling his enemies as agents of fake news. Unencumbered by knowledge, Trump is not simply hostile to those who rely on facts and evidence, he works hard to prevent people from being able to distinguish between truth and falsehoods while undermining the institutions vital to a democracy that enable informed judgments. Trump is addicted to the language of a war culture, one that promotes a culture of aggression and fear in the service of violence. Language for Trump is part of a sustained state of war on the cultural front.

Any resistance to the new stage of American authoritarianism has to begin by analyzing its language, the stories it fabricates, the policies it produces, and the cultural, economic, and political institutions that make it possible. Questions have to be raised about how right-wing educational and cultural apparatuses function both politically and pedagogically to shape notions of identity, desire, values, and emotional investments in the discourses of casino capitalism, white supremacy, and a culture of cruelty. Trump's language both shapes and embodies policies that have a powerful consequences on peoples' lives, and such effects must be made visible, tallied up, and used to uncover oppressive forms of power that often hide in the shadows. Rather than treat Trump's lies and fear-mongering as an expression of merely a petulant and dangerous demagogue, it is crucial to analyze their historical roots, the institutions that reproduce and legitimate them, the pundits who promote them, and the effects they have on the texture of everyday life.

Trump's language has a history that must be acknowledged, made known for the suffering it produces, and challenged with an alternative critical and hope-producing narrative. Such a language must be willing to make power visible, uncover the truth, contest falsehoods, and create a formative and critical culture that can nurture and sustain collective resistance to the diverse modes of oppression that characterize the dark times that have overtaken the United States and, increasingly, many other countries. Progressives need a language that both embraces the political potential of diverse forms racial, gender, and sexual identity and the forms of "oppression, exclusion, and marginalization" they make visible while simultaneously working to unify such movements into a broader social formation and political party willing to challenge the core values and institutional structures of the American-style fascism.[117] No form of oppression, however hideous, can be overlooked. In addition, with that critical gaze there must emerge a critical language about what a socialist democracy will look like in the United States. At the same time, there is a need to strengthen and expand the reach and power of established public spheres as sites of critical learning. There is also a need to encourage artists, intellectuals, academics, and other cultural workers to talk, educate, make oppression visible, and challenge the normalizing discourses of casino capitalism, white supremacy, and fascism. There is no room here for a language shaped by political purity or limited to a politics of outrage. A truly democratic vision has a broader and more capacious overview.

Language is not simply an instrument of fear, violence, and intimidation; it is also a vehicle for critique, civic courage, resistance, and engaged and informed agency. We live at a time when the language of democracy has been pillaged. If fascism is to be defeated, there is a need to make education an essential element of politics, and in part, this can be done with a language that unravels falsehoods, systems of oppression, and corrupt relations of power while making clear that an alternative future is possible. Hannah Arendt was right in arguing that language is crucial in highlighting the often hidden "crystalized elements" that make fascism likely. Language is a powerful tool in the search for truth and the condemnation of falsehoods and injustices. We would do well to heed the words of the great Nobel Prize-winning novelist, J. M. Coetzee, who, in a piece of fiction, states that "there will come a day when you and I will need to be told the truth, the real truth….no matter how hard it may be."[118] Too much is at stake in the current historical conjuncture for the truth not to be told. A critical language can guide us in our thinking about the relationship between older elements of fascism and how such practices are emerging in new forms.[119] The search and use of such a language can also reinforce and accelerate the need for young people and others to continue creating alternative public spaces in which critical dialogue, exchange, and a new understanding of politics in its totality can emerge. Focusing on language as a strategic element of political struggle is not only about the search for the truth, it is also about power — both in terms of grasping how it works and using it as part of ongoing struggles that merge the language of critique with the language of possibility, and theory with action. While a critical language does not translate automatically into collective action, it is the precondition for a politics that is more than a short-lived protest, demonstration, or cathartic display of outrage. A truly critical language provides a segue to not look away and remain silent, but to take the risk of imagining a movement for the elimination of neoliberal capitalism rather than simply a call to reform it.

As Wen Stephenson observes, the writings of Hannah Arendt on totalitarianism are more relevant than ever in such dark times. Stephenson writes:

> … [Arendt] warn[s] against the tendency of her contemporaries to look numbly away, to minimize the horrors, to move on, she insists upon squarely confronting the new facts, if only to try to comprehend them. The kind of comprehension she has in mind, though, would come not by taking refuge in old "commonplaces." It requires … "examining and bearing consciously the burden which our century has placed on us — neither denying its existence nor submitting meekly to its weight."[120]

Without a faith in intelligence, critical education, and the power to resist, humanity will be powerless to challenge the threat that casino capitalism, fascism, and right-wing populism pose to the world. All forms of fascism aim at destroying standards of truth, empathy, informed reason, and the institutions that make them possible. The current fight against a nascent fascism in the United States is not only a struggle over economic structures or the commanding heights of corporate power. It is also a struggle over visions, ideas, consciousness, and the power to shift the culture itself. It is also, as Arendt points out, a struggle against "a widespread fear of judging."[121] Without the ability to judge, it becomes impossible to recover words that have meaning, imagine alternative worlds and a future that does not mimic the dark times in which we live, and create a language that changes how we think about ourselves and our relationship to others. Any struggle for a radical democratic socialist order will not take place if "the lessons from our dark past [cannot] be learned and transformed into constructive resolutions" and solutions for struggling for and creating a post-capitalist society.[122]

Progressives need to formulate a new language, alternative cultural spheres, and fresh narratives about freedom, the power of collective struggle, empathy, solidarity, and the promise of a real socialist democracy. We need a new vision that refuses to equate capitalism and democracy, or to normalize greed and excessive competition, or to accept individual interests tied exclusively to monetary accumulation as the highest form of motivation. We need a language and critical comprehension of how power works to enable the conditions in which education is linked to social change and the capacity to promote human agency through the registers of cooperation, compassion, care, love, equality, and a respect for difference. Ariel Dorfman's ode to the struggle over language and its relationship to the power of the imagination, collective resistance, and civic courage offers a fitting reminder of what needs to be done. He writes:

> We must trust that the intelligence that has allowed humanity to stave off death, make medical and engineering breakthroughs, reach the stars, build wondrous temples, and write complex tales will save us again. We must nurse the conviction that we can use the gentle graces of science and reason to prove that the truth cannot be vanquished so easily. To those who would repudiate intelligence, we must say: you will not conquer and we will find a way to convince.[123]

In the end, there is no democracy without informed citizens and no justice without a language critical of injustice.

Chapter 3

The Politics of Neoliberal Fascism

Every age has its own fascism.
— Primo Levi

Introduction

THE NIGHTMARES THAT have shaped the past and await return slightly just below the surface of American society are poised to wreak havoc on us again. America has reached a distinctive crossroads in which the principles and practices of a fascist past and neoliberal present have merged to produce what Philip Roth once called "the terror of the unforeseen." Since the 1970s, American society has lived with the curse of neoliberalism, or what can be called the latest and most extreme stage of predatory capitalism. As part of a broader comprehensive design, neoliberalism's overriding goal is to consolidate power in the hands of the financial elite. As a mode of rationality, it functions pedagogically in multiple cultural sites to ensure that no alternatives to its mode of governance can be either imagined or constructed. Central to its philosophy is the assumption that the market drives not just the economy but all of social life. It construes profit-making as the essence of democracy and consuming as the only operable form of agency. It redefines identities, desires, and values through a market logic that privileges self-interest and unchecked individualism. Under neoliberalism, life-draining and unending competition is a central concept for defining human freedom.

As an economic policy, neoliberalism creates an all-encompassing market guided by the principles of privatization, deregulation, commodification, and the free flow of capital. Advancing these agendas, it weakens unions, radically downsizes the welfare state, and wages an assault on public services such as education, libraries, parks, energy, water, prisons, and public transportation. As the state is hollowed out, big corporations take on the functions of government, imposing severe austerity measures, redistributing wealth upward to the rich and powerful, and reinforcing a notion of society as one of winners and losers.[124] Put simply, neoliberalism gives free rein to finance capital and seeks to liberate the market from any restraints imposed by the state. At present, governments exist primarily to maximize the profits, resources, and the power of the wealthy. As a political project, neoliberalism empties politics of any substance and denounces any viable notion of the social contract. This is evident as a market society replaces a market economy and the language of politics is replaced by market-based discourses and values. Moreover, neoliberalism produces widespread misery and suffering as it weakens any vestige of democracy that interferes with its vision of a self-regulating market. In a winner-take-all society, the burden of merely surviving prevents many people from sharing in the power to govern.

Theoretically, neoliberalism is often associated with the work of Friedrich August von Hayek and the Mont Pelerin Society, Milton Friedman, and the Chicago School of Economics, and most infamously with the politics of Augusto Pinochet in Chile, President Ronald Reagan in the United States, and Prime Minister Margaret Thatcher in England. Politically, it is supported by various right-wing think tanks such as the Heritage Foundation and by billionaires such as the Koch Brothers. The legacy of neoliberalism cannot be separated from its attempt to impose a new narrative in which the logic of the market is more important than the ideals that define a substantive democracy. Moreover, any efforts to "create a more equal society are [considered] both counterproductive and morally corrosive."[125] In this narrative, capital is the subject of history, everything is for sale, the rich get what they deserve, and those who fail to accumulate wealth and power are dismissed as losers, making it easier to refigure massive inequality as virtuous and responsibility as an individual choice. Neoliberalism not only takes aim at the welfare state, social provisions, and public goods, it also cancels out the future. It has produced with a kind of fraudulent weight an all-consuming narrative that treats human misery as normal and its fictional portrayals of those it considers disposable as the apogee of common sense.

Neoliberalism's hatred of democracy, the common good, and the social contract has unleashed generic elements of a fascist past in which white supremacy, ultra-nationalism, and rabid misogyny come together in a toxic mix of militarism, state violence, and a politics of disposability. Modes of fascist expression adapt variously to different political historical contexts assuring racial apartheid-like forms in the postbellum United States and overt encampments and extermination in Nazi Germany. Fascism — with its unquestioning belief in obedience to a powerful cult figure, violence as a form of political purification, hatred as an act of patriotism, racial and ethnic cleansing, and the superiority of a select ethnic or national group — has resurfaced in the United States. In this mix of economic barbarism, political nihilism, racial purity, free market orthodoxy, and ethical somnambulance, a distinctive economic-political formation has been produced that I term neoliberal fascism.

Neoliberalism as the New Fascism

The war against liberal democracy has become a global phenomenon. Authoritarian regimes have spread from Turkey, Poland, Hungary, and India to the United States and a number of other countries.[126] Right-wing populist movements are on the march spewing forth a poisonous mix of ultra-nationalism, white supremacy, anti-Semitism, Islamophobia, and xenophobia. The language of national decline, humiliation, and demonization fuels dangerous proposals and policies aimed at racial purification and social sorting while hyping a masculinization of agency and a militarism reminiscent of past dictatorships. Under current circumstances, the forces that have produced the histories of mass violence, torture, genocide, and fascism have not been left behind. Consequently, it has been more difficult to argue that the legacy of fascism has nothing to teach us regarding how "the question of fascism and power clearly belongs to the present."[127]

Fascism has multiple histories, most connected either to failed democracies in Italy and Germany in the 1930s or to the overthrow of democratic governments by the military, as in Argentina and Chile in the 1970s. Moreover, the history between fascism and populism involves a complex mix of relations over time.[128] What is distinctive about this millennial fascism is that its history of "a violent totalitarian order that led to radical forms of political violence and genocide" has been softened by attempts to recalibrate its postwar legacy to a liberal democratic register.[129] For instance, in Hungary, Turkey, and Poland — and in a number of other emerging fascist states — the term "illiberal democracy" is used as code to allegedly replace a "supposedly outmoded form of liberal democracy."[130] In actuality, the term is used to justify a form of populist authoritarianism whose goal is to attack the very foundations of democracy. These fascist underpinnings are also expanding in the United States. In Trump's bombastic playbook, the notion of "the people" has become a rhetorical tool to legitimate a right-wing mass movement in support of a return to the good old days of American Apartheid.[131] Trump's right-wing populism is born of and breeds "a culture convulsed of hatred and rancor."[132] It is a worldview organized for repulsion willing to intellectually rationalize the murder of a journalist by Saudi Arabia, the killing of children in Yemen, and the forcible separation of migrant families at the southern border.

Democracy is the scourge of neoliberalism and its ultimate humiliation

As the ideas, values, and institutions crucial to a democracy have withered under a savage neoliberalism, which has been 50 years in the making, fascistic notions of racial superiority, social cleansing, apocalyptic populism, hyper-militarism, and ultra-nationalism have gained in intensity, moving from the repressed recesses of US history to the centers of state and corporate power.[133] Decades of mass inequality, wage slavery, the collapse of the manufacturing sector, tax giveaways

to the financial elite, and savage austerity policies that drove a frontal attack on the welfare state have further strengthened fascistic discourses and redirected populist anger against vulnerable populations
and undocumented immigrants, Muslims, the racially oppressed,
women, LBGTQ+ people, public servants, critical intellectuals, and
workers. Not only has neoliberalism undermined the basic elements
of democracy by escalating the mutually reinforcing dynamics of economic inequality and political inequality — accentuating the downhill
spiral of social and economic mobility — it has also created conditions
that make fascist principles more attractive.

Under these accelerated circumstances, neoliberalism and fascism
conjoin and advance in a comfortable and mutually compatible
movement that connects the worse excesses of capitalism with authoritarian "strong man" ideals — the veneration of war; a hatred of
reason and truth; a celebration of ultra-nationalism and racial purity;
the suppression of freedom and dissent; a culture which promotes
lies, spectacles, scapegoating the other, a discourse of deterioration,
and brutal violence, ultimately erupting in state violence in heteroge-
neous forms. In the Trump administration, neoliberalism is on steroids
and represents a realignment — a convergence of the worse dimensions and excesses of gangster capitalism with the fascist ideals of
white nationalism and racial supremacy associated with the horrors
of the past.[134]

Neoliberal structural transformation has both undermined and refigured "the principles, practices, cultures, subjects, and institution of
democracy understood as rule by the people."[135] Since the early sev-
enties, the neoliberal project has mutated into a revolt against human
rights and democracy, and created a powerful narrative that refigures
freedom and authority so as to legitimate and produce massive inequities in wealth and power.[136] Its practices of offshoring, restructuring
everything according to the dictates of profit margins, slashing progressive taxation, eliminating corporate regulations, unchecked privatization, and the ongoing commercializing of all social interactions
"inflicts alienating misery" on a polity vulnerable to fascist ideals, rhetoric, and politically extremist movements.[137]

Furthermore, the merging of neoliberalism and fascism has accelerated as civic culture is eroded, notions of shared citizenship and
responsibility disappear, and reason and informed judgment are re-

placed by the forces of civic illiteracy. State sanctioned attacks on the truth, facts, and scientific reason in Trump's America are camouflaged as one might expect of the first reality TV president — by a corporate-controlled culture of vulgarity that merges celebrity culture with a non-stop spectacle of violence. As language and politics are emptied of any substantive meaning, an authoritarian populism is emboldened and fills the airways and the streets with sonic blasts of racism, anti-Semitism, and violence. The *New York Times* columnist Michelle Goldberg rightly observes that Trump makes it difficult to hold onto any sense of what is normal given his relentless attempts to upend the rule of law, justice, ethics, and democracy itself. She writes:

> The country has changed in the past year, and many of us have grown numb after unrelenting shocks. What now passes for ordinary would have once been inconceivable. The government is under the control of an erratic racist who engages in nuclear brinkmanship on Twitter … He publicly pressures the Justice Department to investigate his political opponents. He's called for reporters to be jailed, and his administration demanded that a sportscaster who criticized him be fired. Official government statements promote his hotels. You can't protest it all; you'd never do anything else. After the election, many liberals pledged not to "normalize" Trump. But one lesson of this year is that we don't get to decide what normal looks like.[138]

There is more at work here than the kind of crass entertainment that mimics celebrity culture. As Pankaj Mishra argues we live in a world in which there is a "rout of such basic human emotions as empathy, compassion, and pity."[139] This is a world in which "the puzzle of our age is how this essential foundation of civic life went missing from our public conversation."[140] Part of that puzzle undermining civic culture and its institutions can be found in an unprecedented corporate take-over over of the US government and the reemergence of elements of totalitarianism in new forms. At stake here is the power of an authoritarian ideology that fuels a hyperactive exploitative economic order, apocalyptic nationalism, and feral appeals to racial cleansing that produce what Paul Street has called the nightmare of capitalism.[141]

Neoliberalism strips democracy of any substance by promoting an irrational belief in the ability of the market to solve all social problems and shape all aspects of society. This shift from a market economy to a market-driven society has been accompanied by a savage attack on equality, the social contract, and social provisions as wages have been gutted, pensions destroyed, health care put out of reach for millions, job security undermined, and access to crucial public goods such as public and higher education considerably lessened for the lower and middle classes.

In the current historical moment, neoliberalism represents more than a form of hyper capitalism, it also denotes the death of democracy if not politics itself. Defining all aspects of society in economic terms, finance and corporate capital defines all behavior through the lens of neoliberal reason. One consequence is that the most fundamental elements of democracy — including the vocabularies that define it, the spaces of deliberation that make it imaginable, and the formative cultures that create the informed citizens that make it possible — are under siege. Anis Shivani's articulation of the threat neoliberalism poses to democracy is worth quoting at length:

> Neoliberalism believes that markets are self-sufficient unto themselves, that they do not need regulation, and that they are the best guarantors of human welfare. Everything that promotes the market, i.e., privatization, deregulation, mobility of finance and capital, abandonment of government-provided social welfare, and the reconception of human beings as human capital, needs to be encouraged, while everything that supposedly diminishes the market, i.e., government services, regulation, restrictions on finance and capital, and conceptualization of human beings in transcendent terms, is to be discouraged.[142]

What is particularly distinctive about the conjuncture of neoliberalism and fascism is how the full-fledged liberation of capital now merges with an out-and-out attack on the racially oppressed and vulnerable populations considered disposable. Not only do the oppressive political, economic, and financial structures of casino capitalism bear down on people's lives, but there is also a frontal attack on the shared understandings and beliefs that hold a people together. One crucial and distinctive place where neoliberalism and fascism converge is in the undermining of social bonds and moral boundaries. Displacement, disintegration, atomization, social isolation, and deracination have a

long history in the United States, which has been aggressively exploit-
ed and intensified by Trump, taking on a distinctive right-wing 21st
century register. More is revealed here than the heavy neoliberal toll of
social abandonment. There is also, under the incessant pedagogical
propaganda of right-wing and corporate-controlled media, a culture
that has become cruel and cultivates an appetite for maliciousness
that undermines the capacity for empathy, making people willing par-
ticipants in their violent exclusion.

While there is much talk about the influence of Trumpism, there are
few analyses that examine its culture of cruelty and politics of disposability. Such cultures reach back to the founding of the United States
as a settler-colonial society. How else does one explain a long line of
state-endorsed atrocities — the genocide waged against Native Americans in order to take their land, enslavement and breeding of black
people for profit and labor, and the passage of the Second Amendment to arm and enforce white supremacy over those populations?
The legacies of those horrific roots of US history are coded into Trump-
ist slogans, as I mentioned previously about "making America great
again," and egregiously defended through appeals to American excep-
tionalism.

More recent instances indicative of the rising culture of bigoted cruelty and mechanisms of erasure in US politics include the racially motivated drug wars, policies that shifted people from welfare to
workfare without offering training programs or childcare, and morally
indefensible tax reforms that will "require huge budget cuts in safety
net programs for vulnerable children and adults."[143] As Marian Wright
Edelman points out, such actions are particularly alarming and cruel
at a time when "millions of America's children today are suffering from
hunger, homelessness, and hopelessness. Nearly 13.2 million children
are poor — almost one in five. About 70 percent of them are children of
color who will be a majority of our children by 2020. More than 1.2 million are homeless. About 14.8 million children struggle against hunger
in food insecure households."[144]

Trump is both a symptom and enabler of this culture, one that per-
mits him to delight in taunting black athletes, embrace the ideology of
white nationalism, and mocking anyone who disagrees with him. This
is the face of a kind of Wilhelm Reichian psycho-politics with its mix
of violence, repression, theatrics, incoherency, and spectacularized ig-

norance. Trump makes clear that the dream of the Confederacy is still with us, that moral panics thrive within a culture of rancid racism: "a background of obscene inequalities, progressive deregulation of labor markets, and a massive expansion in the ranks of the precariat."[145] All of this suggests that fascism is more than faint memory unrelated to the present moment in American history.

Irish journalist, Fintan O'Toole, warns that fascism unravels the ethical imagination through a process in which individuals eventually "learn to think the unthinkable," — followed, he writes, "by a crucial next step, usually the trickiest of all." He writes:

> You have to undermine moral boundaries, inure people to the acceptance of acts of extreme cruelty. Like hounds, people have to be blooded. They have to be given the taste for savagery. Fascism does this by building up the sense of threat from a despised out-group. This allows the members of that group to be dehumanized. Once that has been achieved, you can gradually up the ante, working through the stages from breaking windows to extermination.[146]

What is often labeled as an economic crisis in American society is also a crisis of morality, of sociality, and of community. Since the 1970s, increasingly unregulated capitalism has hardened into a form of market fundamentalism that has accelerated the hollowing out of democracy through its capacity to reshape the commanding institutions of American society, making it vulnerable to the fascist solutions proposed by Trump. As an integrated system of structures, ideologies, and values, neoliberalism economizes every aspect of life, separates economic activity from social costs, and depoliticizes the public through corporate-controlled disimagination machines that trade in post-truth narratives, enshrine the spectacle of violence, debase language, and distort history. Neoliberalism now wages a battle against any viable notion of the social, solidarity, the collective imagination, the public good, and the institutions that support them. Wendy Brown rightly insists that democracy comes in many forms and does not offer any political guarantees, but without it, there is no acceptable future. She writes:

> Without it, however, we lose the language and frame by which we are accountable to the present and entitled to

make our own future, the language and frame with which we might contest the forces otherwise claiming that future.[147]

The Crisis of Reason and Fantasies of Freedom

As more and more power is concentrated in the hands of a corporate and financial elite, freedom is defined exclusively in market terms; inequality is cast as a virtue, and the logic of privatization heaps contempt upon civic compassion and the welfare state. The fatal after-effect is that neoliberalism has emerged as the new face of fascism.[148] With the 50 year advance of neoliberalism, freedom has become its opposite, a parody of its true meaning. Moreover, democracy — once the arc of civic freedom — now becomes its enemy since democratic governance no longer takes priority over the unchecked workings of the market. Neoliberalism undermines both social ties and the public good and, in doing so, weakens the idea of shared responsibilities and moral obligations. As Zygmunt Bauman argues, "ethical tranquilliza-tion" is now normalized under the assumption that freedom is limited to the right to only advance one's own interests and the interests of the markets.[149] Freedom in the neoliberal playbook disavows any notion of responsibility outside of the responsibility to oneself.

As Wendy Brown makes clear, democracy is now viewed as the enemy of markets and "politics is cast as the enemy to freedom, to order, and to progress."[150] Politics now becomes a mix of regressive notions of freedom and authority whose purpose is to protect market-driven principles and practices. What disappears in this all-encompassing reach of capital is the notion of civic freedom, which is replaced by securiti-zation organized to protect the lawless workings of the profit motive and the savagery of neoliberal austerity policies. Moreover, as freedom becomes privatized, it feeds a lack of interest in politics and breeds moral indifference. Democratic passions are directed towards private pleasures, the demands of citizenship are undermined, and the public sphere withers as self-interest becomes one of the primary organiz-ing principle of society. Under neoliberalism, the spheres of intimacy and interpersonal relations begin to disappear and are replaced by an ideological and economic system that constructs individuals as objects of capital within a system of harsh competitive relations and commercial exchange. As it becomes more difficult for people to think critically, the market provides them with a consumerist model that both infantilizes and depoliticizes people. As the terrain of politics, agency, and social relations loses its moral bearings, the passions of a fascist past are unleashed and society increasingly begins to resemble a war culture, blood sport and form of cage fighting.

In this instance, the oppressed are not only cheated out of history, they are led to believe that under neoliberal fascism there are no alternatives and that the future can only imitate the present. Not only does this position suppress any sense of responsibility and resistance, it produces what Timothy Snyder calls "a kind of sleepwalking, and has to end with a crash."[151] The latter is reinforced by a government that believes that the truth is dangerous and that reality begins with a tweet that signals both the legitimation of endless lies and forms of power that infantilize and depoliticize because they leave no room for standards of language capable of holding power accountable. Even worse, Trump's war on language and truth does more than limit freedom to competing fictions, it also erases the distinction between moral depravity and justice, good and evil. As I have said elsewhere, "Trump's Ministry of Fake News works incessantly to set limits on what is thinkable, claiming that reason, evidence, consistency, and logic no longer serve the truth because the latter are crooked ideological devices used by enemies of the state. 'Thought crimes' are now labeled as 'fake news.'"[152]

Timothy Snyder is right in arguing that "to abandon facts is to abandon freedom. If nothing is true, then no one can criticize power because there is no basis upon which to do so. If nothing is true, then all is spectacle."[153] More startling is the assumption that in an age of deep divisions, exploitation, and precarity what matters is not only whether something is true or false but also the willingness of people to identify with the seductive lure of a consistent fascist narrative in which people willingly suspend "their capacity for distinguishing between the truth and falsehood, between reality and fiction."[154] Hannah Arendt rightly argued that "what was new and dangerous to the American republic was not lying, but a situation in which lies had become indistinguishable from the truth."[155] Needless to say, there is more at stake here than the creation and normalization of a culture of lying and what Walter Benjamin, Guy Debord and others identified as the theatricalization of politics, there is also the threat to democracy itself.

We do not live in a post-truth world and never have. On the contrary, we live in a pre-truth world where the truth has yet to arrive. As one of the primary currencies of politics, lies have a long history in the United States. For instance, state sponsored lies played a crucial ideological role in pushing the US into wars in Vietnam, Iraq, and Afghanistan, legitimated the use of torture under the Bush administration, and covered up the crimes of the financial elite in producing the economic crisis of 2008. Moreover, we have been living the lie of neoliberalism and white nationalism for over forty years and because of the refusal to face up to that lie, the United States has slipped into the abyss of an updated American version of fascism of which Trump is both a symptom and endpoint.

The post-truth society is a state-sponsored diversion and spectacle. Its purpose is to camouflage a moral and political crisis that has put into play a set of brutal neoliberal arrangements. Rather than view truth as the currency of democracy, Trump and his acolytes view it and democracy as the enemy of corporate power and the financial elite. Such arrangements put democracy at risk and create an educational and political project receptive to the political currency of white supremacy. As a master of schlock performance, Trump tweets and speaks largely to his angry resentful base often using crude language in which the threat of violence and repression appears to function for his audience as a source of "romance, pleasure, and fantasy."[156] These core supporters represent, at best, what Philip Roth once called the "uneducated and overburdened." But they also cultivate what Erin Aubry Kaplan calls "the very worst American impulses, from xenophobia to know-nothingism to disdain for social necessities such as public education and clean water … [and their] signature quality is racism."[157]

Restaging Fascism within Democracy

Rather than disappear into the memory hole of history, fascism has reappeared in a different form in the United States, echoing Theodor Adorno's warning: "I consider the survival of National Socialism *within* democracy to be potentially more menacing than the survival of fascist tendencies *against* democracy."[158] Theorists, novelists, historians, and writers that include such luminaries as Hannah Arendt, Sinclair Lewis, Bertram Gross, Umberto Eco, Robert O. Paxton, Timothy Snyder, Susan Sontag, and Sheldon Wolin have argued convincingly that fascism remains an ongoing danger and has the ability to become relevant under new conditions. In the aftermath of the fall of Nazi Germany, Hannah Arendt warned that totalitarianism was far from a thing of the past because the conditions of extreme precarity and uncertainty that produce it were likely to crystalize into new forms.[159]

What Arendt thought was crucial for each generation to recognize was that presence of the Nazi camps and the policy of extermination should be understood not simply as the logical outcome of a totalitarian society or a return of the past, but also for what their histories suggest about forecasting a "possible model for the future."[160] The nightmare of fascism's past cannot escape memory because it needs to be retold over and over again so as to recognize when it is happening again. Talk of a fascist politics emerging in the United States is often criticized as either a naive exaggeration or a failure to acknowledge the strength of liberal institutions. Yet, the case can be made that rather than harbor an element of truth, such criticism further normalizes the very fascism it critiques, allowing the extraordinary and implausible to become ordinary. After decades of the neoliberal nightmare both in the United States and abroad, the mobilizing passions of fascism have been unleashed unlike anything we have seen since the 1930s. Politics has turned pornographic. Culture has become an extension of war, and, as the artist Nicole Eisenman observes, overdrawn [fascistic] "masculine archetypes...drive each cycle of our fresh hell from TeaPartiers to frat guys."[161]

 The architects and managers of extreme capitalism have used the crisis of economic inequality and its "manifestly brutal and exploitative
arrangements" to sow social divisions and resurrect the discourse of
racial cleansing and white supremacy.[162] In doing so, they have not
only tapped into the growing collective suffering and anxieties of millions of Americans in order to redirect their anger and despair through
a culture of fear and discourse of dehumanization, they have also
turned critical ideas to ashes by disseminating a toxic mix of racialized categories, ignorance, and a militarized spirit of white nationalism. The renowned historian of fascism Robert O. Paxton argues in his
Anatomy of Fascism that the texture of American fascism would not
mimic traditional European forms but would be rooted in the language, symbols, and culture of everyday life. He writes:

> No swastikas in an American fascism, but Stars and Stripes
> (or Stars and Bars) and Christian crosses. No fascist salute,
> but mass recitations of the Pledge of Allegiance. These sym-
> bols contain no whiff of fascism in themselves, of course, but
> an American fascism would transform them into obligatory
> litmus tests for detecting the internal enemy.[163]

Given the alarming signs that have come into play under the Trump
administration, it is hard to look away and condone the suppression of
both the history and language of fascism and its relevance for comprehending the United States' flight from the promise and ideals of a substantive democracy. This is not to suggest that the only template for
addressing the legacy of fascism is to point to Nazi Germany, the most
extreme of the fascist states, or, for that matter, to Mussolini's brand of
fascism. Not only does the comparison not work, but it tends to understand fascist ideals only against their most extreme expressions.

While it is true that the United States may not be putting millions in
gas chambers or promoting genocide, there remain, nonetheless,
reworked elements of the past in the present. For instance, there are
already echoes of the past in existing and expanding infrastructures
of punishment — amounting to a carceral state — that have been in
place but have grown exponentially for the past four decades. In fact,
the United States has the largest prison system in the world with over
2.5 million people incarcerated. Astonishingly, this figure does not include immigrant detention centers and other forms of encampment
around the US border with Mexico. The visibility of this state autho-

rized punishing apparatus and its similarity to a fascist history was on display with the caging of young immigrant children who were forcibly separated from their parents at the southern border for months at a time. Immigrant children and family members increasingly are deprived of due process and disappear into a vast gulag of detention centers spread throughout the United States. The "black sites" of the Bush administration have come home and marked another register of extreme violence under the auspices of legal illegalities.

Reports of widespread abuse of imprisoned unaccompanied migrant children separated from their parents received an enormous amount of attention in the mainstream press. Detained under inhumane and cruel conditions, many of these children in government detention centers have been drugged, sexually abused, and subject to a range of inhumane actions. In Texas, a federal judge ordered a Texas detention center to stop forcing children to take psychotropic drugs such as Clonazepam, Divalproex, Benztropine, and Duloxetine in order to control their behavior.[164] *ProPublica* reported that sexual abuse is widespread in detention centers for children and cited "hundreds of allegations of sexual offenses, fights, and missing children."[165] Even the most vulnerable and youngest of children have not been protected from such abuse. For instance, according to *The Nation*, a six-year-old migrant girl who had been separated from her mother and placed in an immigrant detention center under the Trump administration's noxious separation policy was allegedly sexually abused.[166] Needless to say, such actions, policies, and institutions resonate with deeply disturbing events of a dark past for which the violent separation of families was a hallmark feature of fascist cruelty, barbarism, and brutality. The editors of *The Washington Post* stated that Trump's removal of children from their parents represents a form of "bureaucratic barbarism on an epic scale. And in its aftermath, there is no accountability, and scarcely a glimmer of regret, for the suffering it inflicted on human beings."[167] Near the end of 2018, the government shipped, in the middle of the night, hundreds of immigrant children to a barren desert that is the site of a detention tent camp in the border town of Tornillo, Texas.[168] Before it was closed down in December 2018, it held as many as 2700 children. No schooling was provided for them, and they have limited access to legal services. Taylor Levy, a legal coordinator at a non-profit immigrant shelter in El Paso, said that kids she spoke to described tent city as a form of punishment. Levy described "Tornillo [as] prison-camp like."[169] The Trump administration's response to these criticisms has been to call for more funds to expand its detention centers, impose further restrictions on undocumented immigrants, and strip $10 million from FEMA to fund the US Immigration and Customs Enforcement's terroristic practice of detaining and deporting of immigrants.[170]

Some pundits and academics have argued that the huge public outcry against the separation of children from their parents proves that the US is not a fascist society. Actually, all it really proves is that the most extreme policies at work in Trump's America can still provoke moral outrage. But such outrage, when disconnected from warnings to be learned from a fascist past in which similar events took place, is simply an example of an isolated form of protest that ignores historical memory as a tool to understand how elements of a fascist past crystallize today in different forms. One might actually say that Trump's zero tolerance policy was simply a test run for measuring the speed at which he could advance his fascist agenda. It is also important to note that the protest did nothing to get the Trump administration to release hundreds of children who are still being held without their parents, nor has it stopped the terrorist tactics produced by ICE. The new form of fascism updated under the Trump administration does not require the overthrow of democracy in one grand sweep, nor does it mean that the taste for savagery produced in numerous policies of suffering and cruelty won't be resisted by the public in some cases.

It is against this background that I believe that the current debates that discuss whether the United States under Donald Trump is a fascist society are unproductive. The argument against this recognition generally proceeds by claiming that fascism is either a relic of the past, fixed in a certain historical period and having no relevance to the present, or that the differences between Trump's policies and those of Hitler and Mussolini are different enough so as to make any comparison irrelevant. Many commentators denounce any reference between Trump and a Nazi past as exaggerated or inapplicable. In this view, fascism is always somewhere else, relegated to a time and a place that suggests an accommodating distance, one that runs the risk of disconnecting historical memory and the horrors of another age from the possibility of fascism resurrected in a different form, newly attuned to its moment. We live in an age in which there is a terror on the part of critics to imagine the plasticity of fascism.

The Mobilizing Passions of Fascism

Fascism is neither a static nor fixed moment in history, and the forms it takes do not have to imitate earlier historical models. It is an authoritarian ideology and a form of political behavior defined by what the historian Robert O. Paxton calls a series of "mobilizing passions."[171] These include: an open assault on democracy, the call for a strongman, a contempt for human weakness, an obsession with hypermasculinity, an aggressive militarism, an appeal to national greatness, a disdain for the feminine, an investment in the language of cultural decline, the disparaging of human rights, the suppression of dissent, a propensity for violence, disdain for intellectuals, a hatred of reason, and fantasies of racial superiority and eliminationist polices aimed at social cleansing.[172]

The ghost of fascism has to be retrieved from history and restored to a "proper place in the discussions of the moral and political limits of what is acceptable,"[173] especially at a moment when the crisis of democracy cannot be separated from the crisis of neoliberalism. As a heuristic tool to compare different forms of state power, the legacy of fascism offers an opportunity to recognize when authoritarian signposts are on the horizon. For example, under Trump, the spectacle reigns supreme, harking back to an earlier time in history when bravado, armed ignorance, and theatrical performances provided a model of community that squelched memory, domesticated thought, and opened the door for a galvanizing figure's followers to disavow their role as critical agents in favor of becoming passive, if not willful, spectators. With regard to the present, it is crucial to recognize the ascendency of Trump politically within, rather than against, the flow of history.

Fascism in the United States has arrived slowly by subversion from within. Its roots have been on display for decades and emerged most visibly with Bush and then Obama's war on terror. Bush, in particular, embraced unapologetically a raw display of power that permitted torture, domestic spying, secret prisons, kill lists, laws sanctioning indefinite detention and warrantless searches. Obama did little to correct these legal illegalities and endorsed a degree of militarism that was as shameful as it was destructive. As the noted social critic Carl Bogs writes:

> His imperial ventures spanned many countries — Afghanistan, Iraq, Syria, Libya, Somalia along with proxy interventions in Yemen and Pakistan. He ordered nearly 100,000 bombs and missiles delivered against defenseless targets, a total greater than that of the more widely-recognized warmonger George W. Bush's total of 70,000 against five countries... Meanwhile, throughout his presidency, Obama conducted hundreds of drone attacks in the Middle East, ...all run jointly (and covertly) by the CIA and Air Force.[174]

Trump will breathe new life into this legacy of militarism both at home and abroad further extending the underlying militarism of neoliberal fascism. Instead of the sudden appearance on American streets of thugs, brown shirts, purges, and massive state violence — the state violence waged against African Americans notwithstanding — fascism has been resurrected through the enabling force of casino capitalism, which has unleashed and mobilized a range of economic, political, religious, and educational fundamentalisms.

This manifestation of fascism is most obvious in the subversion of power by the financial and corporate robber barons, the taming of dissent, the cultivation of tribal identities, and the celebration of orbits of self-interest and hyper individualism over any sense of common purpose. It is also evident in the convergence and growing power of ultra-nationalism and white supremacy, the privatization of public goods, the transformation of elections into a battle among billionaires, the push towards regulatory rollbacks, especially in the energy industries, and the ongoing production of a culture of greed and cruelty. But, as Wendy Brown makes clear, it is increasingly obvious in a right-wing populist revolt generated by neoliberalism's decimation of "livelihoods and neighborhoods," while "evacuating and delegitimizing democracy," "devaluing knowledge apart from job training" and hastening the "eroding of national sovereignty."[175]

Orthodoxy, especially under Trump, has transformed education into a workstation for ignorance where harsh discipline is metered out to undocumented immigrants, vulnerable populations, Muslims, and others considered disposable. All of this takes place against a political culture that has been utterly corrupted by big money and morally deficient bankers, hedge fund managers, and corporate moguls.[176] The Trump administration has produced a number of scandals suggesting an almost unmatched level of administrative corruption and criminogenic behavior. For instance, former Environmental Protection Agency head Scott Pruitt used taxpayer money to fund an endless number of personal expenses. White House Staff Secretary Rob Porter was forced to leave the White House once it was made public that he physically abused his wife. Treasury Secretary Steve Mnuchin used a military jet on his honeymoon while Secretary of Housing and Urban Development Ben Carson spent $31,000 on a dining set for his office and later placed the blame for the purchase on his wife. Tom Price, the former Health and Human Services Secretary, was fired after spending over $1 million in taxpayer money for using private planes and military aircraft for himself and his family.[177] In addition, many evangelicals and other religious groups support, or are complicit, with a president who sides with white supremacists and trades in the language of viciousness and brutality.[178] As of March 2019, under the Mueller investigation, a growing number of top Trump associates have pleaded guilty to federal crimes. The more notable include Michael Flynn, the president's former national security adviser; George Papadopoulos, a former Trump campaign adviser; Paul Manafort, former Trump campaign chairman; Rick Gates, Mr. Manafort's business partner and deputy campaign chairman; and Mr. Cohen, whose case is being handled by federal prosecutors in Manhattan. The irony here is hard to miss given that Trump rode to power claiming he was going to "drain the swamp" and launch an aggressive attack on government corruption. Instead, he expanded and deepened the swamp, creating a government that brazenly engaged in corrupt practices without any apologies.

Widespread corruption in the Trump administration is matched by a political order that trades in the abuse of power and normalizes acts of cruelty, lawlessness, and racism throughout the social order. The corporate state fueled by a market fundamentalism and a long legacy of racial apartheid has imposed almost incomprehensible cruelty on poor and vulnerable black populations. The merging of neoliberalism and fascist elements of white supremacy and systemic racism is particularly evident in the environmental racism, dilapidated schools, police violence, and air pollution that have come to light recently.[179]

The short list includes going so far as to sacrifice poor black children in Flint, Michigan to the perils of lead poisoning in order to increase profits, subjecting the population of Puerto Rico to unnecessary despair by refusing to provide adequate government services after Hurricane Maria,[180] and creating conditions in which "America's youngest children, some 47 percent [under the age of five] live in low-income or poor households."[181]

As UN Special Rapporteur Philip Alston reports, amid a massive concentration of wealth among the upper one percent in the United States, 40 million people live in poverty and 18.5 million Americans live in extreme poverty. Neoliberal policies are "aggressively regressive" in their promoting of harsh work requirements for welfare recipients, cutting back programs to feed poor children, and a willingness to spend millions to incarcerate young undocumented children.[182] The brutality, if not state terrorism, at work here is evident in recent revelations that not only are more children than ever held in government custody, but that children as young as two years old are appearing in federal immigration courts.[183] All the while, the Trump administration has shifted massive resources to the wealthy as a result of a tax policy that shreds 1.5 trillion dollars from the federal budget.

Since the 1970s, wages have stagnated, banks have cheated millions out of their homes through rigged mortgage policies, and the political power brokers have imposed financial ruin on minorities of class and race.[184] The war against poverty initiated by the Johnson administration had been transformed into a war on poverty by Reagan and has accelerated and achieved its apotheosis under the Trump regime. With a pathological enthusiasm, Trump's morally bereft Republican Congress has cut crucial benefits for the poor such as the food stamp program while also imposing harsh work requirements on Medicare recipients. At work here is the self-serving and vindictive neoliberal belief that government is bad when it gets in the way of markets and does not serve the interest of the rich. What we are witnessing, especially under the Trump administration, is an intensification of a politics of disposability. This speaks to a growing and perverse state sanctioned investment in the degradation and punishment of the most at-risk individuals, those considered other, and those unable to participate in the consumer society. They are part of an ever-expanding army of individuals viewed by the state as disposable and dispatched to the garbage dumps of society.[185]

One consequence is a beleaguered American landscape marked by a growing opioid crisis, the criminalization of peaceful protests, race-based environmental poisoning, shorter longevity rates for middle-age Americans, and an incarceration rate that ranks as the highest in the world.

The war on democracy has also morphed into a war on youth as more and more children are homeless, subjected to mass school shootings, inhabit schools modeled after prisons, and increasingly ushered into the school-to-prison pipeline and disciplinary apparatuses that treats them as criminals.[186] For example, data from the United States Census Bureau indicates that from 2016 to 2017 the rate of poverty among young children, primarily infants and toddlers, rose markedly, especially among black and Hispanic infants. The tragedy of such immiseration goes beyond the data that make such poverty visible. What is often left out of such data is the fact that poverty at this young age can have lifelong effects on all aspects of one's life. Yet, this makes the data produced by the study all the more shocking and shameful. According to *Child Trends*:

> One in five infants and toddlers (19.9 percent of children ages birth through two years) were poor. The disparities in poverty levels among infants and toddlers by race and ethnicity are particularly concerning: in 2017, nearly one in three black infants and toddlers (32.7 percent), and more than one in four Hispanic infants and toddlers (27.3 percent) lived in poverty, compared to approximately one in nine white, non-Hispanic infants and toddlers (11.8 percent). The most dramatic disparities are among infants (up to one year of age). While the overall percentage of infants living in poverty significantly increased between 2016 and 2017 from 17.2 percent to 20.2 percent, the largest increases were among black and Hispanic infants, for whom the poverty rate rose by six and eight percentage points — 28.5 to 34.4 percent and 20.7 to 28.4 percent, respectively.[187]

Rethinking the Politics of Inverted Totalitarianism

What is essential to understand is that neoliberalism is not only a more extreme element of capitalism, it has also enabled the emergence of a radical restructuring of institutional power and in doing so converges with a style of fascism suited to the American context. Sheldon Wolin's book, *Democracy Incorporated*, was one of the first to analyze the transformation of a capitalist democracy into what he called an inverted form of totalitarianism. According to Wolin, the political state was replaced by a corporate state that exploits all but the ruling classes, empties politics of any substance through rigged elections, uses the power of capital to define citizens largely as consumers of products, and applies the power of the corporate state as a battering ram to push through policies that strengthen the power of capital. Echoes of fascism are resonating in the rise of Republican candidates who are unapologetic racists openly running on platforms designed to limit the voting rights of African-Americans. For instance, Brian Kamp, the former Georgia secretary of state and elected Republican governor in 2018 is known for devoting "his time in office to a ruthless campaign of voter suppression."[188]

For Wolin, neoliberalism was the endpoint of a long process "to transform everything — every object, every living thing, every fact on the planet — in its image."[189] He believed that this new right-wing political formation and form of sovereignty in which economics dominated politics was hostile to both social spending and the welfare state. Wolin rightly argued that under neoliberalism, political sovereignty is largely replaced by economic sovereignty as corporate power takes over the reins of governance.

The dire consequence, as David Harvey points out, is that "raw money power wielded by the few undermines all semblances of democratic governance."[190] As George Monbiot points out, congressional candidates who spend the most money win elections, corporations back candidates that support their interests such as less taxation for the rich, and truckloads of dark money disguised as public advocacy rule the airwaves during elections.[191] All kinds of methods are used to prevent millions from voting, many of whom are poor and black. Policy is now fashioned by lobbyists representing big businesses such as the pharmaceutical and health insurance companies, going so far in the case of the drug companies to catalyze the opioid crisis in order to increase their profits.[192]

Wolin's great contribution to theories of totalitarianism lies in his ability to lay bare the authoritarian economic tendencies in neoliberalism and its threat to democracy. What he did not do is associate neoliberalism and its enervating effects closely enough with certain legacies of fascism, and in this absence, he was unable to predict the resurgence of right-wing populist politics in the United States and the ascendant fascist investments in white supremacy, racial sorting, ultra-nationalism, a war on youth, the attack on women's reproductive rights, and a race-inspired eliminationist politics of disposability. What he underemphasized was that neoliberalism impoverished not only society economically while serving the interests of the rich, but it also created a powerful narrative that normalizes political inaction as it shifted the weight and responsibility of all social problems onto the individual rather than the society.[193]

In the age of neoliberal myth-making, systemic deficiencies such as homelessness and precarious employment are now relegated to individual failures, character deficits, and moral turpitude. Correspondingly, notions of the social, systemic, and public disappear, serving to expand the base of those who feel voiceless and powerless, opening them up to the crude and simplistic emotional appeals of authoritarian figures, such as Donald Trump. In truly demagogic fashion, Trump promises a new world order that will be fashioned out of the rhetorical bombast of dehumanization and a weaponized appeal to fear and hate. As the poor and discarded vanish from the political discourse of democracy, they become susceptible to a "volatility and the fury that [mutilates] contemporary politics that thrives on an appetite for authoritarian and fascistic impulses.[194]

Fascism by Trial in the Age of Trump

In a thoughtful analysis, Fintan O'Toole asserts that neoliberalism creates the conditions for enabling what he calls a trial run for a full-blown state of contemporary fascism. He writes:

> To grasp what is going on in the world right now, we need to reflect on two things. One is that we are in a phase of trial runs. The other is that what is being trialed is fascism — a word that should be used carefully but not shirked when it is so clearly on the horizon. Forget "post-fascist" — what we are living with is pre-fascism. Rather than overthrow democracy in one full swipe, it has to be undermined through rigged elections, the creation of tribal identities, and legitimated through a propaganda machine so effective that it creates for its followers a universe of "alternative facts" impervious to unwanted realities... Fascism doesn't arise suddenly in an existing democracy. It is not easy to get people to give up their ideas of freedom and civility. You have to do trial runs that, if they are done well, serve two purposes. They get people used to something they may initially recoil from; and they allow you to refine and calibrate. This is what is happening now, and we would be fools not to see it.[195]

Ultra-nationalist and contemporary versions of fascism are gaining traction across the globe in countries such as Greece (Golden Dawn), Hungary (Jobbik), India (Bharatiya Janata Party), and Italy (the League) and countless others. Needless to say, they have been emboldened by Trump who has both displayed a close admiration for authoritarian leaders such as Russia's Putin, Turkey's Erdogan, and China's Xi Jinping, among others. He recently praised North Korean leader Kim Jong-un for his "intellect and personality" and without irony stated: "He speaks and his people sit up at attention. I want my people to do the same."[196] He has publicly accused Democrats in Congress for not standing following his State of the Union Address and has conducted a foreign policy that trashes Western allies while celebrating authoritarian strongmen.

In addition, Trump consistently promotes extremist policies, surrounds himself with far right-wing ideologues such as former Attorney General Jeff Sessions, John Bolton, and Stephen Miller — all hardliners on just about every issue. Steve Bannon's early presence in the Trump administration was symbolic of the extremism Trump brought to the White House. Bannon, who served as former senior counselor to the president, ran *Breitbart,* a white nationalist tabloid. Now freelancing, Bannon continues to normalize white supremacist ideas in his endless speeches and public appearances. Trump shares Bannon's allegiance to white supremacy and has relentlessly catered to the racial fears and economic anxieties of an abandoned white working class; moreover, he has created a new synergy between his authoritarian demagoguery and an array of fascist groups that include the alt-right, white nationalists, militia groups, and others who embrace his militarism, race-based law-and-order agenda, and his overt contempt of undocumented immigrants and Muslims.[197]

Trump has elevated himself as patron saint of a ruthless neoliberalism. This is evident in the various miracles he has performed for the rich and powerful. He has systemically deregulated regulations that extend from environmental protections to worker safety rules. He has enacted a $1.5 trillion tax policy that amounts to a huge gift to the financial elite and all the while maintaining his "man of the people" posture. He has appointed a range of neoliberal fundamentalists to head major government posts designed to serve the public. Most, like Scott Pruitt, the former head of the EPA and Betsy DeVos, the Secretary of Education, have proved to be either corrupt, incompetent, or often both. Along with the Republican Congress, Trump has vastly increased the Pentagon budget to $717 billion, creating huge financial profits for the military-industrial-defense complex while instituting policies that eviscerate the welfare state and further expand a war machine that generates mass suffering and death.

Trump has reduced food assistance for those who are forced to choose between eating and taking medicine and prevents millions from accessing adequate health care.[198] And last but not least, he has become a cheerleader for the gun and security industries, going so far as to call for the arming of teachers as a way to redress mass shootings in the nation's schools. All of these policies serve to unleash the anti-liberal and anti-democratic passions, fears, anxieties, and anger necessary to mainstream fascism.

Trump's Politics of Disposability

Trump's neoliberalism aligns with fascism particularly through his embrace of white supremacy and his commitment to an expanding notion of disposability. Trump's view of disposability takes on a double register. First, he produces economic policies that support the neoliberal conviction that human beings without economic value — those who make no contribution to the market — are refuse, waste, excess, and have no possible social use. In neoliberalism's survival-of-the-fittest ethos, which amounts to a form of econocide, redundancy becomes code for disposability in economic terms. The only relations that matter are those compatible with economic decision making and the imperatives of capital. As Anis Shivani observes, "anyone not willing to conceive of themselves as being present fully and always in the market," who present a burden to the state, or "refuse to invest in their own future… will be subject to discipline and refused recognition as [a] human being."[199]

Trump extends the logic of redundancy and disposability beyond economic categories to all those others who cannot fit into a white nationalist script. This is the language of the police state — one fashioned by the history of US apartheid. Moreover, the endpoint of the language of white supremacy via a regressive crime policy is a form of social death, or even worse. What is frightening about Trump's racist vocabulary is that it registers a move from the coded language of benign neglect to policies marked by malignant cruelty that legitimates state violence. Trump's allegiance to white supremacy is hard to miss, though many deny it by focusing more on his economic policies than his white supremacist agenda. Ta-Nehisi Coates offers an insightful analysis of Trump's white supremacist ideology:

It is often said that Trump has no real ideology, which is not true — his ideology is white supremacy, in all its truculent and sanctimonious power... His political career began in advocacy of birtherism, that modern recasting of the old American precept that black people are not fit to be citizens of the country they built. But long before birtherism, Trump had made his worldview clear. He fought to keep blacks out of his buildings, according to the US government; called for the death penalty for the eventually exonerated Central Park Five; and railed against "lazy" black employees. "...Trump inaugurated his campaign by casting himself as the defender of white maidenhood against Mexican "rapists," only to be later alleged by multiple accusers, and by his own proud words, to be a sexual violator himself... In Trump, white supremacists see one of their own.[200]

Author John Feffer goes further and argues that Trump's hatred of immigrants is clear not only in his push for "extreme measures to keep them out of the United States: a wall, a travel ban, a zero tolerance family-separation policy" but also in signifying immigrants as a "threat that transcends the political. It's a matter of blood and soil, the touchstones of extreme nationalism."[201] Trump's view of ethnic sorting is also reminiscent of a central policy of earlier forms of fascism. Under Trump's draconian border crackdown and reign of terror implemented by ICE, immigrant families in the language of a fascist past "disappear," are "lost," or are categorized as "deleted family units."[202]

The United States is in a dangerous moment in its history, which makes it all the more crucial to understand how a distinctive form of neoliberal fascism now bears down on the present and threatens to usher in a period of unprecedented barbarism in the not too distant future. In an attempt to address this new political conjuncture, I want to suggest that rather than view fascism simply as a repetition of the past, it is crucial to forge a new vocabulary and politics in order to grasp how neoliberal fascism has become a uniquely American model for the present. One way to address this challenge is to rethink what lessons can be learned by interrogating how matters of language and memory can be used to illuminate the dark forces connecting the past and present as part of the new hybridized political nightmare.

The Language of Fascism

Fascism begins not with violence, police assaults, or mass killings, but with language. Throughout his presidential campaign and presidency, Trump has consistently targeted undocumented immigrants, Muslims, and African-Americans with racist remarks and dehumanizing rhetoric. He constantly criminalizes entire classes of people, calls African-Americans stupid, and repeatedly shames women who have accused him of sexual offenses or with whom he has denied having sexual relations. He has weaponized the language of racism by translating his bigotry into a series of dehumanizing and cruel policies that extend from denying or revoking DACA to separating children from their parents at the southern border, all the while stoking the fuming resentments of white nationalists and other white supremacist groups. This is more than the language of polarization or a strategic dog whistle — it is an overt discourse and theatrical performance in the service of white supremacy and racist violence, a logic largely overlooked by the mainstream press. This ongoing blast of racist invective has made clear Trump's white supremacist beliefs with his ongoing appeal to white nationalists, the alt-right, and other neo-Nazis groups.

Such actions share a legacy with state censorship, the repression of dissent by banishing freedom of speech, and book burning, all of which was part of the playbook of fascist regimes. Ruth Ben-Ghiat is right in stating that each of the words on Trump's censorship list "is part of an ongoing war about the future of our democratic rights to speak and research freely, to control our own bodies and identities, and to live without fear of being targeted by the state because of our faith, skin color, or sexual orientation."[203]

It is worth noting that words are not just about the production of meaning but also about how they generate consequences, especially in light of how such meanings buttressed by state sanctioned relations of power function to encourage and produce acts of violence aimed at those individuals and groups considered less than human.

Some meanings have a force that others don't, especially since power confers authority and can set in motion a range of effects. This is particularly clear, given how Trump uses the power of the presidency, evident in part in how he reacts to critics, especially those who garner some public attention through their criticism of him or his policies. His attempts to squelch dissent take on a rather ruthless register since he often publicly humiliates those who criticize him, threatens their livelihood, and uses language that functions to incite violence against his critics. We have seen too many instances where Trump's followers have beaten critics, attacked journalists, and shouted down any form of critique aimed at Trump's policies — to say nothing of the army of trolls unleashed on intellectuals and journalists critical of the administration.

As a tool of state repression, language holds the potential to open the door to fascism. As Rose Sydney Parfitt observes, "the language, symbols, and logic of fascism are being deployed today more overtly than at any time since the early 1940s."[204] Trump uses language that dehumanizes and makes it more acceptable for individuals to rationalize racist beliefs and practices. Under the Southern Strategy and later in the Clinton, Bush, and Obama administrations, racism was either coded in dog-whistle discourses or rendered unspeakable in the language of color blindness. Trump discarded such formalities by making racist language overt, shockingly deployed as a badge of honor, and pragmatically used as a nod to his base of support.

Trump's racist rhetoric was particularly evident in one race-baiting message tweet following a segment he watched on Fox News regarding violence against white South African farmers. Trump tweeted that he was asking Secretary of State Mike Pompeo to look into the alleged seizure of farms and large scale killing of white farmers in South Africa.[205] The Anti-Defamation League quickly responded by stating that the large-scale killing of white farmers is a long-standing and false white supremacist claim that feeds into the myth of "white genocide." Research by a number of organizations in South Africa indicate that violence against white farmers is at a 20-year low.[206] Trump never retracted his false claim. Commenting on Trump's false claim, Jason Burke and David Smith writing for *The Guardian* noted that:

> It continues a pattern in which he began his presidency with
> a travel ban on several Muslim-majority countries, reported-

ly described African nations as "shithole countries," pushed for a wall along the Mexican border, offered a flat-footed response to last year's hurricane in Puerto Rico and promoted inflammatory and misleading videos from the anti-immigrant group Britain First.[207]

Reminiscent of Nazi tactics to dehumanize enemies, he has called some undocumented immigrants "animals," "criminals," and has used the word "infest" in referring to immigrants on the southern border. Aviya Kushner asserted that Trump's tweet claiming that immigrants will "infest our country" bears an alarming resemblance to the Nazi claim that Jews were carriers of disease.[208] In response to Trump's use of the term "animal" to refer to some immigrants, Juan Cole argues that the Nazis used the term "'animal' as a technical term, Untermensch or subhuman" in referring "to Jews, gypsies, gays, and other groups as well as the slaughter of Russian boys at the Eastern Front." [209] Making them appear as less than human paved the way "toward permitting their elimination."[210] A convergence between Trump's language and the race-based ideology of Holocaust-era Nazis was clearly heard when Trump implied a moral equivalency between the violence perpetrated by white supremacists and neo-Nazis marching in Charlottesville and the presence of peaceful protesters demonstrating for the removal of a Confederate statue. Trump's scapegoating rhetoric of demonization not only dehumanizes racialized others, it also prepares the ground for encouraging hate groups and an intensification of hate crimes.

The FBI has reported that since the 2016 election hate crimes have increased in addition to a disturbing number of stories about Nazi swastikas being painted on school walls, synagogues being firebombed, and a spike in violent attacks on Muslims and foreigners.[211] Trump's use of dehumanizing language demands comparisons with the insidious rhetoric of fascism's past. Not only have his crassness, vulgarity, and humiliating tweets upended traditional standards of presidential comportment (to say nothing of governance), he has also revived a language of malign violence that echoes "the early warning signs of potential genocide and other atrocity crimes."[212]

Fascism, History, and Memory Work

Neoliberal fascism converges with an earlier form of fascism in its commitment to a language of erasure and a politics of disposability. In the fascist script, historical memory becomes a liability, even dangerous, when it functions pedagogically to inform our political and social imagination. This is especially true when memory acts to identify forms of social injustice and enables critical reflection on the histories of repressed others. It was certainly true given the embarrassing backlash that occurred when Ben Carson, the Secretary of Housing and Urban Development, claimed that slaves were immigrants, and when Education Secretary Betsy DeVos stated that black colleges and universities were "pioneers of school choice."[213]

Unsurprisingly, historical memory as a form of enlightenment and demystification is surely at odds with Trump's abuse of history as a form of social amnesia and political camouflage. Once again, Trump's 1930s-era slogan, "America First," marks a regressive return to a time when nativism, misogyny, and xenophobia defined the American experience. This inchoate nostalgia rewrites history in the warm glow and "belief in an essential American innocence, in the utter exceptionality, the ethical singularity and manifest destiny of the United States."[214] Philip Roth aptly characterizes this gratuitous form of nostalgia in his *American Pastoral* as the "undetonated past." Innocence in this script is the stuff of mythologies that distort history and erase the political significance of moral witnessing and historical memory as a way of reading, translating, and interrogating the past as it impacts, and sometimes explodes, the present.

Under Trump, both language and memory are distorted as words are emptied of substantive content and the space of a shared reality crucial to any democracy is eviscerated. History as a context for understanding language in this contemporary fascist script is stripped away in the immediacy of tweeted experience, the thrill of the moment, and the comfort of a cathartic emotional discharge. The danger, as history has taught us, is when words are systemically used to cover up lies, peddle falsehoods, and undermine the capacity to think critically.

In such instances, the public spheres essential to a democracy wither and die, opening the door to fascist ideas, values, and social relations: Trump has sanctioned torture, ripped babies from their parents' arms, imprisoned thousands of young immigrant children, and declared the media along with entire races and religions to be the enemy of the American people. In doing so, he speaks to and legitimates a history in which state violence becomes an organizing principle of governance and perversely a potentially cathartic experience for his followers. At the same time, the corruption of language is often followed by the corruption of memory, morality, and the eventual disappearance of books, ideas, and human beings. For instance, the prominent German historian Victor Klemperer has noted that for fascist dictators the dynamics of state censorship and repression had an endpoint in a politics of disappearance, extermination, and the death camps.

Trump's celebration of the language of disappearance, dehumanization, and censorship is both an echo and an erasure of the horrors and barbarism of another time. His regressive use of language and denial of history must be challenged so that the emancipatory energies and compelling narratives of resistance can be recalled in order to find new ways of challenging the ideologies and power relations that put them into play. Trump's distortion of language and public memory are part of a larger authoritarian politics of ethnic and racial cleansing that sanitizes the genocidal violence waged down on Native Americans, Black slaves, and African-Americans.

Indifferent to the historical footprints that mark expressions of state violence, the Trump administration uses historical amnesia as a weapon of (mis)education, power, and politics, allowing public memory to wither and the architecture of fascism to go unchallenged. What is under siege in the present moment is the critical need to keep watch over the repressed narratives of memory work. The fight against a fascist erasure of history must begin with an acute awareness that memory always makes a demand upon the present, refusing to accept ignorance as innocence.

As reality collapses into fake news, moral witnessing disappears into the hollow spectacles of right-wing media machines and into state sanctioned weaponry aimed to distort the truth, suppress dissent, and attack the critical media. Trump uses Twitter as a public relations blitzkrieg to attack everyone from his political enemies to celebrities who have criticized him.[215] As I mentioned previously, he is particularly malignant in his racist attacks on black athletes such as LeBron James and other prominent black celebrities such as CNN anchor Don Lemon.[216] The merging of journalism as entertainment with a culture addicted to speed, brevity, anonymity, and the pornographic exposure that digitization affords all has emptied speech of any substance or measure of accountability and further legitimates the unspeakable. Language no longer expands the reach of history, ethics, and justice. On the contrary, it now operates in the service of slogans, disposability, and violence. Words are now turned into an undifferentiated mass of ashes, critical discourse reduced to rubble, and informed judgments a distant radioactive horizon.

Under the Trump presidency, neoliberal fascism has restructured civic life into something that valorizes ignorance, avarice, and willful forgetting. In the current Trumpian moment, shouting replaces the pedagogical imperative to listen and reinforces the stories neoliberal fascism tells us about ourselves, our relations to others, and the larger world. Under such circumstances, monstrous deeds are committed under the increasing normalization of civic and historical modes of illiteracy. One consequence is that comparisons to the Nazi past can wither in the false belief that historical events are fixed in time and place and can only be repeated in history books. In an age marked by a war on terror, a culture of fear, and the normalization of uncertainty, social amnesia has become a power tool for dismantling democracy and making its destroyers immune from criticism. Indeed, in this age of forgetfulness, American society appears to revel in what it should be ashamed of and alarmed over.

Even with the insight of history, comparisons between the older orders of fascism and Trump's regime of brutality, aggression, and cruelty are considered by commentators to be too extreme. There is a cost to such caution. As Jonathan Freedland points out, "if the Nazi era is placed off limits, seen as so far outside the realm of regular human experience that it might as well have happened on a distant planet — Planet Auschwitz — then we risk failure to learn its lessons."[217] Knowing how others in the past successfully fought against elected demagogues such as Trump is crucial to a political strategy that reverses impending global catastrophe.

The story of a fascist past needs to be retold not to simply make comparisons to the present, though that is not an unworthy project, but to be able to imagine a new politics in which new knowledge will be built, and as Arendt states, "new insights... new knowledge... new insights, ... new memories, [and] new deeds, [will] take their point of departure."[218] This is not to suggest that history is a citadel of truth that can be easily mined. History offers no guarantees, and it can be used in the interest of violence as well as for emancipation. For instance, as Ariel Dorfman observes,

> When the white supremacist and neo-Nazis marched in Charlottesville, they carried torches in the night in order to "to evoke memories of terror, of past parades of hate and aggression by the Ku Klux Klan in the United States and Adolf Hitler's Freikorps in Germany. The organizers wanted to issue a warning to those watching: that past violence, perpetrated in defense of the "blood and soil" of the white race, would once again be harnessed and deployed in Donald Trump's America.[219]

Trump's selective appropriation of history wages war on the past, choosing to celebrate rather than question fascist horrors. The past in this case is a script that must be followed rather than interrogated. Trump's view of history is at once "ugly and revealing."[220] Such narratives undermine moral witnessing, transform agency into a weapon of violence, and use history as a tool of propaganda. All the more reason why, with the rise of neoliberal fascism, there is a need for modes of historical inquiry and stories that challenge the distortions of the past, transcend private interests, and enable the American public to connect private issues to broader historical and political contexts.

The production of new narratives accompanied by critical inquiries into the past would help explain why people participated in the horrors of fascism and what it might take to prevent such complicity from unfolding again. Comparing Trump's ideology, policies, and language to a fascist past offers the possibility to learn what is old and new in the dark times that have descended upon the Unites States. The pressing relevance of the 1930s is crucial to address how fascist ideas and practices originate, adapt to new conditions, and how people capitulate and resist them as well.

The Disappearing Social

Since the 1970s, the social structure has been under relentless attack by an assemblage of political, economic, and educational forces unleashed by organized neoliberal agendas. All the commanding institutions of corporate capitalism have enshrined a notion of citizenship that reduces individuals to consumers while promoting regressive notions of freedom defined primarily through the practice of commercial exchange. Freedom, in the neoliberal edition, has been transformed into an obsession with self-interest, part of a war culture that ruthlessly pits individuals against each other while condoning a culture of indifference, violence, and cruelty that rejects any sense of political and moral responsibility. This often takes the form of "freedom" to be a racist, homophobe and sexist, to experience the liberty to hate and demonize others and to inflict violence and emotional harm under the guise of freedom of speech. Individual freedoms are given lip service by politicians and intellectuals but little is said about who does not benefit from such freedoms or how the call for individual freedom is sabotoged with a society defined by market relations and massive inequality. Such values also mock any form of dependency or empathy for others.

Atomization, fear, and anxiety are the breeding ground of fascism. Not only do such forces undercut the radical imagination and collective resistance, they situate language and memory in the vise of a politics of depoliticization. Neoliberal fascism insists that everything, including human beings, are to be made over in the image of the market. Everyone is now subject to a paralyzing language of individual responsibility and a disciplinary apparatus that revises downward the American dream of social mobility. Time is now a burden for most people and the lesson to draw from this punishing neoliberal ideology is that everyone is alone in navigating their own fate. Shattered communities increasingly occupy the landscape of America, marked by broken social bonds, rampant atomization, and the toxic influence of an extreme individualism that provides the conditions that gives rise to growing appeal of monstrous demagogues and extremists.

At work here is a neoliberal project to reduce people to human capital and to redefine human agency divorced from the bonds of sociality, equality, belonging, and obligation. All problems and their solutions are now defined exclusively within the purview of the individual. This is a depoliticizing discourse, but not a depoliticized one, that champions mythic notions of self-reliance and individual character in order to promote the tearing up of social solidarities and the public spheres that support them.

All aspects of the social and public are now considered suspect, including social space, social provisions, social protections, and social dependency, especially for those who are poor and vulnerable. Under neoliberalism, social bonds are replaced by market relations, functioning largely to sanctify greed and create legions of individuals suffering from the cruelties imposed by casino capitalism.[221] According to philosopher Byung-Chul Han, the subjects in a "neoliberal economy do not constitute a *we* that is capable of collective action. The mounting egoization and atomization of society is shrinking the space for collective action. As such, it blocks the formation of a counter power that might be able to put the capitalist order in question."[222]

At the core of neoliberal fascism is a view of subjectivity that celebrates a narcissistic hyper-individualism that radiates with a near sociopathic lack of interest in others with whom it shares a globe on the brink of catastrophe. This project is wedded to a politics that produces a high threshold of disappearance and serves to disconnect the material moorings and wreckage of neoliberal fascism from its underlying power relations.

Neoliberal fascism thrives on producing subjects who internalize its values, corroding their ability to imagine an alternative world. Under such conditions, not only is agency depoliticized, but the political is emptied of any real substance and unable to challenge neoliberalism's belief in extreme inequality and social abandonment thereby fostering fascism's deep rooted investment in ultra-nationalism, racial purity, and the politics of terminal exclusion.

We live at a time in which the social is individualized and at odds with a notion of solidarity once described by Frankfurt School theorist, Herbert Marcuse, as "the refusal to let one's happiness coexist with the suffering of others."[223] Marcuse invokes a forgotten notion of the social in which one is willing not only to make sacrifices for others but also "to engage in joint struggle against the cause of suffering or against a common adversary."[224]

One step towards fighting and overcoming the criminogenic machinery of terminal exclusion and social death endemic to neoliberal fascism is to make education a central element of politics, whose aim is to change the way people think, desire, dream, and act. How might language and history adopt modes of persuasion that anchor democratic life in a commitment to economic equality, social justice, and a broad shared vision? The challenge we face under a fascism buoyed by a savage neoliberalism is to ask and act on what language, memory, and education as the practice of freedom might mean in a democracy, what work can they perform, and how civic courage can be nourished by collective action and the ongoing struggle to create a broad-based democratic socialist movement. What work has to be done to "imagine a politics in which empowerment can grow and public freedom thrive without violence?"[225] What institutions have to be defended and fought for if the spirit of a radical democracy is to return to view and survive?

Chapter 4

Twilight of the Social

The undiminished presence of suffering, fear and menace necessitates that the thought that cannot be realized should not be discarded.
— *Theodor Adorno*

DONALD TRUMP'S INCREASINGLY dangerous, incendiary attacks on the media and journalists,[226] his efforts to strip citizenship from naturalized citizens and deport US citizens on the groundless claim that they have fraudulent birth certificates,[227] and his relentless attempts to pressure former Attorney General Jeff Sessions and others to obstruct the rule of law all amount to a lawless grab for power that is pushing the United States further into the abyss of fascism.[228]

The terrors of 20th century fascism have risen once again in the United States but offer a warning less about repeating past mistakes than as a measure of the degree to which the lessons of history have become irrelevant. Politics now moves between what philosopher Susan Sontag once labeled as "unremitting banality and inconceivable terror."[229] The "unremitting banality" is evident in Trump's daily bombardment of reckless tweets in which language becomes a weapon to vilify, humiliate, and demonize government officials, journalists, and critical media outlets. An evil banality is also present in his constant racist rhetoric aimed at undocumented immigrants, Muslims, black athletes, news commentators, and others whom he views as worthy of contempt, insults, and verbal abuse.[230]

In addition to the use of coarse language and an unprecedented display of incivility by a sitting president, there is also a flirtation with violence, the rhetoric of white supremacy, and the language of expulsion and elimination.[231] Trump's embrace of unthinkable terror takes on an even more ominous tone as the language of dehumanization and cruelty materializes into policies that work to expel people from any sense of community, if not humanity itself.

Such policies are evident in Trump's "zero tolerance" policy, now rescinded, that forcibly separated migrant children from their parents and incarcerated them in prison-like cages where many of them were physically and sexually abused.[232] These attacks have not been limited to children. Aída Chávez reports in *The Intercept* that both physical and sexual assaults on immigrants in detention centers have become commonplace and are documented in a number by reliable sources.[233] For instance, *The Intercept* has obtained public records that reveal the systemic nature and scope of violence and sexual abuse involved in the reign of terror inflicted on immigrants at the hands of ICE agents. The Office of the Inspector General has received over 33,000 horrifying complaints by immigrants made against ICE, revealing the underpinnings and wanton lawlessness of a fascist police state.[234] Senator Kirstjen Nielsen has called ICE a "deportation force" and, along with a number of prominent politicians such as New York Mayor Bill de Blasio, has argued that it should be abolished.[235] Cynthia Nixon, the progressive actor who entered the 2018 gubernatorial race in New York, has called ICE "a terrorist organization" and has insisted on its abolition.[236]

The Trump administration's penchant for cruelty is also on full display in its attempt "to terminate Temporary Protected Status for more than 300,000 people from six countries," including refugees from El Salvador, Honduras, and Haiti.[237] The cruel nature of this act of political and moral irresponsibility is evident in the fact that many Honduran survivors of Hurricane Mitch who have been living in the United States for over 20 years will now have to return to Honduras and face a number of hardships if not potential violence. Not only will this mean 86,000 Honduran immigrants who have now lost their legal status will be deported from the US, but also 53,500 of their US-born children.[238] In addition, we can add to this list the fact that Trump has also rescinded protections for "800,000 young undocumented immigrants, known as Dreamers."[239] Trump's acts of domestic terrorism appear to intensify with each new policy and executive order. For instance, in August 2018, the Trump administration began the process of depriving undocumented immigrants of due process, threatening to deport them immediately when they cross the border "without a trial or an appearance before a judge."[240]

The degree and transparency of Trump's racism are even more well-defined in his plan to punish legal immigrants for accepting public benefits to which they are entitled, such as food stamps and public housing.[241] Moreover, his rule would authorize federal officials to revoke legal resident status from immigrants who accept such assistance. The guiding force behind this anti-immigrant movement in the Trump administration is hardliner and white supremacist sympathizer, Stephen Miller, who takes delight in proposing legislation that makes "it harder for legal immigrants to become citizens or get green cards if they have ever used a range of popular public welfare programs, including Obamacare."[242]

Legislation that denies immigrants citizenship because they receive public assistance reveals a level of state violence, if not a form of domestic terrorism, that increasingly characterizes the onslaught of Trump's policies. More recently, he has suggested the death penalty is an appropriate punishment for drug dealers, a plan which takes its cues from Filipino President Rodrigo Duterte's drug war which has resulted in deaths of over 20,000 alleged drug users and dealers since 2016, many of whom live in poor communities.[243]

Meanwhile, as part of his broader attack on human life and the conditions that make it possible, Trump has rolled back many of the Obama-era policies designed to curb climate change; he has reversed environmental protections such as the banning of pesticides in wildlife refuges and he has dismantled federal rules regulating American coal plants that are "designed to curtail coal emissions of carbon dioxide and methane that contribute to climate change."[244]

In a case that highlights Trump's war on youth and his ongoing attempts to destroy the social bonds that sustain a democracy, the

United States government attempted to scrap a research-based United Nations-World Health Organization resolution that encouraged breast-feeding. Supporting the interests of infant formula manufacturers, American officials first sought to use language that would water down the resolution. When that failed, they threatened smaller countries such as Ecuador that supported it. Patti Rundall, a policy director supporting the bill, observed that the actions by the Trump administration were "tantamount to blackmail."[245] Rundall's criticism becomes even more alarming given a 2016 study in *The Lancet* that documented how "universal breast-feeding would prevent 800,000 child deaths a year across the globe and yield $300 billion in savings from reduced health care costs and improved economic outcomes for those reared on breast milk."[246]

Slow Violence, Fast Violence

Trump's discourse and policies represent a profound attack on the collective values crucial to a democracy and present a constant assault not just on economic and political institutions but also on the formative culture, public foundations, and educational apparatuses necessary to nurture critically active and engaged citizens. Trump's assault on social obligations, social responsibility, and the social fabric is a fundamental element of his espousal of neoliberal fascism.[247] This new political arrangement operates in its most lethal form as a form of "slow violence," which, in Princeton University scholar Rob Nixon's terms, is a "a violence that occurs gradually and out of sight, a violence of delayed destruction that is dispersed across time and space, an attritional violence that is typically not viewed as violence at all."[248]

"Slow violence" destroys the formative cultures that make human suffering visible, covers over authoritarian impulses behind the calls for national greatness, and exposes the danger of surrendering freedom for security. At the core of this violence, which has intensified under neoliberal fascism, is an attack on those social forces that defend the welfare state and engage in an ongoing struggle to make concrete the possibilities of democratic socialism. Under neoliberal fascism, chauvinism, and militarism work hand in hand with the unleashing of the forces of brutal self-interest and a growing illiteracy that undermines both public values and a collective struggle against what sociologist C. Wright Mills once called "a politics of organized irresponsibility."[249] "Slow violence" is often difficult to gauge because it is often concealed beneath policies that promote more overt and distinct forms of violence.

Fast violence opens up the ground from under one's feet. Fast violence is visible in the spectacularized drama of Trump's imperious and insulting tweets, producing high profile assaults on democratic institutions such as the courts, media, and rule of law. Such violence embraces the theatrical, feeds off the spectacle, and aims at high shock value. One recent example of the fast violence of cultural politics was the almost unthinkable announcement by the Trump administration that Betsy DeVos was planning — at a time when underprivileged schools lack the most basic resources and support services — to use federal funds, designed to benefit programs aimed at underserved students, to train and arm teachers, in spite of an established federal policy that prohibits using such funds to arm educators.[250]

Of course, the hidden agenda legitimated in this proposed policy is that schools attended largely by poor students are sites defined in the image of war, should be modeled after prisons, and necessitate being governed through harsh criminalizing policies that often feed the school-to prison-pipeline. The endpoint of such policies moves between pushing poor black and brown youth into the criminal justice system and abolishing these public institutions or turning them into cash cows by privatizing them. The larger goal is to destroy education as a democratic public sphere whose mission is to create an educated citizenry necessary for the workings of a vibrant modern democracy — citizens with self-determination, the capacity to be thoughtful, to participate in shaping public life, solve social problems, and serve the common good. The state-sponsored violence at work here imperils the rule of law and works to unravel alleged democratic institutions, such as the courts and media, which some believe provide an impregnable firewall against Trump's authoritarianism. Taken together, "slow" and "fast" violence under the Trump regime share a cultural politics that erodes memory, substitutes emotion for reason, embraces anti-intellectualism, increases the harshness of rugged individualism and thrives in the glow of what economist Paul Krugman terms a "white nationalism run wild."[251]

State violence has become the organizing principle shaping all aspects of American society. At the heart of such violence is a full-fledged attack on notions of the social and public space that make critical thought, dialogue, and the individual and collective pursuit of what critical theorist and urban historian Mike Davis calls public affluence over private wealth possible.[252] In an age of precarity, the dominant ethos is that we are individually responsible for any problems we face, regardless of the systemic conditions that produce them. Under such circumstances, pressing social problems are removed from the inventory of public concerns and ethical considerations. The endpoint is the replacement of the welfare state and social investments with the punishing state and what Jonathan Simon has called "governing through crime."[253] On a more existential level, the loss of any sense of common purpose leads to a distrust in the promise of collective struggles, if not democracy itself, and leaves a society vulnerable to the withering of civic culture and the institutions that support it. This is all too evident in the Trump administration's mode of governance founded on a harsh racially-charged regime of law and order that is as repressive as it is corrupt.[254] Locked into an "abyss of failed sociality," the American public finds it increasingly difficult to challenge the assumption that the rule of the strong man and markets is all that is needed to solve all individual and social problems.[255] When public values are invoked, to paraphrase Walter Benjamin, they appear less for their recognizability and relevance for the present and more as a symbol for what has been irrevocably lost.[256]

Public values have been reduced to nostalgic reminders of another era — associated, for example, with the New Deal or the Great Society — in which the social contract was seen as crucial to meeting the needs of postwar Americans and fundamental to a substantive democratic order. Rather than viewed as a legacy that needs renewal, visions of the public good are consigned to the distant past, a passing curiosity — perhaps worth viewing but not worth struggling to revive as either an ideal or a reality. What is "new" about the long decline of public values in U.S. society is not that they are again under attack but that they have become weakened to the point of no longer provoking a massive oppositional social movement in the face of more daring and destructive attacks by the Trump administration. When such values are attacked, the targets are groups who for decades have been largely immune to such attacks because they embody the most cherished ideals associated with democratic public service — immigrants, public school teachers, public servants, poor youth of color and labor unions. This suggests that the precondition for any viable sense of individual and collective resistance must reclaim the social as part of a democratic imaginary that makes education central not only to social change but also to the struggle to democratize the very character of American politics and public discourse.

Neoliberalism's Attack on Social Bonds

In the aftermath of the horrors of World War II, Theodor Adorno remarked that while it becomes difficult to live in the shadow of a history in which there seemed to be no end to terror, it is impossible to evade the past — both because "it lingers on after" its own alleged death and because a "willingness to commit the unspeakable survives in people as well as in the conditions that enclose them."[257] Adorno, in this case, was referring to the survival of fascist elements within democracies consoled by the false belief that history could not repeat itself. With the rise of "illiberal democracy" and a resurgent embrace of an unapologetic authoritarianism across the globe, it is clear that not only has the struggle over democratic laws become more urgent than ever, but the formative culture that creates the social fabric and critical agents, habits, and dispositions necessary to sustain and strengthen such a democracy is in peril. The crisis of democracy has taken a lethal turn in the United States.

Over the last 40 years, neoliberalism has produced the most extreme elements of casino capitalism, emphasizing austerity policies designed to accumulate wealth and profits for the financial and corporate elite regardless of social costs and the enormous price paid in human suffering and misery. These included draconian policies such as slashing government spending for health care, gutting retirement benefits, and reducing services mostly for the poor. At the same time, neoliberalism has unleashed and legitimized the mobilizing paroxysms of neo-fascist discourse. Neoliberalism merges a cruel form of contemporary capitalism with elements of white supremacy, ultranationalism, and elimination policies that echo the horrors of a fascist past. Neoliberalism's attack on social justice and the common good coupled with its production of economic conditions that trample on human needs and produce massive inequality in wealth and power mobilizes the violent energies of a right-wing populism and white supremacist anxieties "about loss of status and social dominance."[258]

In the neoliberal narrative, people are reduced to merchandise and expected to imitate rather than challenge corporate values. In this view, culture becomes a pedagogical weapon whose aim is to convince people that imagining an alternative future is impossible. In this fascist version of this script, people are largely considered either extensions of capital or disposable and ultimately subject to racial cleansing, terminal exclusion, or worse. Within this convergence of neoliberal rationality and alarming echoes of a fascist history, Trump has emboldened the discourse of border walls, racial purging, nativism, and militarism along with nonstop attacks on people of color, immigrants, women, LBGTQ+ people, environmentalists, and more.[259]

As Trump's war against democracy intensifies, the speed and onslaught of policies that carry the ghosts of a monstrous past become more difficult to grasp given the endless shocks to the body politic and a plethora of spectacularized earthquakes that follow each succeeding blow to the values, social relations, and institutions that make a democracy possible. While the horrors of a fascist past are easy to recall, it is much more difficult at the current moment to learn from history how to resist a culture tied to extreme forms of nationalism, white supremacy, systemic racism, militarism, police violence, the politics of disposability, and an expanding culture of cruelty. Equally difficult is thoughtful consideration of how the mechanisms of neoliberal fascism work to undermine modes of social solidarity, the social contract, social obligations, and social relations while sustaining in the public mind "conditions that are hostile to any kind of democratic liberties."[260] Years of pressure brought on by neoliberalism's emphasis on competition, a winner-take-all set of values, and the forces of privatization have damaged collective values. This constant battle against any viable democratic notion of the social has also weakened social ties with others and reinforced notions of privilege that bolster a culture of cruelty and a disdain for vulnerable populations.[261]

How does a culture whose mission is to keep democracy alive give way to political, economic, and pedagogical arrangements that normalize a hatred of democracy? What role does neoliberal culture play as an educational force to construct policies that undermine human rights and pose a threat to the dignity of politics? How does neoliberalism use corporate-controlled cultural apparatuses to destroy the communal cohesion necessary to nurture support for the common good, shared democratic values, and a compassion for others? How do the ideological workstations of neoliberal fascism work to configure all of social life in economic terms? How does neoliberalism's regressive embrace of individual responsibility work to reduce all social problems to personal failings and, in doing so, empty politics of any substance while undermining a grammar of ethics and the moral bearings needed to distinguish good from evil?

These questions point to the terror of the unforeseen that is at the heart of the neoliberal formation which has emerged under the Trump administration as a new and frightening political development. As the political sphere is corrupted by ever-greater concentrations of wealth and power, the institutions, cultures, values, and ethical principles that make a democracy possible begin to disappear. Political theorist Wendy Brown is insightful on the breakdown of democracy in the troubled present and points to forces that threaten democracy from within by hollowing out its most crucial public institutions. She writes:

> Neoliberalism generates a condition of politics absent democratic institutions that would support a democratic public and all that such a public represents at its best: informed passion, respectful deliberation, and aspirational sovereignty, sharp containment of powers that would overrule or undermine it…. Democracy in an era of enormously complex global constellations and powers requires a people who are educated, thoughtful, and democratic in sensibility.[50] This means a people modestly knowing about these constellations and powers; a people with capacities of discernment and judgment in relation to what it reads, watches, or hears about a range of developments in its world; and a people oriented toward common concerns and governing itself.[262]

Neoliberal ideology and its attack on social bonds, critical thinking, and democratic values have a long legacy and have accelerated in intensity since the late 1970s. Education in the wider culture is dominated by corporate interests and has become a weapon and disimagination machine. As a form of pedagogical oppression, neoliberalism instrumentalizes learning, reduces education to training, and produces subjects defined by the social relations and values of the market place. Substituting market values for democratic values, it has economized and commercialized all social relations and subordinated human needs to the imperatives of profit making. In an age when self-interest and unchecked individualism are heralded as the essence of agency, democratic relations and ideals, if not human nature, have become difficult to both imagine and recognize. As the longings for wealth, status, and power were elevated to the status of national ideals, the mood in America turned dark in a climate marked by despair, a culture of fear aimed at scapegoated populations, skyrocketing inequalities in wealth and power, and a vision that morphed into cynicism, anger, and resentment. The American dream gave way as a cruel illusion when the hopes of social mobility, a better future, and economic prosperity for all disappeared in the aftermath of the financial crisis of 2008.[263]

As social bonds deteriorate under obscene notions of privatization, business deregulations, and an expansion of the precariat, there is a growing moral panic engineered by white nationalists and those who substitute traditional forms of economic nationalism for what might be called cultural sovereignty. In this instance, community is now defined through a "mix of neoliberalism, cultural chauvinism, anti-immigrant anger, and majoritarian rage as the major model" of governance. An attack on cultural differences has become the driving force of a toxic form of neoliberal fascism that mixes the cruelty of a market-driven system with an embrace of racial purity and social cleansing.

This demagogic pursuit of power driven by a hatred of democracy is reinforced by the dismantling of public goods, tax policies that produce massive inequalities, the expansion of military power, the rise of voter suppression policies, and the corrosive imbalance between freedom and security. It is also reinforced through a neoliberal formative culture that has redefined the very nature of subjectivity, desire, and agency in reductive market terms. This becomes evident in the educational force of a neoliberal culture that defines the citizen as the consumer of commodities, uses economic calculations to measure the worth of the good life, rewards entrepreneurship as the driving force of human agency, and reduces politics to the empty spectacle of voting in election cycles. Under neoliberal fascism, we are citizens with alleged individual and political rights but without economic and social rights.

As neoliberalism is normalized, self-secure in its proclaimed motto and self-fulfilling prophecy that there is no alternative, it becomes difficult to imagine a society, social relations, and a self that is not defined through the rationality, logic, and values of the market. In this conception, capitalism and the market are synonymous, and human beings can only be conceived as human capital. Rather than be called to think critically, share power, and exercise one's imagination, human beings are reduced to pawns to be manipulated by financial markets. Literary critic and political analyst Anis Shivani rightly observes that neoliberalism argues that everything is to be imagined and constructed through the lens of the market and the wishes of the financial elite. He writes:

> One way to sum up neoliberalism is to say that everything — everything — is to be made over in the image of the market, including the state, civil society, and of course human beings. Democracy becomes reinterpreted as the market, and politics succumbs to neoliberal economic theory, so we are speaking of the end of democratic politics as we have known it for two and a half centuries. As the market becomes an abstraction, so does democracy, but the real playing field is somewhere else, in the realm of actual economic exchange — which is not, however, the market. We may say that all exchange takes place on the neoliberal surface.[264]

Cynicism now replaces optimism as matters of responsibility are reduced exclusively to matters of individual choice, if not character, nurtured by regressive notions of self-enrichment while any notion of the social, dependency, or care for the other is viewed as both a weakness and an object of contempt. A mix of social amnesia, punitive justice, and a theater of cruelty now drive policy decisions increasingly accepted by segments of the public that either refuse or are incapable of connecting private troubles and worries with broader systemic forces. According to late sociologist Zygmunt Bauman, what is broken under such circumstances is

> the link between public agenda and private worries, the very hub of the democratic process ... with each of the two spheres rotating by now in mutually isolated spaces, set in motion by mutually unconnected and uncommunicating (though certainly not independent!) factors and mecha-

nisms. To put it simply, it is a situation in which people who have been hit don't know what has hit them — and have little chance of ever finding out.[265]

Under neoliberal fascism, a plague of privatizations weakens democratic culture and promotes a flight from any sense of political and social responsibility. As the high priest of neoliberalism on steroids, Trump embodies the ideology of unchecked self-interest and voracious greed while supporting the corporate mantra that the public good is a site to be colonized and democracy functions largely as the enemy of private interests, commercial values, and market liberties.

Neoliberalism Fuels the Trump Administration's Neo-Fascist Agenda

Policies conducive to the most extreme elements of casino capitalism have become the testing ground for seeing how far, for instance, the Trump administration can advance its neo-fascist agenda. Solutions that echo the extreme cruelty of a sordid past have pushed the United States closer to a full-fledged American fascism that makes clear its hatred of immigrants, the poor, black people, indigenous people, Muslims, and others who do not fit into the racist logic at work in Trump's call to "Make America First."

Yet, there is more at work here than the proliferation of neoliberal policies that breathe new life into white supremacist ideologies, privatize public goods, limit the power of unions, deregulate the public sphere, and hollow out the state by shifting massive amounts of capital through regressive tax policies to big corporations and the ultra-rich.

Under neoliberalism, politics is tied to the discourse of exclusion and powerlessness and is viewed along with democracy as the enemy of a market that views itself above the influence of the rule of law, accountability, ethics, governance, and the common good.[266] As legal scholar Eva Nanopoulos observes, in the current historical moment, the specific forms of contemporary fascism have to be understood "in

the wider context of their relationship to neoliberalism and the neoliberal crisis."[267] What is especially important to grasp is how neoliberalism has reconfigured the state to maximize the disintegration of
democratic social bonds and obligations, especially through neoliberal policies that test how far a demagogic administration can push
a public into accepting practices that are as cruel as they are unimaginable. This logic is now being carried to extremes under Trump as he
is constantly redrawing the lines of what is possible in violating human
rights and promoting an ever-widening labyrinth of cruelty, destruction, and disposability.

Some of the most distinctive features of neoliberal fascism include
the disintegration of the social, the collapse of a culture of compassion, and the dissolution of public spheres that make democracy
possible. Individual existence is now defined through the circulation
of commodities and the elevation of self-interest to a national ideal.
This amounts to what Marx and Engels once called "the icy water of
egotistical calculation."[268] One consequence is the expansion of an
ongoing plague of social atomization, alienation, existential despair,
and a collective sense of powerlessness. Evidence for the latter can
be found in the ongoing opioid crisis, which killed 42,000 people in
2016,[269] the increasing mortality rate for uneducated white men,[270] the
growing lack of confidence in American institutions,[271] the desperation
experienced by families living on the brink of poverty trying to make
ends meet each month,[272] and the heartbreak and despair among the
6.5 million children and their families living in extreme poverty.[273] In
addition, the mutually informing forces of anomie, despair, and powerlessness produce the conditions for the growth of right-wing populism, racism, ultra-nationalism, militarism, and fascism.

As the reach of neoliberal ideology spreads throughout society, it
works to trivialize democratic values and public concerns, enshrines
a militant individualism, celebrates an all-embracing quest for profits,
and promotes a form of Social Darwinism in which misfortune is seen
as a weakness and the Hobbesian rule of a "war of all against all" replaces any vestige of shared responsibilities or compassion for others.
This punishing script constitutes an often-unrecognized form of state-
sanctioned terrorism that numbs many people just as it wipes out the
creative faculties of imagination, memory, and critical thought. Under
a regime of privatized utopias, hyper-individualism, and ego-centered

values, human beings slip into a kind of ethical somnolence, indifferent to the plight and suffering of others. Under such circumstances, civic culture is replaced with a turbo-charged culture of consumerism and self-absorption. One consequence is the withering of institutions that nurture shared values and a respect for the common good. In the midst of extreme inequality and poverty, shared values disappear and in a time of growing authoritarianism are replaced by shared resentments and fears. Neoliberalism produces a unique form of modern terrorism that trades on fear, insecurity, and anomie. The late Frankfurt School theorist Leo Lowenthal refers to it as a form of mass repression and self-preserving numbness that amounts "to the atomization of the individual." He writes:

> The individual under terrorist conditions is never alone and always alone. He becomes numb and rigid not only in relation to his neighbor but also in relation to himself; fear robs him of the power of spontaneous emotional or mental reaction. Thinking becomes a stupid crime; it endangers his life. The inevitable consequence is that stupidity spreads as a contagious disease among the terrorized population. Human beings live in a state of stupor, in a moral coma.[274]

Implicit in Lowenthal's commentary is the assumption that as democracy becomes a fiction, the moral mechanisms of language, meaning, and morality are undermined. In addition, a culture of atomization, precarity, intolerance, and brutishness reinforces an ethos of cruel indifference promoted through a relentless volley of ruthless policies that test how far the most extreme elements in the convergence of neoliberalism and fascism can be promoted by the Trump administration without arousing mass outrage and resistance. As my colleague David Clark remarks, the existential despair promoted by neoliberal fascism works overtime to dissuade the public from developing "a critical vocabulary that is up to addressing and resisting a truly dismal moment in history, steeped as it is in unapologetic forms of aggression and committed to the destruction of political life. We find ourselves in the talons of those who would murder the future."[275] This raises a key question for addressing education as central to politics. That is, how education can be enlisted to fight what the cultural theorist Mark Fisher once called neoliberalism's most brutal weapon: "the slow cancellation of the future."[276]

As I mention throughout this book, the disintegration of social bonds, social ties, and emancipatory modes of solidarity and collective struggle are intensified through an endless series of political and ethical shocks produced by the Trump administration. Such shocks are designed to weaken the ability of citizens to resist the ongoing barrage of attacks on the moral indexes and values central to a democracy. They are also designed to normalize neoliberal fascist terrorist tactics dispelling the notion that such practices are ephemeral in the 21st century.

In its willingness to demonstrate such terror, the state mobilizes fear and unchecked displays of power in order to convince people that the president is above the law and that the only viable response to his increasingly cruel policies is individual and collective resignation. This is an exercise of power without a conscience — a form of violence that revels in the passivity, if not moral infantilism, it wishes to produce in its citizens. Echoes of this view were obvious in Trump's comment, later claimed to be a joke, that he wants "[his] people" to listen to him the way North Koreans listen to North Korean dictator Kim Jong-un. As the president stated on the Fox News Channel program *Fox & Friends,* "He speaks, and his people sit up at attention. I want my people to do the same."[277] Trump's war against the social and ethical imagination is part of a larger politics designed to destroy those social ties and public spheres that would encourage a sense of responsibility and compassion toward others, especially those considered the most vulnerable. This is a form of terrorism that celebrates self-interest, bare survival, and a regression to a kind of Social Darwinism and political infantilism. Lowenthal again is on target in his comment that this form of terrorism is equivalent to a form of self-annihilation. He writes:

> Terrorism wipes out the causal relation between social conduct and survival and confronts the individual with the naked force of nature — that is, of denatured nature — in the form of the all-powerful terrorist machine. What the terror aims to bring about, and enforces through its tortures, is that people shall come to act in harmony with the law of terror, namely, that their whole calculation shall have but one aim: self-perpetuation. The more people become ruthless seekers after their own survival, the more they become psychological pawns and puppets of a system that knows no other purpose than to keep itself in power.[278]

Surely, this is obvious today as all vestiges of social camaraderie give way to a form of Social Darwinism with its emphasis on ruthlessness, cruelty, war, violence, hyper-modes of masculinity, and a disdain for those considered weak, dependent, alien, or economically unproductive.

Central to developing any viable notion of the social is a rethinking of the critical institutions and shared spaces in which matters of morality, justice, and equality become central to a renewed understanding of politics. There is a need to reimagine where public spaces, connections, and public commitments lie beyond the domain of the private and how they can be constructed as part of a broader effort to create engaged and critical citizens willing to fight for an emergent democratic politics. Central here is a renewed perception of education as the crucial site in which the intertwined dynamics of individual agency and democratic politics merge. Politics in this sense is connected to a discourse of critique and possibility in which a plurality of memories, narratives, and identities come together in defense of a common good and a comprehensive politics that brings together personal and public meanings, discourses, and connections.

The political philosopher Hannah Arendt's fear about the extinguishing of the public realm, along with pragmatist John Dewey's apprehension about the loss of a public sphere where visions, power, politics, and the ethical imagination can be brought to life, are no longer abstract concerns. Such trepidations have become a reality in the age of Trump. Amid the current attack on the foundations of social solidarity and the bonds of social obligation, public values are running the risk of becoming irrelevant. In a society in which it has become commonplace to believe that one has no responsibility for anyone other than oneself, the social is downsized to accommodate a culture of hate, xenophobia, and cruelty. If democracy is to survive, especially in a time of tyranny, it is crucial to speak out and refuse the comfort of silence. Donald Harward, the former president of Bates College, though specifically addressing educators, offers up a warning about being silent in the face of the current fascist turn in the US that applies to all individuals and civic institutions concerned about democracy. He states:

> Ignorance, hatred, racism, misogyny, and deceit are not part
> of a public dialogue that will create the kind of education
> our institutional missions champion or the democracy our

country should promise — and should be striving to, even haltingly, realize. The comments that deceive and offend (and the supportive, pernicious silence that echoes them) are repugnant. In a democracy, they must be called out ... As educators and as educational institutions, we cannot risk failing to speak — to assert what we do value and to challenge deceit, ignorance, and bigotry at a time when the very fabric of our democracy is frayed, if not unraveling. We cannot risk silence.[279]

Keeping the Struggle for a Radical Democracy Alive

There will be no democracy without a formative culture to construct the questioning agents capable of dissent and collective action. Nor will the struggle for a radical democracy get far without a vision that can replace representative politics with a politics and mode of governing based on a participatory politics. Wendy Brown touches on some of the elements of a visionary politics in which power and governance are shared collectively. She writes:

> ... a left vision of justice would focus on practices and institutions of popular power; a modestly egalitarian distribution of wealth and access to institutions; an incessant reckoning with all forms of power — social, economic, political, and even psychic; a long view of the fragility and finitude of non-human nature; and the importance of both meaningful activity and hospitable dwellings to human flourishing ... The drive to promulgate such a counter rationality — a different figuration of human beings, citizenship, economic life, and the political — is critical both to the long labor of fashioning a more just future and to the immediate task of challenging the deadly policies of the imperial American state.[280]

The great philosopher of democracy, Cornelius Castoriadis, adds to this perspective the idea that for democracy to work, people have to have a passion for public values and social participation alongside the ability to access public spaces that guarantee the rights of free speech, dissent, and critical dialogue. Castoriadis recognized that at the heart of such public spaces is a formative culture that creates citizens who are critical thinkers capable of "putting existing institutions into question so that democracy again becomes [possible] in the full sense of the term." For Castoriadis, people should not be merely given the right to participate in society; they also should be educated in order to participate in it in a meaningful and consequential manner. According to Castoriadis, the protective space of the social becomes crucial when it functions as an educational space whose aim is to create critical agents who can use their knowledge and skills in order to participate in a wider struggle for justice and freedom. At the center of Castoriadis's defense of education is a defense of the public realm where, to paraphrase Hannah Arendt, freedom can find the worldly space to make an appearance. According to Castoriadis, education was not only an essential dimension of justice and politics, but also democracy itself.

One precondition for bringing Trump's neoliberal fascism to a halt is the recognition that democracy cannot exist without knowledgeable citizens who have a passion for public affairs, and who believe that critical consciousness is one precondition through which politics must pass in order to render individuals fit for the kind of collective struggles that offer the possibility for change. Education is more than a struggle to create individuals who can think and understand themselves and their relationship to themselves and others, it is also a condition for any viable notion of autonomy, self-governing, and agency. It is difficult to talk about producing the social bonds necessary in any democracy without viewing civic education, literacy, and learning as acts of resistance. Education has to become central to politics in which new narratives can be developed that refuse to equate capitalism with democracy, hope with the fear of losing and surviving, and the separation of political equality from economic equality.

In doing so, education has to be turned into "instrument of political power,"[281] a way of reading against the conditions that produced a fascist past whose remains are with us once again. In the current historical moment, a society of gated communities, walls, and prisons has torn asunder any sense of shared citizenship, making it more and more difficult to imagine a sense of collective identity rooted in compassion, empathy, justice, and shared obligations to each other. Against this tattering of public space, it is crucial to develop a lofty vision that refuses to give up on the radical imagination and the willingness to fight for a world in which an emancipatory kind of struggle and politics is possible.

Such a politics must move beyond exhibiting outrage towards the regime of neoliberal fascism emerging in the United States and across the globe toward a model for the future. It must also take seriously the notion that there is no democracy without a critical formative culture that can enable the critical power and modes of collective support necessary to sustain it. That is, it must develop a relationship between civic education and political agency, one in which the liberating capacities of language and politics are inextricably linked to the civic beliefs, public spaces, and values that mark a democratic embrace of the social. This is especially urgent at a time when civic culture is being eradicated and commanding visions of an alternative future are disappearing. Politics must once again become educative and education must become central to politics.

As a vehicle for social change, education registers the political, economic, and cultural elements that can be used to reclaim a critical and democratic notion of community and the social relations and values that make such communities possible.[282] The challenge is to create a new and revitalized language of politics, the social, and the common good that can move from the abstract to the practical through the power of a mass social movement that recognizes the tactical importance of what Pierre Bourdieu describes in *Acts of Resistance* as "the symbolic and pedagogical dimensions of struggle."[283]

I am not suggesting that education or public pedagogy in the broadest sense is going to offer political guarantees in creating individuals and movements who can fight against the current attacks on democracy, but there will be no effective resistance without making education fundamental to any political struggle. In his essay "On Politics" in *The Sociological Imagination*, the late sociologist C. Wright Mills captures the spirit of this sentiment in his comment on the value of the social sciences:

> I do not believe that social science will 'save the world' although I see nothing at all wrong with 'trying to save the

world' — a phrase which I take here to mean the avoidance of war and the rearrangement of human affairs in accordance with the ideals of human freedom and reason. Such knowledge as I have leads me to embrace rather pessimistic estimates of the chances. But even if that is where we now stand, still we must ask: if there are any ways out of the crises of our period by means of intellect, is it not up to the social scientist to state them? ... It is on the level of human awareness that virtually all solutions to the great problems must now lie.[284]

If progressives are going to redeem a democratic notion of the social, they need to rethink what it means to take on the challenge of changing how people think about and relate to themselves and others along with the conditions that bear down on their lives. Such efforts speak to possibilities for nurturing modes of civic literacy and critical modes of learning and agency. It also points, as the late Tony Judt observed, to the need to forge a "language of justice and popular rights [and] a new rhetoric of public action."[285] Revitalizing a progressive agenda should be addressed as part of broader social movement capable of reimagining a radical democracy in which public values matter, the ethical imagination flourishes, and justice is viewed as an ongoing struggle. In a time of dystopian nightmares, an alternative future is only possible if we can imagine the unimaginable and think otherwise in order to act otherwise.

II. LANDSCAPES OF TERROR AND STRUGGLE

Chapter 5

Neoliberalism and Higher Education in a Time of Tyranny

We decide whether we love the world enough
to assume responsibility for it
— Hannah Arendt

HIGHER EDUCATION, in our politically desperate age, is threatened by a legacy of anti-intellectualism that it does not dare to name. This inheritance has an eerie resonance with an authoritarian past that asserts itself, in part, with a growing belief among the American public that education is "bad for America" and that it is at odds with Trump's vision of making America great again.[286] The Trump administration, along with other conservative institutions, needs education to fail in a very particular way because it needs democracy to fail. Hostile to its role as a public good, avenue for social mobility, and as a crucial civic institution, the Trump regime is attempting through the logic of a weaponized neoliberalism to reshape education with an intense emphasis on privatization, commodification, deregulation, training, and managerialism.[287]

Some elements of the corporate world and ruling elites are also committed to undermining the democratic mission of higher education. For instance, high tech companies such as Google and Apple no longer

require job "applicants to have a college degree." [288] This lack of support for higher education is also evident in the title of a recent industry
article "Apple HR couldn't care less if you have a college degree."[289] In
this regressive view, education is described exclusively in economic
terms and is beholden to the assumption that only corporations and
market-driven interests have the right to define both the purpose of
education and what type of education is needed by students. Under
such circumstances, higher education is threatened for its potential
role as a public sphere capable of educating informed citizens who
can resist diverse forms of oppression, interrogate power relations,
and exercise civic courage.

Under the reign of neoliberalism, the mission of higher education has
changed dramatically since the 1970s in the United States. No longer
viewed as a democratic public sphere committed to the values of
equality, justice, freedom, and inclusion, it has been transformed into
an entrepreneurial institution that mirrors the logic of the market and
the values of corporations. The goal of producing critical, thoughtful,
socially responsible, and broadly educated citizens has given way to
churning out student investors, competitive financiers, and savvy consumers. Training for the market is the new modus operandi of higher
education. Academic success is defined by how much one expands
one's future financial portfolio. Rather than viewed as a medium for
egalitarianism, social mobility, and a crucial institution for producing an educated citizenry, higher education is increasingly defined
as a corporate entity, reduced to the dystopian demand for accumu-
lating capital, profits, and a business model of governance. As Terry
Eagleton once noted, "By and large, academic institutions have shifted from being the accusers of corporate capitalism to being its ac-
complices ... The real problem today is that universities have largely
ceased to play their classical role as sources of critique."[290] Under such
circumstances, democracy itself has been economized, refigured,
and turned into a slogan and marketing ploy for promoting economic
growth.

Higher education has become complicitous with the ongoing legitimation and dissemination of the market as a model for governing all
of social relations. As such, academic knowledge and modes of inter-
action and communication have been disconnected over time from
the vocabulary of community, compassion, equality, and justice and
replaced by the antiseptic discourse of deregulation, efficiency, cap-

ital flows, economic growth, outsourcing, commercialization, privatization, and a survival-of-the-fittest ethos. Students are motivated to accept not only profit accumulation as a model of human activity, but to view themselves as a species of human capital. As Wendy Brown points out:

> In a neoliberal era when the market ostensibly takes care of itself ... government [is] both responsible for fostering economic health and as subsuming all other undertakings (except national security) to economic health ... This formulation means that democratic state commitments to equality, liberty, inclusion, and constitutionalism are now subordinate to the project of economic growth, competitive positioning, and capital enhancement. These political commitments can no longer stand on their own legs and ... would be jettisoned if found to abate, rather than abet, economic goals.[291]

Byung-Chul Han has argued that "every age has its signature afflictions" and, in this case, the current historical moment is notable for its embrace of a culture of generalized fear, its war on labor, its attack on the welfare state, its devaluation of social goods, and its ongoing attack on youth and higher education.[292] The criminogenic machinery of power has reached the highest levels of the US government and, in doing so, it is changing the language of educational reform while making it difficult for faculty and students to resist their own erasure from modes of self-governance and a critical education. New forms of racist discrimination, unbridled commodification, and exclusion rooted in a retreat from ethics, the social imagination, and democracy itself weakens the role higher education might take in an age of increasing tyranny.

Against the force of a highly militarized mode of casino capitalism in which state violence and a resurgence of white supremacy are at the center of power, higher education is being weakened in its ability to resist the authoritarian machinery of social death now shaping American society. The modern loss of faith in the merging of education and democracy needs to be reclaimed, but that will only happen if the long legacy of struggle over education is once again brought to life as part of a more comprehensive acknowledgment of education being central to politics itself.

II

Donald Trump's ascendancy in American politics has made visible a plague of deep seated civic illiteracy, a corrupt political system, and a contempt for reason that has been decades in the making; it also points to the power of a neoliberal political and economic project that has resulted in the withering of civic attachments, the undoing of civic culture, the decline of public life, and the erosion of any sense of the value of the social contract. Galvanizing his base of true-believers in post-election demonstrations, the world is witnessing how a politics of bigotry and hate is transformed into a spectacle of fear, divisions, and disinformation. Under President Trump, the scourge of mid-20th century authoritarianism has returned not only in the menacing plague of populist rallies, fear-mongering, hate, and humiliation, but also in an emboldened culture of war, militarization, and violence that looms over society like a rising storm.

The reality of Trump's election may be the most momentous development of the age because of its enormity and the shock it has produced. The whole world is watching, pondering how such a dreadful event could have happened. How have we arrived here? What forces have allowed education to be undermined as a democratic public sphere, capable of producing the formative culture and critical citizens that could have prevented such a catastrophe from happening in an alleged democracy? We get a glimpse of this failure of civic culture, education, and civic literacy in the willingness and success of the Trump administration to empty language of any meaning, a practice that constitutes a flight from historical memory, ethics, justice, and social responsibility. Under such circumstances and with too little opposition, the government has taken on the workings of a disimagination machine, characterized by an utter disregard for the truth, and often accompanied, as in Trump's case, by "primitive schoolyard taunts and threats."[293] In this instance, Orwell's "Ignorance is Strength" materializes in the Trump administration's weaponized attempt not only to rewrite history, but also to obliterate it. What we are witnessing is not simply a political project but also a reworking of the very meaning of education both as an institution and as a cultural force.

Truth is now viewed as a liability and ignorance a virtue. Under the auspices of this normalized architecture of alleged common sense, literacy is now regarded with disdain, words are reduced to data, and science is confused with pseudoscience. All traces of critical thought appear at the margins of the culture as ignorance becomes a central feature of American society. For instance, two thirds of the American public believe that creationism should be taught in schools and a majority of Republicans in Congress do not believe that climate change is caused by human activity, making the US the laughingstock of the world.[294] Politicians endlessly lie knowing that the public is addicted to exhortation, emotional outbursts, and sensationalism, all of which mimics celebrity culture. Image selling now entails lying on principle, making it easier for politics to dissolve into entertainment, pathology, and a unique brand of criminality. The corruption of both the truth and politics is abetted by the fact that the American public has become habituated to overstimulation and lives in an ever-accelerating overflow of information, images, and culture of immediacy. Experience no longer has the time to crystalize into mature and informed thought. Opinion now trumps reason and evidence-based arguments. News has become entertainment and echoes reality rather than interrogating it. Popular culture revels in the spectacles of shock and violence.[295]

Defunded and corporatized, many institutions of higher education have been all too willing to make the culture of business the business of education, and the transformation has corrupted their mission. As a result, many colleges and universities have been McDonaldized as knowledge is increasingly viewed as a commodity resulting in curricula that resemble a fast-food menu and is instrumentalized and divorced from its pursuit of truth and democratizing influences.[296] As neoliberalism replaces the language of politics with the market-driven vocabulary of managerialism, the promise of shared power and governance disappears. One consequence is that faculty are subjected increasingly to a Wal-Mart model of labor relations designed "to reduce labor costs and to increase labor servility."[297] Students fare no better and are now relegated to the status of customers and clients. On a larger scale, the educational force of the wider culture has been transformed into a spectacle for violence and trivialized entertainment and a tool for legitimating ignorance. As education in the broadest sense becomes bereft of democratic content yet remains central to politics itself, it removes democratic values and a compassion for the other from the ideology, policies, and institutions that now control American society.

I am not arguing simply about the kind of anti-intellectualism that theorists such a Richard Hofstadter, Ed Herman, Noam Chomsky, and Susan Jacoby have documented, however insightful their analyses might be. I am pointing to a more lethal form of illiteracy that has become a scourge and a political tool designed primarily to make war on language, meaning, thinking, and the capacity for critical thought. Chris Hedges is right in stating that "the emptiness of language is a gift to demagogues and the corporations that saturate the landscape with manipulated images and the idioms of mass culture."[298] Words such as love, trust, freedom, responsibility, and choice have been deformed by a market logic that narrows their meaning to either a commercial relationship or a reductive notion of getting ahead. We don't love each other, we love our new car, and we turn the mall into a temple of worship. Instead of loving with courage, compassion, and desiring a more just society, we love a society saturated in an enervating materialism. Freedom now means removing one's self from any sense of social responsibility so one can retreat into privatized orbits of self-indulgence and unbridled self-interest.

This new form of illiteracy does not simply constitute an absence of learning, ideas, or knowledge. Nor can it be solely attributed to what has been called the "smartphone society."[299] On the contrary, it is a willful practice and goal aimed at actively depoliticizing people and making them complicit with the forces that impose misery and suffering upon their lives. At the same time, illiteracy bonds people and offers the pretense of a community bound by a willful denial of facts and its celebration of ignorance. How else to explain the popular support for someone like Donald Trump who boldly proclaims "I love the poorly educated!"[300] Or, for that matter, the willingness of his followers to put up with his contemptuous and boisterous claim that science and evidence-based truths are "fake news," his dismissal of journalists who hold authority accountable as the "opposition party," and his willingness to bombard the American public with an endless proliferation of peddled falsehoods that reveal his contempt for intellect, reason, and truth. What are we to make of the fact that a person who holds the office of the presidency has praised Alex Jones publicly and thanked him for the role he played in his election victory? Jones is a conspiracy trafficker who runs the website Infowars and believes that September 11th was an "inside job" and that the massacre of children at Sandy Hook was faked.

Illiteracy no longer marks populations predominantly immersed in poverty with little access to quality education; nor does it only suggest the lack of proficient skills enabling people to read and write with a degree of comprehension and fluency. More profoundly, illiteracy is also about refusing to act from a position of thoughtfulness, informed judgment, and critical agency. Illiteracy has become a political weapon and form of political repression that works to render critical agency inoperable and restages power as a mode of domination. Illiteracy serves to depoliticize people because it becomes difficult for individuals to develop informed judgments, analyze complex relationships, and draw upon a range of sources to understand how power works and how they might be able to shape the forces that bear down on their lives. Illiteracy provides the foundation for being governed rather than how to govern.

This mode of illiteracy now constitutes the modus operandi of a society that both privatizes and kills the imagination by poisoning it with falsehoods, consumer fantasies, data loops, and the need for instant gratification. This is a mode of illiteracy and education that has no language for relating the self to public life, social responsibility, or the demands of citizenship. It is important to recognize that the prevalence of such manufactured illiteracy is not simply about the failure of colleges and universities to create critical and active citizens; it is about a society that eliminates those public spheres that make thinking possible while imposing a culture of fear in which there is the looming threat that anyone who holds power accountable will be punished.[301]

At the present moment when democracy is under increasing attack across the globe, the attack on education as a common good and literacy as the basis for producing informed citizens is less of a failing on the part of education, as many conservative pundits claim, than a deliberate policy to prevent critical thinking on the part of both teachers and students. At stake here is not only the crisis of a democratic society, but a crisis of education, memory, ethics, and agency.[302]

What happens to democracy when the President of the United States labels critical media outlets as "enemies of the people" and derides the search for truth by endlessly tweeting lies and misrepresentations? What happens to democracy when individuals and groups are demonized on the basis of their religion? What happens to a society when critical thinking and facts become objects of contempt and are disdained in favor of raw emotion or undermined by an appeal to what US Counselor to the President Kellyanne Conway calls "alternative facts"? What happens to a social order ruled by an "economics of contempt" that blames the poor for their condition and subjects them to a culture of shaming? What happens to a public that retreats into private silos and becomes indifferent to the use of language in the service of a panicked rage that stokes anger but not about issues that matter? What happens to a social order when it treats millions of illegal immigrants as disposable, potential terrorists, and criminals? What happens to a country when the presiding principles of a society are violence and self-interest? What happens is that democracy withers and dies, both as an ideal and as a reality.

In the present moment, it becomes particularly urgent for educators and concerned citizens all over the world to protect and enlarge the formative cultures and public spheres that make democracy possible. The attack on the truth, honesty, and the ethical imagination makes it all the more imperative for educators to think dangerously, especially in societies that appear increasingly amnesiac — that is, countries where forms of historical, political, and moral forgetting are not only willfully practiced but celebrated. All of this becomes more threatening at a time when a country such as the United States has tipped over into a mode of authoritarianism that views critical thought as both a liability and a threat.

Not only is manufactured illiteracy obvious in the presence of a celebrity culture that collapses the distinction between the serious and frivolous, but it is also visible in the proliferation of anti-intellectual discourses and policies among a range of politicians and anti-public intellectuals who are waging a war on science, reason, and the legacy of the Enlightenment. How else to explain the present historical moment with its mounting collapse of civic culture and the future it cancels out? What is to be made of the undermining of civic literacy and the conditions that produce an active citizenry at a time when massive self-enrichment and a gangster morality at the highest reaches of the

US government undermine the public realm as a space of freedom, liberty, dialogue, and deliberative consensus?

Authoritarian societies do more than censor; they punish those who engage in what might be called dangerous thinking. At the core of thinking dangerously is the recognition that education is central to politics and that a democracy cannot survive without citizens who are informed, capable of thinking critically, and willing to act on their convictions and commitments. Critical and dangerous thinking is the precondition for nurturing both the ethical imagination and formative culture that enable members of the public to learn how to govern rather than be governed. Thinking with courage is fundamental to a notion of civic literacy that views knowledge as central to the pursuit of economic and political justice. Such thinking incorporates a critical framework and set of values that enable a polity to deal critically with the use and effects of power, particularly through a developed sense of compassion for others and the planet. Thinking dangerously is the basis for a formative and critical culture that expands the social imagination and makes the practice of freedom operational. Thinking dangerously is the cornerstone of not only critical agency and engaged citizenship, but the foundation for a democracy that matters.

Once again, any viable attempt at developing a democratic politics must begin to address the role of education and civic literacy as central not only to politics itself but also to the creation of individuals capable of becoming critical social agents willing to struggle against injustices and fight to reclaim and develop those institutions crucial to the functioning and promises of a substantive democracy. One place to begin to think through such a project is by addressing the meaning and role of higher education and education in general as part of the broader struggle for and practice of freedom.

Across the globe, a deluge of free-market fundamentalism is using the educational forces of the wider culture that include diverse cultural apparatuses such as the mainstream media, alternative screen cultures, and the expanding digital platforms to reproduce a culture of privatization, deregulation, and commercialization while waging an assault on the historically guaranteed social provisions and civil rights provided by the welfare state, higher education, unions, women's health centers, and the judicial system, among others, all the while undercutting public faith in the defining institutions of democracy.

This grim reality has been called by Alex Honneth a "failed sociality" characteristic of an increasing number of societies in which democracy is waning — a failure in the power of the civic imagination, political will, and open democracy.[303] It is also part of a politics that strips the social of any democratic ideals and undermines any recognition of education and pedagogy as an *empowering* practice necessary for the formation of critical citizens — a practice which acts directly upon the ability to understand, and when necessary transform, the conditions that bear down on everyday existence and public life.

As the language of democracy disappears, it becomes more difficult to raise questions about what role education and educators should take on in the struggle for social justice, equality, and freedom at a time marked by the radical resurgence of a range of anti-democratic forces. In a time of increasing tyranny and legitimized violence, where are the institutions that can produce the ideas, critical intellectuals, and social movements that can make their voices heard in the struggle for a substantive democracy?

One of the challenges facing the current generation of educators, students, and others is the need to address the question of what education should accomplish in a society at a historical moment when it is about to slip into the dark night of authoritarianism. What work do educators have to do to create the economic, political, and ethical conditions necessary to endow young people and the general public with the capacities to think, question, doubt, imagine the unimaginable, and defend education as essential for inspiring and energizing the citizens necessary for the existence of a robust democracy? In a world in which there is an increasing abandonment of egalitarian and democratic impulses, what will it take to educate young people and the broader polity to challenge authority and question how power works in the interest of tyranny? This is a particularly important issue at a time when higher education in the United States and other countries is being defunded and students are being punished with huge tuition hikes and crippling financial debts, all the while being subjected to right-wing policies and a pedagogy of repression that have taken hold under the banner of reactionary and oppressive educational reforms pushed by right-wing billionaires and hedge fund managers.[304]

Given the crisis of education, agency, and memory that haunts the current historical conjuncture, educators need a new language for addressing the changing contexts and issues facing a world in which there is an unprecedented convergence of resources — financial, cultural, political, economic, scientific, military, and technological — increasingly used to exercise powerful and diverse forms of control and domination. Such a language needs to be self-reflective and directive without being dogmatic and needs to recognize that pedagogy is always political because it is connected to the acquisition of agency. In this instance, making the pedagogical more political means being vigilant about "that very moment in which identities are being produced and groups are being constituted or objects are being created."[305] At the same time, it means educators need to be attentive to those practices in which critical modes of agency and particular identities are being denied.

In part, this suggests developing educational policies and practices that both inspire and energize people to challenge the growing number of anti-democratic practices and policies under the global tyranny of casino capitalism.[306] Such a vision suggests resurrecting a democratic project that provides the basis for imagining a life beyond a social order that is immersed in massive inequality, wages endless assaults on the environment, and elevates war and militarization to the highest and most sanctified of national ideals. Under such circumstances, education becomes more than an obsession with accountability schemes, an audit culture, market values, and an unreflective immersion in the crude empiricism of a data-obsessed market-driven society. In addition, such a project rejects the notion that colleges and universities should be downgraded to sites for training students for the workforce — a reductive vision now being imposed on public education by high tech companies such as Facebook, Netflix, and Google along with an increasing group of conservative foundation pundits such as libertarian and George Mason University professor, Bryan Caplan. [307] If high tech companies and billionaires such as PayPal founder Peter Thiel encourage what they call the entrepreneurial mission of education, which is code for collapsing education into training, anti-public intellectuals such as Caplan believe that higher education is just a waste of time for students and that the only type of schooling that matters is vocational.[308] No grand ideas here.

Central here is a notion of pedagogy that should provide the conditions for students to recognize how to use the knowledge they gain both to critique the world in which they live and, when necessary, to intervene in socially responsible ways in order to change it. Critical pedagogy is about more than a struggle over assigned meanings, official knowledge, and established modes of authority: it is also about encouraging students to take risks, act on their sense of social responsibility, and engage the world as an object of both critical analysis and hopeful transformation. In this paradigm, pedagogy cannot be reduced only to learning critical skills or theoretical traditions but must also be infused with the possibility of using interpretation as a mode of intervention, as a potentially energizing practice that gets students to both think and act differently

I think that J.M. Coetzee, the Nobel Prize winner, is right in criticizing the current collapse of education into training when he points out that "all over the world, as governments retreat from their traditional duty to foster the common good and reconceive of themselves as mere managers of national economies, universities have been coming under pressure to turn themselves into training schools equipping young people with the skills required by a modern economy."[309]

What is lost in this instrumentalized view is that students are not just workers but also citizens, and education is about more than training. Learning skills for the workplace is no excuse for purging from education what it means to teach students how to think critically, embrace the common good, exercise a sense of social responsibility, and support a world of values, feelings, and actions that together form the ethical and political foundation necessary for a democratic society.[310] Yes, we must educate young people with the skills they need to get jobs, but as educators we must also teach them to learn "to live with less or no misery [and] to fight against those social sources" that cause war, destruction of the environment, "inequality, unhappiness, and needless human suffering."[311]

At issue here is the need for educators to recognize the power of education in creating the formative cultures necessary to challenge the various threats being mobilized against the ideas of justice and democracy while also fighting for those public spheres, ideals, values, and policies that offer alternative modes of identity, thinking, social relations, and politics. But embracing the imperative of making education meaningful in order to make it critical and transformative also means recognizing that cultural apparatuses such as the mainstream media and Hollywood films are teaching machines and not simply sources of information and entertainment. Such sites should be viewed as spheres of struggle that need to be removed from the control of the financial elite and monopolistic corporations that use them as workstations for propagandizing a culture of vulgarity, self-absorption, and commodification while eroding any sense of shared citizenship and civic culture.

There is an urgent political need for the United States, among other countries, to understand what it means for an authoritarian society to weaponize and trivialize the discourse, vocabularies, images, and aural means of communication in a variety of education and cultural sites and also to grasp that a market-driven discourse does not provide the intellectual, ethical, and political tools for civic education.[312] Such language is used to relegate citizenship to the singular pursuit of unbridled self-interest, legitimate consuming as the ultimate expression of one's identity, and portray essential public services as doing little but reinforcing and weakening any individual responsibility while using the vocabulary of war, militarization, and violence to address a vast array of social problems often faced by citizens and others.

I do not believe it is an overstatement to argue that education can all too easily become a form of symbolic and intellectual violence, one that assaults rather than educates. Examples of such violence can be seen in the forms of an audit culture and empirically driven teaching that dominates higher education, especially in the United States, but also increasingly in other countries such as the United Kingdom, Hungary, and Turkey. These educational projects amount to pedagogies of repression and serve primarily to numb the mind and produce what might be called dead zones of the imagination. These are pedagogies that are largely disciplinary and have little regard for contexts, history, making knowledge meaningful, or expanding what it means for students to be critical and engaged social agents. Of course, the ongoing corporatization of the university is driven by modes of assessment that often undercut teacher autonomy, treat knowledge as a commodity, students as customers, and impose brutalizing structures of governance on higher education. Under such circumstances, education defaults on its democratic obligations and becomes a tool of corporate interests and market-driven values, all the while deadening the capacity to think otherwise in order to act otherwise.

One of the fundamental challenge facing educators within the current age of an emerging authoritarianism worldwide is to create safe educational spaces for students to address "how knowledge is related to the power of self-definition" and social agency.[313] Education, in this sense, speaks to the recognition that any pedagogical practice presupposes some notion of the future, prioritizes some forms of identification over others, upholds selective modes of social relations, and values some modes of knowing over others. Moreover, such an education does not offer guarantees as much as it recognizes that its own visions, policies, and practices are grounded in particular modes of authority, values, and ethical principles that must be constantly debated for the ways in which they both open up and close down democratic relations.

The notion of a neutral, objective education is an oxymoron. Education and pedagogy do not exist outside of ideology, values, and politics. Ethics on the pedagogical front demands an openness to the other, a willingness to embrace a culture of questioning and dialogue, and an ongoing critical engagement with texts, images, events, and other registers of meaning as they are transformed into pedagogical practices both within and outside of the classroom. Education is never innocent and is always implicated in relations of power and specific visions of the present and future. This suggests the need for educators to rethink the cultural and ideological baggage they bring to each educational encounter; it also highlights the necessity of making educators ethically and politically accountable and self-reflective for the stories they produce, the claims they make upon public memory, and the images of the future they deem legitimate. Understood as a form of educated hope, education in this sense is not an antidote to politics, a nostalgic yearning for a better time, or for some "inconceivably alternative future." Instead, it is an "attempt to find a bridge between the present and future in those forces within the present which are potentially able to transform it."[314]

When viewed as an important democratic public sphere, education can provide opportunities for educators, students, and others to redefine and transform the connections among language, desire, meaning, everyday life, and the material relations of power as part of a broader social movement to reclaim the promise and possibilities of an open society. In an age when authoritarianism is spreading across the globe, it should come as no surprise that many governments consider any notion of critical education dangerous because it creates the conditions for students and the wider public to exercise their intellectual capacities, cultivate the ethical imagination, and embrace a sense of social and ethical responsibility.

One of the most serious challenges facing administrators, faculty, and students in colleges and universities is the task of developing a discourse of both critique and possibility. This means developing discourses and pedagogical practices that connect reading the word with reading the world, and doing so in ways that enhance the capacities of young people to translate their hidden despair and private grievances into public transcripts. At best, such transcripts can be transformed into forms of public dissent or what might be called "a moment of 'rupture'" — one that has important implications for public action in a time of impending tyranny and authoritarianism.[315] In taking up this project, educators and others should attempt to create the conditions that give students the opportunity to acquire the knowledge and courage necessary to make desolation and cynicism unconvincing and hope practical.

Democracy begins to fail and political life becomes impoverished in the absence of those vital public spheres such as public and higher education in which civic values, public scholarship, and social engagement allow for a more imaginative grasp of a future that takes seriously the demands of justice, equity, and civic courage. Democracy should be a way of thinking about education, one that thrives on connecting equity to excellence, learning to ethics, and agency to the imperatives of social responsibility and the public good. The question regarding what role education should play in democracy becomes all the more urgent at a time when the dark forces of authoritarianism are on the march all across the globe. As public values, trust, solidarities, and modes of education are under siege, the discourses of hate, racism, rabid self-interest, and greed are exercising a poisonous influence in many societies and are most evident in the discourse of Donald Trump and his merry band of anti-intellectuals and white nationalists. Civic illiteracy collapses the distinction between opinion and informed arguments, erases collective memory, and becomes complicit with the growing criminalization of a range of behaviors and the increasing militarization of places such as public schools and society itself.

Yet, all across the globe, there are signs of hope. Young people are protesting against student debt; environmentalists are aggressively fighting corporate interests; teachers in a variety of countries extending from Canada and Brazil to the United States are waging a brave fight against oppressive neoliberal modes of governance; young people are bravely resisting and exposing state violence in all of its forms; prison abolitionists are making their voices heard, and once again, the threat of a nuclear war is being widely discussed. In the age of financial and political zombies, finance capitalism has lost its ability to legitimate itself in a warped discourse of freedom and choice. Its poisonous tentacles have put millions out of work, turned many black communities into war zones, destroyed public education, undermined the democratic mission of higher education, flagrantly pursued war as the greatest of national ideals, turned the prison system into a default welfare institution for punishing minorities of race and class, produced massive inequities in wealth, income, and power, pillaged the environment, and blatantly imposed a new mode of racism under the silly notion of a post-racial society.

III

I want to go back to a central concern of this chapter by raising the question of how as educators we begin a meaningful conversation about how to redefine and reclaim the mission of colleges and universities as democratic public spheres? In doing so, I want to address in general terms the importance of what I have called the need for a new language of governance accompanied by a reclaiming of the discourse of civic courage and the ethical imagination, all of which I believe are central to any viable notion of change that I am suggesting. This is especially crucial at a time when higher education in the United States is under attack by a savage form of casino capitalism. Regarding the politics of governance, I have argued both explicitly and implicitly that educators, students, and others concerned about the fate of higher education need to mount a spirited attack against the managerial takeover of the university that began in the late 1970s with the emergence of a market fundamentalism called neoliberalism, which is an economic system that argues that market principles should govern not just the economy but all of social life, including politics and education. Neoliberalism thins out politics, reducing it to the language, power, and values of the market while turning it over to the rule of the ultra-rich, big corporations, and Wall Street billionaires. In doing so, it hollows out both the social state and public life through policies that massively increase inequalities of wealth and power, which further destroy the institutions, including public and higher education, which provide the foundations for informed, critical, and engaged forms of citizenship.

As an ideology and policy, neoliberalism has produced cruel austerity measures, defunded public institutions, pushed through skyrocketing tuition hikes, and created what amounts to a culture dominated by metrics and increasingly devoid of humanistic values.[316] Central to such a recognition is the need to struggle against a university system developed around the reduction in faculty power, the replacement of a culture of cooperation and collegiality with a shark-like culture of competition, the rise of an audit culture that has produced a very limited notion of accountability and evaluation, and the narrow and harmful view that colleges "should operate more like private firms than public institutions, with an onus on income generation."[317] In addition, any movement for reforming colleges and universities must both speak out against modes of governance that have reduced faculty to the status of part-time employees and join the fight to take back the governing of the university from the new class of managers and bureaucrats that now outnumber faculty in the United States.

Regarding the discourse of civic courage and the ethical imagination, I have argued that informed citizens are crucial to a democracy and that the university must play a vital role in creating the formative cultures that make such citizens possible. In part, this would mean creating intellectual spaces free of coercion and censorship and open to multiple sources of knowledge in the pursuit of truth, the development of critical pedagogies that inform, energize, inspire, empower and promote critical exchanges and dialogue. These should be spaces in which education focuses on "dispositions and qualities, on human flourishing, and on the fulfilment of individual potential."[318] Education in the more critical sense aims to overcome the moral disregard and undermining of the social and ethical imagination that accompany those deadening repressive pedagogies rooted in utterly instrumental approaches to teaching and learning. These are educational zones that accelerate the deadening of the mind, social responsibility, and the ability to imagine a future different from the present.

There is also the need for providing faculty not only with time and resources necessary for critical teaching and meaningful scholarship but also with full-time employment and protections while viewing knowledge as a public asset and the university as a public good. More is at stake here than protecting job security and providing faculty with the resources and support that enable them to teach, research, and engage in viable forms of public service. There is also the necessity of protecting their right to academic freedom and freedom of speech. Job insecurity and casual labor conditions reinforce a culture of fear, suspicion, and surveillance that silences faculty members and weakens their role in connecting their teaching, scholarship, and service with important and often controversial issues.[319]

With these issues in mind, I want to conclude by pointing to a few initiatives, though incomplete, that might mount a challenge to the current oppressive historical moment in which many societies and their respective colleges and universities find themselves.[320] First, there is a need for what can be called a revival of the social imagination and the defense of the public good in order to reclaim higher education's egalitarian and democratic impulses. This call would be part of a larger project "to reinvent democracy in the wake of the evidence that, at the national level, there is no democracy — if by 'democracy' we mean effective popular participation in the crucial decisions affecting the community."[321] One step in this direction would be for young people, intellectuals, scholars, and others to go on the offensive against a conservative led campaign "to end higher education's democratizing influence on the nation."[322] Higher education should be harnessed neither to the demands of the warfare state nor to the instrumental needs of corporations. Clearly, in any democratic society, education should be viewed as a right, not an entitlement. Educators should mobilize nationally to produce a conversation in which higher education can be defended as a public good and the classroom as a site of deliberative inquiry, dialogue, and critical thinking. Educators need to ask difficult questions about what type of education is responsible for the abandonment of democratic impulses in the United States and the rise of widespread racism, ignorance, and the normalization of lies, deceit, and misinformed arguments. The mission to reclaim higher education as a democratizing force in which administrators, students, and faculty can press the claims for economic and social justice, take risks, and further the frontiers of the critical knowledge and inquiry is an important stratagem for addressing the broader educational challenge to create a social movement in defense of public goods.

Second, I believe that educators need to consider defining pedagogy, if not education itself, as central to producing those democratic public spheres capable of creating an informed citizenry capable of thoughtful action. Pedagogically, this points to modes of teaching and learning willing to sustain a culture of questioning and enable pedagogical practices through what Kristen Case calls moments of classroom grace.[323] Pedagogies of classroom grace point to the conditions for students and others to interrogate commonsense views of the world and begin to question, however troubling, their sense of agency, relationship to others, and their relationships to the larger world. This can be linked to broader pedagogical imperatives that ask why we have wars, massive inequality, a surveillance state, and a range of other problems. There is also the issue of how everything has become commodified, along with the withering of a politics of translation that might otherwise prevent the collapse of the public into the private. Central to the notion of classroom grace is the question of what role the university, revered historically for its commitment to truth and reason, can play to generate pedagogical spaces responsible for safeguarding the interests of young people and educate future generations of adults to fulfill their social, political, economic, and ethical responsibility to create and sustain a genuine democracy. Surely, one must reject the neoliberal emphasis on methods, standards, and metrics as the organizing principle of pedagogy in a time of legitimized violence and growing authoritarianism.

These are not merely methodical considerations but also moral and political practices because they presuppose the creation of students who can imagine a future in which justice, equality, freedom, and democracy matter. In this instance, the classroom should be a place to think critically, ask disquieting questions, and engage with troubling knowledge, even though that may mean transgressing established norms and bureaucratic procedures. Such pedagogical practices are rich with possibilities not only for recognizing the classroom as a space that ruptures, engages, unsettles, and inspires, but also for extending the meaning of learning to wider cultural apparatuses in which education functions often by stealth to shape subjects, identities, and social relations, often so as to mimic the values of a market-driven society.

Education in this instance must provide the conditions for faculty to develop the moral courage to invent in a time of growing tyranny a pedagogy that addresses "the fragility of peace," society's growing addiction to violence, and the civic vacuum that now feeds a state and corporate culture of fear, precarity, and militarization.[324]

Education as democratic public space cannot exist under modes of governance dominated by a business model in which only corporate CEOs are hired as university presidents; it undermines its democratic mission of the university when tenure-line faculty positions are filled with contract labor, students are treated as customers, and learning is increasingly defined in instrumental terms removed from community needs. In the US, over 70 percent of faculty occupy non-tenured and part-time positions, many without benefits and salaries so low that they qualify for food stamps. It gets worse. In some parts of the United States, adjunct faculty are now hired through temp agencies. Faculty need more security, full-time positons, autonomy, and the support needed to function as professionals. While not all countries emulate this model of faculty servility, it is part of a neoliberal machinery that has increasingly gained traction across the globe.

Third, educators need to develop a comprehensive educational program that would include teaching students how to live in a world marked by multiple overlapping modes of literacy extending from print to visual culture and electronic cultures. It is not enough to teach students to be able to interrogate critically screen culture and other forms of aural, video, and visual forms of representation. They must also learn how to be cultural producers. This suggests expanding the parameters of literacy and educating students to develop skills necessary for them to both produce and work in alternative public spheres such as online journals, television shows, newspapers, zines, and any other platform in which different modes of representation can be developed.

Such tasks can be accomplished by mobilizing the technological resources and platforms that many students are already familiar with. It also means working with one foot in existing cultural apparatuses in order to promote unorthodox ideas and views that would challenge the affective and ideological spaces produced by the financial elite who control the commanding institutions of public pedagogy in North America. As I mentioned earlier, what is often lost by many educators and progressives is that popular culture is a powerful form of education for many young people and yet it is rarely addressed as a serious source of knowledge. As Stanley Aronowitz has observed, "theorists and researchers need to link their knowledge of popular culture, and culture in the anthropological sense — that is, everyday life, with the politics of education."[325]

Fourth, academics, students, community activists, young people, and parents must address the ongoing struggle for the right of students to pursue a free, formidable, and critical education removed from the influence, if not domination, of corporate values. This means faculty and young people should have more influence in the shaping of education and what it means to expand and deepen the practice of freedom and democracy. Put simply, educators need to be attentive to their students' histories, needs, aspirations, and hopes. At the very least, if higher education is to be taken seriously as a public good, it should be tuition-free, at least for the poor, and affordable for the affluent. This is not a radical demand and is not unprecedented as countries such as Germany, France, Norway, Finland, and Brazil already provide this service for young people. While university education is free in much of the world, the combined student debt is close to $1.5 trillion, which is almost identical to the tax break Trump gave to big corporations and the ultra-rich.

Accessibility to higher education is especially crucial at a time when young people have been left out of the discourse of democracy. They are the new disposable populations who lack meaningful jobs, a decent education, hope, and any semblance of a future better than the one their parents inherited. Facing what Richard Sennett calls the "specter of uselessness," they are a reminder of how finance capital has abandoned any viable vision of the future, including one that would support future generations. This is a mode of politics and capital that eats its own children and throws their fate to the vagaries of the market. The ecology of finance capital only believes in short term investments because they provide quick returns. Under such circumstances, young people who need long term investments are considered a liability. If any society is in part judged by how it views and treats its children, the United States by all accounts is truly failing in a colossal way.

Moreover, if young people are to receive a critical and comprehensive education, academics might consider taking on the role of public intellectuals, capable of the critical appropriation of a variety of intellectual traditions while relating their scholarship to wider social problems. This raises questions about the responsibility of faculty to function as intellectuals relating their specialized knowledge to wider social issues, thinking hard about "how best to understand how power works in our time" and how education might function in the interest of economic and social justice.[326]

Fifth, in a world driven by data, specialisms, and the increasing fragmentation of knowledge, educators need to enable students to develop a comprehensive vision of society that "does not rely on single issues."[327] This is not to suggest that single-issue oriented movements are not relevant as much as to suggest that they are inadequate in struggling against oppression in all of its forms. As Katrina Forrester observes, "There should be no contradiction between single issue struggles such as women's rights and providing an alternative economic and political vision for America."[328] It is only through an understanding of the wider relations and connections of power that young people and others can overcome uninformed practice, isolated struggles, and modes of singular politics that become insular and self-sabotaging. In short, moving beyond a single-issue orientation means developing modes of analyses that connect the dots historically and relationally. It also means developing a more comprehensive vision of politics and change, an issue I will explore in more detail in the conclusion.

Sixth, another serious challenge facing educators who believe that colleges and universities should function as democratic public spheres is the task of developing a discourse of educated hope. Informed hope goes beyond critique extending it into the realm of the possible. Critique is important for breaking through the hold of commonsense assumptions that legitimate a wide range of injustices. It is also crucial for making visible the workings of unequal power and the necessity of holding authority accountable. But critique is not enough, and lacking a discourse of possibility can lead to a stultifying sense of despair or, even worse, a damaging cynicism. A faith in politics speaks to imagining a life beyond commodities, profits, and branding, and combines a realistic sense of limits with a lofty vision of demanding the impossible. Reason, justice, and change cannot blossom without hope because it taps into our deepest experiences and longing for a life of dignity with others, a life in which it becomes possible to imagine a future that does not mimic the present. I am not referring to a romanticized and empty notion of possibility, but to a notion of informed and realistic political imaginary that faces the concrete obstacles and realities of domination while continuing the ongoing task of "holding the present open and thus unfinished."[329]

The discourse of possibility not only looks for productive solutions, it also is crucial in defending those public spheres which authoritarianism has not yet colonized with a predatory class of unethical zombies — who are producing dead zones of the imagination that even Orwell could not have envisioned while waging a fierce fight against the possibilities of a democratic future. One only has to look at the United States, Turkey, the Philippines, and Hungary to realize that the time has come to develop a political language in which civic values, social responsibility, and the institutions that support them become central to invigorating and fortifying a new era of civic imagination, a renewed sense of social agency, and an impassioned international social movement with a set of strategies to challenge the neoliberal nightmare engulfing the planet.

The dark shadow of authoritarianism may be spreading, but it can be stopped. And that prospect raises serious questions about what educators, youth, intellectuals, and others are going to do today to make sure that they do not succumb to the authoritarian forces circling so many countries across the globe, waiting for the resistance to stop and for the lights to go out. My friend, the late Howard Zinn rightly insisted that hope is the willingness "to hold out, even in times of pessimism, the possibility of surprise." To add to this eloquent plea, I would say, that history is open, and it is time to think otherwise in order to act otherwise, especially if as educators we want to imagine and fight for alternative futures and horizons of possibility.

Chapter 6

Shooting Children in the Age of Disposability: Beyond the Spectacle of American Carnage

The paradox of education is precisely this - that as one begins to become conscious one begins to examine the society in which he is being educated.
— James Baldwin

DONALD TRUMP may have once startled Republican lawmakers with his sudden and unexpected support for background checks and other gun control measures, but a closer look at his comments to lawmakers reveals his continued adherence to the core of the pro-gun script that he has been following all along.[330] At his meeting with lawmakers on February 28, 2018, Trump buckled down on the idea that the real problem is the existence of gun-free zones, arguing that eliminating gun-free zones will "prevent [mass shootings] from ever happening, because [the shooters] are cowards and they're not going in when they know they're going to come out dead."[331]

The president's repeated efforts to disparage the idea of gun-free zones fit with the earlier call for arming teachers by one of his most powerful financial and ideological backers — the dark knight of gun violence, NRA leader Wayne LaPierre. Meanwhile, Trump has shown no interest in preventing school shootings by hiring more teachers, teacher aids, support staff, and psychologists. In fact, after the demonstrations over the Parkland, Florida school shooting died down, Education Secretary Betsy DeVos suggested that federal funding could be taken from the federal Every Student Succeeds Act to purchase firearms and provide training for public schools teachers and school staff. Stiff opposition prevented DeVos from turning her suggestion into policy, but she did state that it is perfectly legal to allow school districts to use federal funds to purchase guns. Lily Eskelsen García, head of the National Education Association, responded to DeVos's comments stating that it is "ill-conceived, preposterous, and dangerous. Arming teachers and other school personnel does nothing to prevent gun violence."[332] Dewey Cornell, a University of Virginia professor who studies school shootings and safety issues, rightly observes that "the proposal to arm teachers might be emotionally appealing after a school shooting, but it is not practical or realistic. We should place more emphasis on preventing shootings than preparing for shootings. Prevention must start long before a gunman shows up at school. Instead of more guards, we need more counselors."[333]

The key issue involved in preventing school shootings is to identify troubled students before they commit a violent act while at the same time addressing the myriad political, economic, and cultural forces and corporate interests outside of the school that make millions from producing and normalizing violence in the United States. Violence is both a dogmatic religion and a source of huge profits for the purveyors of mass destruction and extends from private defense contractors and those industries producing and selling guns and ammunition to a culture industry that trades in the spectacle of violence.[334]

Trump's initial call for a comprehensive gun bill may have made for "captivating" television, but it rattled NRA lobbyists and initiated a tsunami of calls to their allies on Capitol Hill. Nothing surprising in this reaction. It gets worse. Chris Cox, the top lobbyist for the NRA, met with Trump a few days after Trump made his remarks and suggested in a tweet that the president had backed away from his apparent embrace of gun control. Moreover, there is little confidence following Trump's remarks that Republicans would even remotely endorse legislation for meaningful gun control.[335] The NRA has five million members and an annual revenue of $348 million and "paid five million dollars to lobbyists last year."[336] There is no indication that the time and money the NRA has spent buying off cowardly politicians will prove ineffectual.[337]

The deeply troubling call for eliminating gun-free zones and arming teachers comes at a time when many schools have already been militarized by the presence of police and the increasing criminalization of student behaviors. Moreover, the debate over school violence often ignores the ways in which violence is built systemically into the public school. This includes not only the consequences of underfunding and its effects on essential school programs such as free lunches for poor kids, but also zero tolerance policies that criminalize a range of student behaviors reinforcing what is often called the school-to-prison pipeline. In addition, there are numerous states that explicitly allow teachers and administrators to administer physical force to students. Many of the children who are the objects of such violence that ranges from paddling and physical restraints to being placed in seclusion suffer from some type of disability.[338]

Suggesting that teachers be armed and turned into potential instruments of violence extends and normalizes the prison as a model for schools while increasing the potential expansion of the school-to-prison pipeline.[339] What is being left out of this tragedy is that the number of police in schools has doubled in the last decade from 20 percent in 1996 to 43 percent today. Moreover, as more police are put in schools, more and more children are brutalized by them. There is no evidence that police presence in schools has made them any safer. Instead, more and more young people have criminal records, are being suspended, or expelled from school, all in the name of school safety, particularly poor students of color. As Sam Sinyangwe, the director of the Mapping Police Violence Project, observes:

> The data ... that does exist ... shows that more police in schools leads to more criminalization of students, and especially black and brown students. Every single year, about 70,000 kids are arrested in school.... [Moreover] since 1999, 10,000 additional police officers have been placed at schools, with no impact on violence. Meanwhile, about one million students have been arrested for acts previously punishable by detention or suspension, and black students are three times more likely to be arrested than their white peers. [340]

Trump's proposal to arm teachers suggests that the burden of gun violence and the crimes of the gun industries and politicians should fall on teachers' shoulders, foolishly imagining that armed teachers would be able to stop a killer with military grade weapons and disregarding the risk of teachers shooting other students, staff, or faculty in the midst of such a chaotic moment. But it does more — it also damagingly shifts the image of school, as a site of critical teaching and learning, to a militarized institution organized around fear and mistrust. At the same time, it offers the image of the teacher less as a mentor, caregiver, and role model than as a soldier in the war on terror, a warrior, and an "armed representative of the state, with the legal right to take someone's life."[341] As Benjamin Balthaser observes, the proposal to arm teachers "is not about helping students, but turning the student-teacher relationship from one of trust and respect into one of violence."[342] Organizing public education around a culture of fear, mistrust, and security makes it easier to turn schools into armed fortresses that normalize pedagogies of repression.

In addition, the proposal to arm teachers points to the insidious fact that mass shootings and gun violence have become so normalized in the United States that, as Adam Gopnik points out, "we must now be reassured that, when the person with the AR-15 comes to your kid's school, there's a plan to cope with him." [343] Such statements make visible a society rife with the embrace of force and violence. How else to explain the fact that, at the highest levels of government, horrendous acts of violence, such as mass shootings involving school children, are now discussed in terms of containing their effects rather than eliminating their causes. This is especially troubling in light of the fact, as *The New York Times* reports, that after a "gunman killed 20 first graders and six adults with an assault rifle at Sandy Hook Elementary School in 2012 … there have been at least 239 school shootings nationwide. In those episodes, 438 people were shot, 138 of whom were killed."[344] Moreover, as violent crime rates go down, the number of children who are the objects of gun violence keeps going up. For example, according to the *Gun Violence Archive,* 667 children and 2,841 teens were injured or killed by gun violence in 2018.[345]

The culture of fear surrounding school shootings is more than an ideological ruse to sell firearms, it is also the bedrock of a growing attempt to turn school shootings into a growth industry for the companies that market school safety equipment.[346] According to Tiffany Hsu, reporting in *The New York Times*, "In 2016, the 'sales of security equipment and services to the education sector reached $2.7 billion, up from $2.5 billion in 2015, according to data from IHS Markit.'"[347] As expected, after the Parkland shooting, the demand for such services is expanding rapidly. Everything from palm scanners and metal detectors to $120 ballistic panels that kids can put in their backpacks are being advertised by the security industries. Yet, there is little evidence that these security technologies and services actually work.[348] As the RAND Corporation reports, "Many schools have turned to technology — including entry control equipment, metal detectors, and video surveillance systems — as a way to prevent, intervene in, respond to, and protect schools from violent acts and risks to students' safety. But rigorous research about the effectiveness of these technologies is virtually nonexistent."[349]

Then Governor Rick Scott of Florida, a Republican, argued soon after the Parkland shooting: "We've got to invest in metal detectors, we've got to invest in bulletproof glass, we've got to invest in steel doors, we've got to invest in upgraded locks. We've got to do everything we can to make sure that somebody that wants to harm any one of our students can never do it again."[350] Under pressure from protesting students, Scott belatedly signed a gun reform law that raised the minimum age to purchase a firearm to 21 from 18, provided more than $69 million for mental health assistance in schools, and sets aside a budget of "$67 million for arming some teachers if both the local school district and local sheriff's department agree."[351] The bill also bans "the sale or possession of bump fire stocks, give[s] law enforcement greater power to seize weapons and ammunition from those deemed mentally unfit, and [provides] additional funding for armed school resource officers."[352]

While the bill represents a moderate break from NRA policies, it does not go far enough and fails to ensure comprehensive criminal background checks or to ban assault rifles, like the AR-15. In the end, this is a deceptive and disingenuous move to address gun violence in America. Not only does it fail to address the underlying causes of such violence, it also ignores the need for providing adequate funds for schools to employ human resources and needed support systems, which would include a range of services that address harmful issues such as poverty, racism, homelessness, and overcrowded classrooms while providing neighborhood outreach programs, more guidance teachers, mental health counselors, and social workers. Of course, the one-sided emphasis on security is also a rationale for turning political immaturity, moral cowardice, and social irresponsibility into a virtue while embracing violence as an organizing principle for a nation in decline. The insidious ideology behind the call for more technologies that promote security and school safety is motivated mostly by the corporate drive for profits and has little to do with addressing the epidemic of gun violence in the United States. Such technologies also provide the bedrock of the surveillance state and speak less to the real need for security than for the ongoing need to impose a digital gaze that threatens freedom itself.[353]

The call for arming teachers and for ramping up security gloss over the diverse ways in which gun violence disproportionally impacts black people and ignore different political demands for addressing violence from black and white student movements. Before Parkland, there was the killing by the police of a number of black children such as Mike Brown, Jordan Davis, Trayvon Martin, Tamir Rice, Freddie Gray, and Jordan Edwards. The broader anti-racist argument that whiteness is a site of terror and violence is almost completely absent from the debate around putting armed police in the schools and arming white teachers, many of whom teach in segregated schools. This is especially tragic given what appears to be the ongoing shooting by white police of unarmed black children and youth. The killing of children casts a wide net in the United States and is not limited to school shootings. The exclusive focus on school security and the Parkland school shootings obscure this issue. It too easily obscures the fact that black children are not viewed as innocent but often seen by the police as a threat.[354] In this logic, the underlying causes of mass shootings and gun killings disappear, and the measure emphasized for dealing with such violence reproduces an act of political and moral irresponsibility in its call to curtail or contain such violence rather than address the underlying causes of it.

We live in an age in which the politics of disposability has merged with what Jeffrey St. Clair has called the spectacle of "American Carnage."[355] America is addicted to violence and the figures around gun deaths that point to a self-inflicted carnage make clear such a cruel reality. For instance, Bob Hennelly points out that "since 1968, nearly 1.4 million Americans have been killed by guns — as compared to a total of 1.17 million Americans killed in every war this nation has fought since its founding."[356] The machineries of social death and misery are the outgrowth of a mode of casino capitalism in which more and more people are considered waste, expendable, and excess. The politics of disposability now couples with acts of extreme violence as pressure grows to exclude more and more people from the zones of visibility, justice, and compassion. This is also true for children, especially black children. Violence against children in the United States has reached epidemic proportions. As Marian Wright Edelman points out:

> Pervasive gun violence against children is a uniquely shameful all-American epidemic. Consider that since 1963, over three times more children and teens died from guns on American soil than US soldiers were killed by hostilities in wars abroad. On average, 3,426 children and teens — 171 classrooms of 20 children — were killed by guns every year from 1963 to 2016. And gun violence comes on top of other major threats of global violence that threaten our children.[357]

A culture of cruelty, silence, and indifference to the needs of children, built through the efforts of conservative media politicians and the gun industry and lobby, has become a central and ethically disturbing feature of American society. This is a culture of political corruption and social abandonment that "has a remarkable tolerance for child slaughter, especially the mass murders of the children of others."[358] This culture of violence has a long history in the United States and has become increasingly legitimated under the Trump regime, a regime in which lawlessness and corruption combine to ignore the needs of children, the poor, elderly, sick, and vulnerable. Drawing from James Baldwin, the story of violence in America is the story of America: "it is not a pretty story," and it is a crisis that is reproduced rather than addressed by calling for reforms limited to safety and security.[359] Violence in America is far deeper than something that can be solved through gun control.

In the age of neoliberal brutality, protecting guns and profits has become more important than protecting the lives of young people. And this is only one register of the degree to which the threshold of violence has been exceeded in ways that were once considered unimaginable. What does it mean when children live with the daily fear of being assaulted, especially as their behavior on the streets, schools, and workplaces is being criminalized? Black and brown youth have long been the subject of moral panics in the United States and increasingly they have found themselves within a vast array of institutions that views them as a dangerous threat and subjects them to the punishing industries. Over time, violence has increasingly seeped into too many spaces where children should find comfort and safety. As Edelman observes, this generation of children has "quickly learned a sad truth many adults already knew: There is no safe space in America."[360] She writes:

> Gun violence saturates our children's lives and relentlessly threatens them every day. It has romped through their playgrounds; invaded their birthday parties; terrorized their Head Start classrooms, childcare centers, and schools; frolicked down the streets they walk to and from school; danced through their school buses; waited at the red light and bus stop; lurked behind trees; run them down on the corner; shot them through their bedroom windows, on their front porches, and in their neighborhoods. Gun violence has taught, entertained, and tantalized them incessantly across television, movie, and video game screens and the internet. It has snatched away their parents, aunts, uncles, cousins, brothers, sisters, friends, and teachers; sapped their energy and will to learn; and made them forget about tomorrow.[361]

As is apparent from its policies, values, and celebration of profits over the needs of children, American society no longer views young people as a worthy social investment or the promise of a decent future. On the contrary, as John and Jean Comaroff note in *Frontiers of Capital: Ethnographic Reflections on the New Economy*, instead of becoming a primary register of the dreams of a society, youth have become "creatures of our nightmares, of our social impossibilities, and our existential angst."[362]

With young people viewed largely as a liability, the institutions that they inhabit have been discarded as citadels of critical thinking and social mobility. As a result, such institutions, particularly public education, have become zones of social abandonment — often modeled after prisons — that appear to exist in a state of perpetual danger and fear, especially for students marginalized by race and class and for whom violence operates routinely and in multiple ways. Children are now defined largely as consumers, clients, and fodder for the military or the school-to-prison pipeline. As a result, their safety is now enmeshed with the weaponized discourse of surveillance, and security personnel and police patrol their corridors. Horrific shootings boost the ratings and profit margins of the mainstream press, undercutting these news outlets' will and ability to use their resources to address the culture and political economy of violence that now amounts to a form of domestic terrorism in the United States.

As Brad Evans and I have argued in *Disposable Futures: The Seduction of Violence in the Age of the Spectacle*, violence has now become the organizing principle for society in general.[363] It is also worth noting that the spectacularization, marketing, and commodification of violence powerfully mediates both how the American public understands the relations of power that benefit from the production of violence at all levels of society and how the visceral suffering that is produced can be neutralized in a culture of immediacy and "alternative facts." How does one judge an ecosystem of violence shaping society and every-day life at a time when facts, evidential standards in reasoning, and moral reasoning are being abandoned? Truth, facts, and evidence are now subordinate to feelings, emotion, and opinions.[364] This is a script for fascism, a politics that ignores reality and enshrines violence. As a form of entertainment, violence now saturates popular culture. As Dr. Norman Herr observes, by the time a child finishes elementary school, they have witnessed 8,000 murders on TV, and by the time they are 18, they have seen 200,000 violent acts.[365] Of course, this figure does not include the extreme violence that has crept into and become normalized in Hollywood films, video games, and the daily news.

The politics of distraction is embedded in the logic that has become a trademark of the Trump administration. At the same time, it creates more profits for the gun industries and makes clear that many people, including children, have no safe spaces in the US. The message to students is clear. They are not worth protecting if they threaten the profits of the industries that trade in violence and the purses of the politicians who have become the lackeys for them. Rather than engage young people and other gun rights advocates in a debate about gun control, some conservatives mimic the discourse of humiliation and lies used relentlessly by Trump in claiming that "bereaved students were being manipulated by sinister forces, or even that they were paid actors."[366]

As objects of moral and social abandonment, young people are beginning to recognize that the response to their calls for safety, well-being,

and a future without fear is cruel and cynical. In addition, their struggle against gun violence makes clear that the Trump administration,
the NRA, and the industries that trade in instruments of violence and
death are waging a war against democracy itself. The call to arm teachers also speaks to the Trump administration's efforts to further milita-
rize and expand the weaponization not only of the armed forces but
also of spaces in which large numbers of students congregate. In his
call to arm 20 percent of all teachers, Trump is suggesting that 640,000
teachers be trained and given guns. *The Washington Post* estimates
that the costs of training teachers sufficiently could reach as high as
$718 million while the cost of providing teachers with firearms could
amount to an additional $251 million.[367] According to *The Post,* "the
full-price, more expansive training and the full-price firearm … creeps
past $1 billion."[368] Furthermore, putting 640,000 more guns in schools
is not only a reckless suggestion, it also further enriches the profits of
gun makers by adding millions of dollars to their bottom line. Why not
invest this amount of money in providing support staff and services
for students — services that could meaningfully support those facing
mental health issues, bullying, homelessness, and poverty?

When combined with a culture of fear and a massive government investment in a carceral state, the politics of disposability eerily echoes
the damaging legacy of a fascist past in the US, with its celebration
of violence, concentration of power in the hands of the few, massive
inequities in wealth, and militarization of all aspects of society. There
is no defense for weapons of war to be sold as commodities to either
children or anyone else. Gun violence in the US is not simply about
a growing culture of violence, it is about the emergence of a form of
domestic terrorism in which fear, mistrust, lies, corruption, and financial gain become more important than the values, social relations, and
institutions that write children into the script of democracy and give
them an opportunity to imagine and struggle for a future that embraces human rights, the rule of law, and the institutional and governing
structures that strengthen democracy. How else to explain that Trump
in his capacity as the President of the United States constantly demon-
izes and threatens politicians, journalists, and individuals who reject
his demagoguery?

Playing to his base at a rally in Montana in 2018, Trump celebrated
a congressman who had criminally assaulted a reporter who asked
him a question. Republican Greg Gianforte responded to a question

Guardian reporter Ben Jacobs asked him about health care by body slamming him. Trump praised Gianforte at the rally stating "Any guy that can do a body slam, he's my kind of guy."[369] Trump's praise for Gianforte's actions have been viewed by many as code for encouraging violence by his base against journalists, politicians, and others. Astonishingly, Trump's heated rhetoric follows a number of attacks on journalists, including by all-accounts the horrific torture and killing by the Saudi government of Saudi journalist Jamal Khashoggi.

A war culture now permeates American society — extending from sports events and Hollywood films to the ongoing militarization of the police and the criminalization of everyday behaviors such as violating a dress code or doodling on a desk.[370] War has become a permanent element of everyday life, deeply etched into our national ideals and social relations. And those responsible for the bloodshed it produces appear immune from social criticism and policies that limit their power.

The issue of violence in the United States appears as a toxin that threatens to poison every aspect of society. This suggests that the debate about school shootings is not simply about gun violence; it is about a form of neoliberal fascism that has tipped over into a dangerous moment in American history. What does it mean politically when the highest measure of how a society judges itself ethically and politically is no longer about how it treats its children? Violence on a grand scale certainly has produced a high sense of moral outrage within the US public at times, but not over the fate of young people for whom the future is being cancelled out.

People in the US need a new language to talk about violence in order to interrogate its many registers and the threads that tie them together. One important thread is the politics of disposability and financialization that is central to capitalist violence. School violence cannot be understood outside of the deeply inordinate influence of money and power in US politics. Nor can it be removed from a history of violence in which the discourse of dehumanization allowed the barbarism of lynching to become a sport, an act of genocide against Native Americans to be celebrated as part of a mythic past. The call to model schools after prisons would have to be examined against the rise of the punishing state and the Trump administration's celebration of a "law and order" regime. The anger fueling what might be called white rage would have to be analyzed against the gutting of jobs, wages, pensions, health care benefits, and the massive growth of inequality in wealth and power in the United States. US society has become an abyss in which violence, disposability, and the logic of social abandonment and terminal exclusion work against the interests of most children and for the interests of the rich and powerful. Weapons now operate in the service of what might be called the necro-power of casino capitalism. How else to explain the fact that there are more than 13,000 homicides a year in the United States, or that seven teens are killed with guns on average daily, yet the response on the part of politicians is either silence and inaction or a more aggressive push to put more guns in circulation?

A cult of militarism has dragged extreme violence into the very soul of the US and has become a source of pride rather than alarm and anger. This depraved transformation is accelerated by a crisis of agency in which every relation is reduced to an exchange relation, one in which, as political theorist Wendy Brown has argued, "everything from learning to eating become matters of speculative investments — ranked, rated, balanced in your portfolio." [371] When the only self available to the public is rooted in the discourse of entrepreneurship, it is not surprising for a society to produce generations of people indifferent to the effects of mass violence, unsympathetic to the growing multitudes of disposable individuals and groups, and unmoved by a culture of deepening collective cynicism. Casino capitalism has hardened large segments of the American public into moral and political callousness. One consequence is an indifference to a society in which the killing of children is routine.

Mass shootings and gun violence in America cannot be abstracted from what I call the death of the social, which involves the collapse of an investment in the public good, the ongoing destruction of democratic values, and the undermining of civic culture. As the state is reduced to its military and police functions, public space becomes a space of violence, surveillance, and a location for the unthinkable. A toxic mix of rugged individualism, untrammeled self-interest, privatization, commodification, and culture of fear now shapes American society, leaving most people isolated, unaware of the broader systemic forces shaping their lives, and trapped in a landscape of uncertainty and precarity that makes them vulnerable to having their anxieties, anger, and rage misdirected.

All too often, the only discourse available for them to deal with their problems is provided by the disingenuous vocabulary of fear and security delivered in the call for gun ownership, the allure of violence as an antidote to their individual and collective anxieties, and a hateful appeal to racism, Islamophobia, and demonization.

The highjacking of freedom and individual responsibility by extremists is corrosive and rots society from within, making people susceptible to what C. W. Mills describes as "organized irresponsibility" in his book *The Politics of Truth*. [372] The right-wing attack on the welfare state, community, and democracy functions to dissolve crucial solidarities, undermine mutual responsibilities, and dissolve bonds of social obligation. In the absence of the discourse of community, compassion, and mutual respect, fear and violence have become the new currency mediating social relations at all levels of society. Massive inequality, widespread immiseration, loss of social provisions, and a culture that feeds on fear and hatred of the other refigures democracy as the enemy of the people. Under such circumstances, self-rule and collective governance are thwarted, popular sovereignty disappears, and the radical constraints imposed by neoliberalism reduce choice to a toxic contest between winners and losers. In a society in which the war of all against all prevails, the call for more guns is symptomatic of the shredding of the social fabric, the hardening of society, the evisceration of public trust, and a ratcheting up of a political and economic investment by the ruling elite in the machinery of cruelty, inequality, and militarism. Neoliberal fascism creates a predatory sink-or-swim culture that denies the larger social good, disdains "losers," embodies a pathological disdain for community, and trades in the vocabulary of a hyper-masculine bully parading as the strongman.

Violence in the United States is part of a wider politics of disposability in which the machineries of social and political death accelerate the suffering, hardships, and misery of children. For too long, youth have been written out of the script of justice and democracy. Gun violence, mass shootings, and state violence are simply the most visible elements of a culture that organizes almost every aspect of civil society for the production of terror and fear and views young people within the specter of uselessness and indifference.

Fortunately, the students from Parkland, Florida, are refusing to be silent about gun violence and are fighting back, shunning the coarse language used by apologists for systemic violence while embracing new forms of social solidarity and collective struggle. But it must be remembered, black youth are fighting back against gun violence as well, though these students do not get the attention white students get. Yet, these students are also standing up, making their voices heard and are not willing to be written out of the discourse of democracy and social and racial justice. They are refusing the violence that accompanies a politics of disposability as a form of state terrorism while refusing to be viewed as excess, collateral damage or as a by-product of the violence produced by the police, NRA, and the arms industries.

Young people in Parkland are saying "No" to being rendered voiceless and "Yes" to undermining those cowardly politicians like Marco Rubio and Rick Scott who are lackeys of the gun industry and the NRA. They don't want prayers in the face of the ongoing mass shootings taking the lives of young people on a weekly basis. They want justice. These young people are unwilling to privatize hope or allow the ethical imagination and their sense of moral outrage and social responsibility to be tranquilized. They are not only outraged over the brutal actions of the defenders of gun violence and the epidemic of police violence, they feel betrayed. Betrayed, because they have learned that the power of state violence, the gun industries, and the politicians who defend them do not consider their lives worthy of protection and a future free of violence. They recognize that US society is unusually violent and that they are a target. Moreover, they are arguing convincingly that mass shooting in the United States have a direct correlation with the astronomical number of guns present in this country.[373] But there is more at stake here than an epidemic of gun violence. There is the central idea of the US as defined by carnage — violence that extends from the genocide of Native Americans and slavery to the rise of mass incarceration and the instances of state violence against blacks, undocumented workers, and Muslims now sweeping across the US.[374]

At least for the moment, young people are refusing to live with a modern system of violence that functions as a form of domestic terrorism. Engaged in a form of productive unsettling and collective dissent, they are fighting back, holding power accountable, and giving birth to a vibrant form of political struggle. The Parkland students in particular have gained the attention of the liberal establishment, and they have called for a number of liberal reforms such as a ban on assault rifles and the strengthening of background checks for purchasing guns.

Yet, however liberal these reforms are, the boldness of their anti-gun student movement and their perseverance to continue their struggle in the face of sustained attacks by conservatives and some liberals suggest that both the gun lobby and industries as well as Trump as president are vulnerable and can be defeated.[375] As Natasha Lennard points out:

> The Parkland teenagers organizing the "March for Our Lives" rallies and walkouts have already shown a tenacity and strength that goes far beyond the Democratic Party line. They have been unabashed about shaming NRA-backed politicians to their faces on national television — stomping where kowtowing journalists dare not tread.[376]

Moreover, it is remarkable that some major corporations are withdrawing their support for the NRA; the consumer campaign to boycott NRA's business partners is widening, and national support for gun control of some form has reached its highest level in years, given the power that the gun industry and lobbyists have wielded historically in stifling any dissent, resistance, or oppositional legislation.[377] At the same time, the liberal goals of the Parkland students are not radical enough and must address the more far-reaching demands against state terrorism and gun violence produced by the Black Lives Matter movement and other radical minority student movements.[378] The grassroots movement started by the Parkland students must join with the youth movements started by a range of minority youth. Abolishing assault rifles and keeping guns out of the hands of criminals and the mentally unbalanced must be connected to getting guns off the streets and addressing those social and economic conditions that have weakened "social inhibitions against the use of violence."[379] These would include: the ongoing militarization of schools modeled after prisons, the increasing criminalization of a range of social behaviors such as homelessness and truancy, the expansion of the mass-incarceration state, the rise of debtors prisons, the arming of the police with military style weapons, the growing inequality in wealth and power, the impoverishment of the inner cities, and the open assault on democratic institutions in support of the common good.

The political and cultural distinctiveness of the current generation of black and white survivors is clear in their use of social media, their willingness to speak out, their planned marches, their civic courage, and their unwillingness to continue to live with the fear and insecurity that have shaped most of their lives.[380] Young people are beginning to recognize that there are no commanding visions in America, when civic culture is being eradicated by the unchecked power of finance capital, civic education has given way to a reductionist notion of training, and communal values and social ties have been replaced by shared fears and a culture of unbridled individualism and cruelty. Mass entertainment functions primarily to infantilize and depoliticize everything it touches as it turns audiences primarily into consumers and every relationship into an act of commerce and harsh competition. Economic Darwinism has produced a hardening of the social order — a kind of self-righteous coldness that takes delight in the suffering of others, abandons the social contract, and views young people as a liability because they are a reminder of how casino capitalism has shed itself of any responsibility for the future. Young people are refusing to live in a world in which democracy is viewed with disdain, economic impoverishment the new normal, and a survival-of-the-fittest culture has replaced bonds of trust with the bonds of fear and suspicion and stripped life of the most basic necessities. As part of a nation-wide protest in March 2018, thousands of young people walked out of their schools and rallied against gun violence suggesting that young people may be on the verge of a social awakening in the United States, one that integrates the diverse registers of violence that impact and cut across class, racial, ethnic, religious, and gender divisions. Hopefully, this moment of collective resistance will expand, become more inclusive, and will transform itself into a movement fighting to reclaim the promises of a radical democracy.

Since the *March for Our Lives* rally, a number of young people went on a bus tour speaking at various town halls and other venues in order to spur voter turn out in order to get people to vote on legislation enacting various gun control measures. Moreover, young people are opening up local chapters around the country in order to convince the public to fund efforts to develop anti-gun violence programs. Such efforts speak to the ongoing attempts by young people to both create mass movements to resist gun violence and produce new political formations in the interests of expanding and deepening a gun-free democratic society.

Chapter 7

Striking for Justice:
Teachers and Students
Protesting Neoliberal Violence

*Even in the darkest of times we have the right
to some illumination.*
—Hannah Arendt

SINCE DONALD TRUMP'S ELECTION in November 2016, there have been few occasions to feel hopeful about politics. The crisis of politics and democracy is on full display with what appears to be an endless number of gun shootings, the proliferation of mac-jobs, ballooning consumer debt, climate denialism, unchecked toxic masculinity, systemic police violence, and racialized mass incarceration. While there is no shortage of mass cynicism, there are also spectacular demonstrations of resistance and a proliferation of causes for hope as brave students from Parkland, Florida, and equally courageous teachers throughout the United States have lead throughout 2018 mass movements of demonstrations, walkouts, and strikes. Before exploring the possibilities of this pregnant moment, it is important to take the measure of where we stand now.

Teachers and students aside, the United States has been in the midst of a crisis of values, ethics, and politics that has been decades in the making. Produced largely by a neoliberal system that has subordinated all aspects of social life to the dictates of the market, this assault has stripped assets from the civic sphere and produced untenable levels of inequality. What we are now living through is the emergence of new political formations in which neoliberalism has generated both progressive resistance, but also, and more often than not, it has produced and mobilized growing expressions of fascism. The evidence abounds.

The nation state has been transformed into a corporate state reconfiguring political power to serve the interest of the rich and big corporations. Like previous forms of fascist rule, the state offers both legal and extra-legal protections for those economic, political, and social relations that favor and enable entitlements for those groups that increasingly find liberal democracy burdensome — the financial elite, big corporations, nativists, white nationalists, and religious fundamentalists. For example, under the Trump administration, a range of structural transformations have been executed that include cutting taxes to benefit the rich, privatizing public services, deregulating business practices, rolling back of environmental protections, lessening workplace safety standards, and packing the Supreme Court with rightwing ideologues, e.g., Judge Brett Kavanaugh. These governmental projects point to attempts on the part of the Trump regime to enable the current restoration and legitimation of white supremacy, racial hierarchies, and the unleashing of what Robert O. Paxton has called the mobilizing passions of fascism — which range from the call for a purer community and the beauty of violence to the need for the authority by a natural leader and the belief that one's group is a victim.[381]

Rather than rein in Wall Street and invest in large scale infrastructure projects, as Trump promised during his presidential campaign, he has distributed more wealth upward to the one percent, cut social provisions for the poor, expanded the military budget, bolstered a reactionary politics with a vicious and reactionary brand of white supremacy and ultra-nationalism, and shamelessly embraced a heavy dose of crony capitalism. Feminist writer and educator Nancy Fraser has spelled out the fascistic elements in his reactionary politics. She writes, once Trump was elected, he:

> … proceeded to double down on [his] reactionary politics …
> hugely intensified and ever more vicious. The list of his provocations and actions in support of invidious hierarchies of

status is long and chilling: the travel ban in its various versions, all targeting Muslim-majority counties, ill-disguised by the cynical late addition of Venezuela; the gutting of civil rights at Justice (which has abandoned the use of consent decrees) and at Labor (which has stopped policing discrimination by federal contractors); the refusal to defend court cases on LGBTQ rights; the rollback of mandated insurance coverage of contraception; the retrenchment of Title IX protections for women and girls through cuts in enforcement staff; public pronouncements in support of rougher police handling of suspects of 'Sheriff Joe's' contempt for the rule of law, and the 'very fine people' among white supremacists who ran amok at Charlottesville … The upshot is not reactionary populism but hyper-reactionary neoliberalism.[382]

At the same time, the state has waged a relentless war against social bonds, social welfare, and the obligations of social conscience. Caught in the crosshairs of the neoliberal ideological and financial juggernaut have been those public spheres, social formations, and crucial ways of life that make possible the formative cultures, civic virtues, and knowledge that produce critical and engaged democratic citizens. At the heart of such an agenda is a war on equality, justice, freedom, civic literacy, and critical thinking itself. The shredding of the landscape and fabric of democracy coupled with the seeding of social pathologies of white rage, racism, nativism, and the degradation of language have been well documented, especially with the onset of the Trump presidency.[383]

Also documented have been the ongoing attacks on women's reproductive rights, public servants, undocumented workers, and the transformation of poor black and Latino neighborhoods into war zones. In addition, visceral examples of state violence have been reproduced in the endless public narratives of misery that testify to the consequences of lost jobs, the elimination of social provisions, the attack on the welfare state, increasing poverty and inequality, declining health care benefits, and the growing militarization of society. For the last 45 years, neoliberalism has evolved into a new kind of fascism wielding the savage tools of austerity in the service of a predatory and cruel capitalism while imposing on most Americans a deadly precarity and survival-of-the-fittest logic that reinforces the pernicious forces of uncertainty, fear, insecurity, and despair.

But there is more at stake here than the emergence of new and more aggressive forms of state violence, economic domination, white supremacist logics, and an ensuing culture of cruelty — there is also a range of ideological and pedagogical practices aimed at both depoliticizing and undoing the possibilities for critical forms of individual and social agency. For instance, neoliberalism's distorted notion of freedom is entwined within a narrow notion of market-based choice and a flight from social responsibility that undermine the notions of a militant hope and collective struggle. Moreover, freedom in the neoliberal rulebook is linked to the impersonal forces of the market and serves to privatize needs and further isolated and separate individuals from each other. Neoliberalism preaches freedom from constraint, which is code for elevating self-interest over social responsibility and justifying a society of winners and losers while diverting the obligations of citizenship to the freedom to consume.[384] As George Monbiot observes, freedom under neoliberalism is a kind of newspeak for the crushing of personal and social agency, the public imagination, and democracy itself. He writes:

> The freedom that neoliberalism offers, which sounds so beguiling when expressed in general terms, turns out to mean freedom for the pike, not for the minnows. Freedom from trade unions and collective bargaining means the freedom to suppress wages. Freedom from regulation means the freedom to poison rivers, endanger workers, charge iniquitous rates of interest and design exotic financial instruments. Freedom from tax means freedom from the distribution of wealth that lifts people out of poverty.[385]

This notion of freedom places a stranglehold on democracy that not only undermines the rights of citizens, it also unleashes forms of misdirected rage and anger. This truncated and dangerous notion of freedom is fuelled and abetted by a depoliticizing cynicism and war-against-all logic that easily morphs into an ugly form of "libertarian freedom to speak and enact the power of white male supremacy against principles of equality and policies of social justice that neoliberalism itself cast as illegitimate and, worse, totalitarian."[386] It also casts every relationship as a marketable transaction and, in doing so, devalues any notion of sociality that is not defined in terms of a commercial transaction. The marketplace makes a mockery of freedom and responsibility by offering up the claim that the United States is a meritocracy and that one's fate in life is defined by a society that rewards merit. In this discourse, winners and losers are defined by character, resilience, grit, and intelligence. This is simply code for ignoring the advantages the rich are born into, the vast machinery of inequality that decides in advance who the winners are, and a rationale for connecting what might be called surplus powerlessness to an intense ideology of self-blaming.[387] Social needs no longer occupy a dominant space of public articulation because the institutions that support the social contract are withering while impoverished social relations breathe new life into forces that grow more cruel, meaner, degraded, and humiliating. Under Trump, privatization, commodification, punishment, and a culture of cruelty have become the defining features of politics.[388]

In the current historical moment, the discourses of racial purification, law and order, and disposability have moved from the fringes to the center of society and the consequences are both the near death of the social contract and the acceleration of a social order in which bonds of trust have been replaced by the bonds of fear, bigotry, and hatred. Correspondingly, the forces of privatization, deregulation, and commodification have reinforced an anemic notion of self-help for populations who struggle to survive on a daily basis. While at the same time, the neoliberal juggernaut promotes infantilization and depoliticization for the rest, which is too easily transformed by demagogic politicians and pundits into politics of misdirected fury, a narrative of self-blame, and a sense of individual helplessness.

Under this new form of American fascism, there is more than a war on the social and those constitutive values and public spheres that make a democracy possible — there is also a range of structural transformations that extend from cutting taxes to benefit the rich and eliminating all elements of the commons, on the one hand, to the offshoring of major industries and the financialization of all aspects of society on the other hand.[389] This becomes clear when we look at the consequences of the right-wing policy of cutting taxes, which are designed in the long run as an excuse to roll back all vestiges of the social state by weakening or gutting altogether social security, Medicare, Medicaid, and numerous other social provisions. Letting the market decide is code for neoliberal fascism and translates into power and wealth for the few and poverty for the many.

Vast cultural apparatuses controlled by the financial and corporate elite function as forms of pedagogical regulation to privilege market relations, mold market-based identities in the discourse of common sense, and erase activities not related to the practice of commercial exchange. As Doreen Massey observes, neoliberalism produces a worldview, ideological scaffolding, and vocabulary that shapes desires and attempts to reproduce everything in the image of the market; the market becomes "a powerful means by which subjectivities are constructed and enforced." She writes:

> There is a whole worldview — and economic theory ... It is one in which the majority of us are primarily consumers, whose prime duty (and source of power and pleasure) is to make choices. The so-called truth underpinning this [worldview] — which has been brought about in everyday life through managerial instruction and the thoroughgoing renaming of institutional practices in their allowed forms of writing, address and speech — is that, in the end, individual interests are the only reality that matters; that those interests are purely monetary; and that so-called values are only a means of pursuing selfish ends by other means. And behind this in turn, the theoretical justification of this now nearly-dominant system is the idea of a world of independent agents whose choices, made for their own advantage, paradoxically benefit all. Moreover, for this to 'work,' no individual agent can have sufficient power to determine what happens to the whole.[390]

As I have argued throughout this book, neoliberalism is more than an economic policy and set of political ideas — it is also a powerful narrative and story that defines who we are and how we should act. As an ideology, it disowns structural problems and systemic forms of oppression and preaches a survival-of-the-fittest ethos that teaches people that they are on the own, utterly responsible for whatever problems, failures, and misfortunes they may face. Failure, regardless of the cause, now becomes a rationale for self-hatred, shame, and often misdirected anger.

This is a powerful force for depoliticization because it undermines any sense of collective agency and reduces politics to the discourse of self-blame. In the face of widespread poverty, insecurity, inequality, and precarity, the poor are told to try harder. And when they are not told to try harder, they are pitted against each other through the polarities of race and class. One consequence is that the poor, vulnerable, and disadvantaged begin to blame themselves for their circumstances and resent others, especially racial and religious others, who exhibit what are viewed as individual failings or debasing differences. As Monbiot observes, this is a toxic and punishing ideology. He writes:

> If you do not have a job, the relentless whisper tells you, it is not because of structural unemployment. If your credit card is maxed out, it is not because of the impossible costs of housing but because you are feckless and improvident. If your children are unfit, it is not because their school has sold its playing field but because you are a bad parent. In a world governed by competition, those who fall behind come to be defined and self-defined as losers. [The] poor are the new deviants, who have failed both economically and morally, and are now classified as social parasites.[391]

What has often been lost on those who have courageously charted this growing assault on modes of critical agency, self-determination, democracy, and the accompanying rise of a neoliberal brand of fascism in America is perhaps its most debilitating legacy — the long standing and mutually reinforcing attacks on both public education and young people. As schools have been transformed into zones of economic and political abandonment, they have been increasingly modeled after prisons, sites that crush the imagination, and subject to pedagogies of oppression purged of the experiences, values, and creativity necessary for students to expand and deepen their knowledge and imagination. Moreover, as state and corporate violence engulfs the entire society, schools increasingly become subject to forms of violence that in the past existed normally outside of their doors.

Mass shootings now occur with mind numbing regularity, the police patrol school corridors, student infractions are increasingly treated as criminal problems, and security firms profit from a culture of fear and insecurity — all of which dramatically undermines the symbolic and material conditions for teaching and learning to take place. Until recently, this war on public education understood as part of a larger war on public goods and democracy has been ignored, especially in light of its implications for making visible what Hannah Arendt has called the "'crystalized elements' of totalitarianism that forged together ... make fascism possible."[392] The intensified attacks on schooling and education in the last decade make clear that the rudiments of anti-intellectualism, sanctioned ignorance, and civic illiteracy central to a fascist politics are still with us, though they have developed into new forms.[393] The poisonous possibilities and emergence of such forms are particularly dangerous in light of the rise of a number of anti-democratic tendencies in the United States.

In what follows, I explain that it is crucial not only to connect together the recent actions of mass opposition that have emerged in the form of widespread teacher strikes and the growing student opposition to gun violence, but also to place these movements within a wider theoretical and political context in order to understand the new political and economic formations and types of violence at work in creating the conditions that have given rise to these forms of opposition in the first instance. I also want to situate actions of protest within a broader analysis of state violence and how it functions as a thread that braids together and runs through these diverse protest movements.

II

Public schools are at the center of the manufactured breakdown of the fabric of everyday life. They are under attack not because they are failing, but because they are public — a reminder of the centrality of the role they play in making good on the claim that critically literate citizens are indispensable to a vibrant democracy. Moreover, they symbolize the centrality of education as a right and public good whose mission is to provide young people with the knowledge, skills, values, and public concerns that enable them to exercise those modes of leadership and governance in which "they can become fully free to claim their moral and political agency."[394] Public education is a threat to the advocates of authoritarianism because it invokes an ethical imperative, which as Hannah Arendt put it in "The Crisis of Education," reminds us "whether we love the world enough to assume responsibility for it."[395] Rather than a business enterprise and commodity to be bought and sold, teachers and students across the country are re-claiming education as a public good and a human right, a protective space that should be free of violence, and open to critical teaching, informed judgments, and thoughtful modes of inquiry. Not only is it a place to think, engage in critical dialogue, encourage human poten-tial, and contribute to the vibrancy of a democratic polity, it is also a place in which the social flourishes in that students and teachers learn to think and act together. All the more reason for public schools to be viewed as dangerous, if not a direct challenge to Trump's version of illiberal democracy.

Public schools have surely become a threat to the alt-right, political demagogues, religious fundamentalists, and the conservative rul-ing elite because thinking itself is considered dangerous. Moreover, learning how to think critically and how to mediate charged appeals to one's emotions define democratic education, which opens up the space of translation, one that enables students to make power ac-countable, embrace diverse forms of civic literacy capable of chal-lenging the various threats to justice and democracy, and develop the capacities necessary for them to be responsible to themselves, others, and the larger society. Education is especially dangerous when it does the bridging work between schools and the wider society, between the self and others, and allows students to translate private troubles into broader systemic considerations. Schools are dangerous because they make visible the crucial notion that teaching and learning at best recognize, to quote Richard J. Bernstein, that "democracy is 'a way of life,' an ethical ideal that demands *active* and *constant* attention. And if we fail to work at creating and re-creating democracy, there is no guarantee that it will survive."[396]

Democracy involves a reflective faith in the capacity of all human be-ings for intelligent judgment, deliberation, and action if the proper so-cial, educational, and economic conditions are to be furnished. This is the deeper message behind the students' opposition to gun violence and the message behind the teacher strikes — all of whom are de-manding safe spaces for learning, smaller classes, respectable work-ing conditions, reasonable pensions, sufficient resources, and decent salaries. The striking teachers and protesting Parkland students are telling a different story about education, one that refuses the domi-nant narratives that have produced what I referred to in chapter 4 as a form of "slow violence" against public education and the people it serves.[397] As Nixon observes, "slow violence" is "a violence that occurs gradually and out of sight, a violence of delayed destruction that is dispersed across time and space, an attritional violence that is typically not viewed as violence at all."[398]

Evidence of the largely ignored consequences of "slow violence" in America's schools is obvious in a number of statements from teachers made to David Smith, a writer for *The Guardian*, in which they talked about the unspeakable conditions their students had to endure.[399] Emily James, a teacher in Brooklyn, New York, spoke for many teachers in stating: "Our students are often hungry, or don't sleep, or come from shelters or homes with a single parent … Our buildings are infested with cockroaches and rodents and many air conditions don't work. Our furniture is old and broken."[400] Alyssa Arney, a 46-year-old teacher in San Francisco, argued that many teachers "spend our days feeding children, doing their laundry, filling out forms, and providing basic support services. Students cannot learn when their most fundamental needs are not being met — and teachers can't teach when they're acting as the social safety net."[401] The "slow violence" that has been waged against schools, with the exception of mass shooting events themselves, is neither "immediate in time, explosive and spectacular … nor [does it erupt] into instant sensational visibility."[402]

On the contrary, the accumulated consequence of decades-long defunding is either hidden, unseen, or denied by politicians and a wider public. And low wages for teachers has been utterly normalized. Of course, one could also argue that even when such violence is spectacularized as in the Sandy Hook school and Parkland, Florida, shootings, the underlying causes and absence of legislative consequences that produce and reproduce such violence remain hidden beneath the most immediate calls for gun regulations and other surface reforms. What both the striking teachers and protesting students are saying is that the crisis of public schooling and the war on youth are related, and this can no longer be ignored. What is particularly promising about these widespread protest movements is that they have the potential to move public consciousness towards a wide-ranging recognition in which the assaults on public schooling will be understood as part of a larger war on schools, on youth, and on the very possibility of teaching and learning — and that these struggles cannot be separated.

III

Insisting on the right to teach, the right to learn, and the right to view schools as valued public good have been radical acts. How did we get to this present moment? Deindustrialization, the tax revolt of the 1970s, and the increasing attack on the social contract and welfare state imposed new burdens on public education at the end of the 20th and beginning of 21st centuries. Schools were increasingly underfunded even as inner cities descended into poverty, class sizes increased, poor students dropped out, and schools became more segregated by class and race. Teachers were increasingly deskilled and lost control over the conditions of their labor as lifeless accountability schemes and mind-numbing testing regimes were passed off as reform initiatives under the Reagan, Bush, Clinton, and Obama administrations.

These reforms, while allegedly appealing to educational ideals, especially the assumption that they would help economically underprivileged students, did just the opposite and turned schools largely into imagination crushing citadels of boredom and conformity. Reagan's 1983 report, A *Nation at Risk*, claimed schools were not just failing but embodied a rising tide of mediocrity and held the potential for a looming disaster. The report attacked teacher unions, claimed teachers were lazy, and opened the door for charter schools, deregulation, and tax cuts.[403] Bush's educational policy, the No *Child Left Behind Act of 2001*, further embraced defining schools through market forces, which did a great deal to leave many children behind. The Bush administration's educational perspective was made explicit in comments made by then education secretary Roderick Paige. Paige stated that the country's biggest teachers' union, the National Education Association, was like a "terrorist organization."[404] Unfortunately, Obama educational policy, Race to the Top, simply provided more of the same dead-end approaches to education that had crippled public education for decades. According to renown education critics such as Professors Kenneth Saltman and David Berliner along with former assistant Secretary of Education under Reagan, Dianne Ravitch, Obama followed "the same punitive cycle of high-stakes testing and accountability ushered in under the presidency of George W. Bush — and … these policies are actually hurting students."[405]

What is different under the Trump administration is that today's teachers and students are facing not only a crisis of schooling but also a crisis of education in the broader sense. Trump is upfront in stating without apology that he loves both the uneducated and being uneducated. Not only does he disparage any display of critical intelligence, whether in the critical media, courts, or on-line culture, he has made it clear with his education secretary, Betsy DeVos, the billionaire and utterly clueless charter school advocate, that he holds the very notion of public education as a crucial democratic public sphere in low regard. In a meeting with 2018 teachers of the year, DeVos stuck to her anti-public school, anti-teacher script by stating that she hoped that teachers "would take their disagreements and solve them not at the expense of kids and their opportunity to go to school and learn."[406] In part, this is code for a broader narrative in which conservatives and liberals for years have been blaming teachers exclusively for students who drop out of school, end up in the criminal justice system, perform poorly academically, and distrust authority, among other issues.[407] As if such failures are entirely the fault of teachers, regardless of the defunding of schools, the rise of overcrowded classrooms, the increase in widespread poverty, the starving of the public sector, accelerated attacks on public servants, the transformation of cities into ghost towns, the smashing of teacher unions, and the creation of labor conditions for teachers that are nothing short of deplorable. No surprises here. DeVos appears to have a penchant for reaching for the low hanging rhetorical fruit when it comes to commenting on public schools, teachers, and students.

The ideological assault against public schools, teachers, and students is now in full force given the alliance among big corporations, billionaires such as the Koch brothers, conservative foundations, business lobbying groups such as the American Legislative Exchange Council (ALEC), and the Trump administration that aims to privatize public schools, increase tax breaks for the rich (thereby depriving schools of essential revenue), substitute privately run charter schools for public schools, support voucher programs, cut public services, endorse on-line instruction, and redefine public schools around issues of safety and security, further situating them as armed camps and as extensions of the criminal justice system.[408] The question here is why would

corporations, politicians, hedge fund managers, and a horde of billionaires want to destroy public education and inflict irreparable harm
on millions of children? Gordon Lefer, a professor at the University of
Oregon, has argued brilliantly that America is a country in decline,
characterized by a rise in economic inequality, families unable to support themselves, increased hardships for workers, the decline of social
provisions, the evisceration of public goods, restricted voter rights,
lowered employment standards, and an ongoing attack on social safety nets and a dwindling middle-class.[409] Lefer believes that the war on
schools is rooted in a terrifying set of neoliberal policies and that big
business is determined to dismantle public education. He argues:

> Big corporations are ... worried about how to protect them-
> selves from the masses as they engineer rising economic
> inequality [and] they try to avoid a populist backlash ...
> by lowering everybody's expectations of what we have a
> right to demand as citizens ... When you think about what
> Americans think we have a right to, just by living here, it's re-
> ally pretty little. Most people don't think you have a right to
> healthcare or a house. You don't necessarily have a right to
> food and water. But people think you have a right to have
> your kids get a decent education.[410]

Public schools are no longer sites whose purpose is to prepare young
people for the promise of social and economic mobility. Instead, after
decades of neoliberal policies, they are defined increasingly by both
the threat of gun violence and mass shootings and a current of violence in which the grim conditions of austerity deprive teachers of decent salaries, adequate resources, and a viable degree of autonomy. A
related register of violence bears down on students not only through
cruel neoliberal policies of disinvestment, but also by way of a growing
security state in which every "school is geared for terror," every student
is treated as a suspect or target, and every student has to navigate a
climate of fear as "they move through their classrooms."[411] As Sophie
McClennen observes:

> Students are treated as either lazy, entitled, or dangerous ...
> research showed that in 2013, 59 percent of black students
> and 32 percent of white students received corporal punish-
> ment. When they aren't being paddled, they are being shot
> at. Since the 1999 Columbine shooting, 150,000 students

have witnessed a school shooting. Teen depression rates are on the rise, as are suicide rates, which are up 24 percent over a 15-year period.[412]

State- and corporate-sponsored violence is the thread that connects the student and teacher movements along with the cruel logic according to which both teachers and students can be treated as disposable. Indeed, both groups are subject to a form of neoliberal authoritarianism in which economic practices are removed from ethical considerations and social costs, memory is removed from an archive of resistance, and violence is now the organizing principle of society. The rise of the punishing state is coupled with an unchecked and extreme form of capitalism and culture of violence in which the ideological project of neoliberalism holds sway over both the meaning and mission of schooling and all other public spheres, if not the entirety of social life. The ruthless, anti-democratic elements of this neoliberal project, which constitute the underlying conditions of oppression faced by both teachers and students, is succinctly outlined by Naomi Klein who observes that neoliberal ideology is an all-encompassing project of deprivation, punishment, and greed which decrees:

> that the market is always right, regulation is always wrong, private is good and public is bad, and taxes that support public services are the worst of all … Neoliberalism is shorthand for an economic project that vilifies the public sphere and anything that's not either the workings of the market or the decisions of individual consumers … Under the neoliberal worldview, governments exist in order to create the optimal conditions for private interests to maximize their profits and wealth … The primary tools of this project are all too familiar: privatization of the public sphere, deregulation of the corporate sphere, and low taxes paid for by cuts to public services, and all of this locked in under corporate-friendly trade deals … Moreover, the flipside of neoliberal economic policies that exile whole segments of the population from the formal economy has been an explosion of the state apparatus aimed at control and containment: militarized police, fortressed borders, immigration detention, and mass incarceration.[413]

What is happening to public schools in the United States is not unlike what is happening to countries throughout the globe that are caught in the crosshairs of neoliberal shock therapies imposed by international corporations such as the International Monetary Fund, the World Bank, and the European Central Bank. In return for these cash strapped countries to receive crucial monetary relief, especially in light of the economic crash of 2008, they have been forced to hand over the power to control their major economic institutions, have been required to impose cuts on pensions, health care, salaries, and crucial social provisions, while also being forced to deregulate and financialize the commanding structures of their societies. In light of such policies, public spheres such as schools have been gutted, the future cancelled out, and the "paralyzing death-spiral of austerity" has given rise to an apocalyptic populism producing conditions ripe for the rise of deeply authoritarian movements and a politics of despair.[414] Until recently, alternative visions appeared only as a faint ray of light in a swirling and destructive sandstorm. The recent waves of opposition that have occurred in 2018 hold the promise of both a new vision for the future and a new set of political alignments to make it possible.

IV

Against the current frontal assault on public education and the rights of teachers and students, a new wave of opposition has developed around the nation's schools that has provoked the public imagination and mobilized mass numbers of students, educators, and the public at large. Teachers have been walking out, striking, and demonstrating in states across the country. In the past year, 400,000 teachers in nine states have gone on strike, affecting over 5 million students from the initial strike in West Virginia to demonstrations in Colorado, Kentucky, Chicago, Arizona to the work stoppage in Sacramento, California , where hundreds of teachers went on strike, teachers are protesting against not only low salaries but also related issues such as school defunding (prompted by regressive tax measures designed to benefit the rich and corporations), overcrowded classroom, and rising health premiums. The successful West Virginia strike was especially notable because it was one of the biggest "work actions in recent US history, rebuffing austerity and, at points, even the wishes of their union leaders."[415] Teachers in West Virginia were under increasing attack by a GOP controlled legislature and their Republican governor, billionaire coal baron, Jim Justice, who colluded to force teachers to pay increasingly higher premiums for their health care, put up with large classes, and endure "increasingly unlivable conditions — including attempts to force them to record private details of their health daily on a wellness app [while allowing] them no more than an annual one percent raise — effectively a pay cut considering inflation — in a state where teacher salaries ranked 48th lowest out of 50 states."[416] At the end of a nine-day strike, they negotiated a five percent pay increase from the state.

Similar strikes followed in Oklahoma, Kentucky, Arizona, and beyond, and even more strikes took place at the beginning of the 2018 fall school year.[417] While all of these strikes addressed issues specific to their states, they shared a number of issues that revealed a broader attempt to undermine public education. In all of these states, teachers made paltry wages nearly $13,077 below the nationwide average of $58,353 and well below the nationwide high of New York at $79,152.[418] Many teachers had to work two or three extra jobs simply to be able to survive. In a number of cases, their pension plans were being weakened and in "all of these states … teachers generally earn less and have fewer benefits than other college graduates."[419] Growing pay inequities stretch across two decades for most teachers as they "are contributing more and more toward health care and retirement costs as their pay falls further behind. Teacher pay (accounting for inflation) actually fell by $30 per week from 1996 to 2015 while pay for other college graduates increased by $124."[420]

There is a direct line between spending cuts for schools and a decrease in taxes for the rich and big corporations. In Oklahoma, taxes had not been raised since 1990; in 2010, the Republican governor passed "huge breaks for the oil and gas companies": and in 2015, the tax rate was reduced to two percent with the "cost to the state … estimated at $300 to $400 million per year."[421] Schools were shockingly underfunded and the consequences for both teachers and students have been devastating. Eric Blank observes that:

> Since 2008, per-pupil instructional funding has been cut by 28 percent — by far the worst reduction in the whole country. As a result, a fifth of Oklahoma's school districts have been forced to reduce the school week to four days. Textbooks are scarce and scandalously out of date. Innumerable arts,

languages, and sports courses or programs have been elim-
inated. Class sizes are enormous ... Many of Oklahoma's
695,000 students are obliged to sit on the floor in class ...
Over a decade of neglect by the legislature has given our students broken chairs in classrooms, outdated textbooks that
are duct-taped together, four-day school weeks, classes that
have exploded in size and teachers who have been forced to
donate plasma, work multiple jobs, and go to food pantries
to provide for their families," said the Oklahoma Education
Association in a statement.[422]

All of the states engaged in wildcat strikes, demonstrations, and protests have been subject to similar toxic austerity measures that have
come to characterize a neoliberal economy. Once these teachers realized that the terrible conditions under which they worked were not
only commonplace in other schools and states and that many other
groups of teachers had reached a boiling point, they were ready to
act regardless of whether they had the support of their unions. This
was another important thread running through demonstrations. The
strikes were not initiated by the leadership in the unions, and when
they did act, they were too slow to be consequential. As working conditions for teachers deteriorated and the assault on public schools
reached fever pitch, teachers bypassed their unions while using the
social media to speak to other teachers, communicate across national boundaries, and educate a wider public.[423] In spite of a number of
attacks by conservative politicians such as Kentucky Gov. Matt Beven,
who stated that teachers were displaying "a thug mentality," the striking teachers gained broad popular support. It is hard to miss the irony
here of the neoliberal promoters of austerity labeling teachers as losers, given that many teachers have extra jobs to support themselves,
use their own money to provide books and basic resources, in some
cases even toilet paper for their students.

Recent findings by the National Center of Educational Statistics found
that 94 percent of teachers pay out of their own pockets for school
supplies — such as notebooks, pens, and paper — which amounts
on average to $480 annually.[424] The real losers in this situation are the
democratically elected politicians who defund public schools, deskill
teachers, force students to put up with repressive test taking pedagogies "while whittling away at [teacher] salaries, supplies, tenure
arrangements, and other union protections ... lengthening teaching

hours, [and] reducing vital prep periods."[425] This is a neoliberal script for the social abandonment of public goods, the termination of the democratic ethos, and the precondition for the rise of an American version of fascism.

The use of the social media by the teachers was particularly effective in getting their message out. Individual teachers talked publicly about having to donate blood, visit food pantries, and teach with textbooks that were ten years old. Images of broken chairs and desks, rodents infesting classrooms, and students complaining about books that were held together with tape offered a compelling visual archive of not only dilapidated schools, impoverished classrooms, and over-burdened students, but also a political system in which Republican governors and legislators were willing to implement economic poli-cies that slashed the taxes of the rich and big corporations at the ex-pense of public schools, teachers, and students. Arizona is another case in point. Not only does it have the worst teacher pay in the na-tion, it is also a state that lacks collective bargaining rights.[426] Debbie Weingarten offers a succinct summary of the effects of budget cuts on Arizona schools, teachers, and students:

> During the Recession, the Arizona state legislature cut $1.5 million from public schools, more than any other state, leaving Arizona schools more than $1 billion short of 2008 funding. There's no toilet paper, there's no soap, and our textbooks are like 15 years old. Arizona currently ranks 49th in the country for high school teacher pay and 50th for el-ementary school teacher pay. When adjusted for inflation, teacher wages have declined more than 10 percent since 2001. Per-student spending in Arizona amounts to $7,205, compared with the national average of $11,392. There are currently 3,400 classrooms in Arizona without trained or cer-tified teachers, and the state has over 2,000 teacher vacan-cies.[427]

Arizona teachers ended their strike after a six-day walkout, and while they did not get everything they demanded, the state gave them a "20 percent raise by 2020 and invest[ed] an additional $138 million in schools."[428] Most importantly, the Arizona teacher strike along with other strikes and teacher walkouts proved not only the power of orga-nized labor prompted by the radical initiatives of teachers willing to fight for their rights, even if the unions do not support them, but also the growing support of a public unwilling to allow neoliberal fascism to destroy all vestiges of the public good, especially schools. As Jane McAlevey observes:

> Remarkably, these strikes have garnered overwhelming support from the public, despite years of well-funded attacks on teachers' unions. In a recent NPR/Ipsos poll, just one in four respondents said they think teachers are paid enough, and three-quarters said teachers have the right to strike. Remarkably, this support cut across party lines. "Two thirds of Republicans, three-quarters of independents and nearly 9 in 10 Democrats" support the teachers' right to strike, the poll showed.[429]

V

The teacher strikes and walkouts are particularly important because they dovetailed with the protest led by students against school shootings and the increasing resurgence of gun violence in our nation's streets. Here "slow violence" intersects with spectacular violence in the near collapse of meaningful conditions of teaching and learning. What is promising is that protests in both cases suggests that support for grassroots organizing is growing. In addition, they indicate that any real changes are not going to come from right-wing politicians who have sold their souls to the corporations and ultra-rich but from everyday people sick and tired of such deplorable conditions in the nation's schools. Refusing to confine their protests to the immediate needs of their professions or the immediate threats of violence, these teachers and students have chosen to make their voices heard while challenging the wider conditions that are waging war on public goods and doing so by making visible what each of these groups has in common in terms of the oppressive conditions they face and the modes of political action they might share. It is worth noting that the striking and protesting teachers have repeatedly called for more funding for schools in order to provide students with decent conditions for learning as well as quality support services and higher salaries for staff.

At the same time, the Parkland students protesting gun violence have argued that the issues they are addressing have their roots in forms of state violence and political and economic disenfranchisement. Young people are outraged at the mass shootings taking place in their schools, the endless lock down drills they have to endure, the increasing presence of police in school corridors, and the fact "that 97 children have been killed and 126 injured in mass shootings in schools since 1989." Since the February 14, 2018, shooting at Stoneman Douglas High School in Parkland, Florida, in which 17 students and teachers were killed, hundreds of thousands of students have held protests across the United States and have sparked worldwide rallies against gun violence. Refusing to be silenced by politicians and legislators bought and sold by gun lobbies such as the National Rifle Association, young people have called for a vision of social justice rooted in the belief that they can not only challenge systemic oppression but can change the fundamental nature of an oppressive social order. They recognize that they have not only been treated as disposable populations written out of the script of democracy, they also are capable of using the new tools of social media and other digital modes of communication as tools of persuasion in order to critique and challenge the deadening political horizons preached by the mainstream media and established politicians such as Senator Marco Rubio and President Trump.

In protesting against the mass shootings in their schools as well as the reign of state terror in the larger society, student leaders such as Emma Gonzales, Cameron Kasky, David Hogg, Alex Wind, Jaclyn Corin, and too many others to name have exhibited a degree of civic courage and political action that exposes the moral cowardice and political corruption of the various special interests supporting the selling of high-powered weapons in the United States. What is so promising about this movement is that not only are students exposing the politicians and gun lobbies that argue against gun control and reframe the gun debate while endangering the lives of young people, they have also energized millions of youth by encouraging a sense of individual and collective agency. They are asking their peers to both mobilize against gun violence, to vote in the 2018 mid-term November elections, and to be prepared for a long struggle against the underlying ideologies, structures, and institutions that promote death-dealing violence in the United States. As Charlotte Alter pointed out in *Time Magazine*, "They envision a youth political movement that will address many of the other issues affecting the youngest Americans. Hogg says he would like to have a youth demonstration every year on March 24, harnessing the power of teenage anger to demand action on everything from campaign-finance reform to net neutrality to climate change."[430] What is remarkable about this statement is that it makes clear that these young people recognize that the threat they face in the United States goes far beyond the gun debate and that what they need to address is a wider culture of cruelty, silence, and indifference to the needs, lives, and hopes of young people. Violence comes in many forms, much of which is hidden, some of which is spectacularized, and most of which is cultivated, valued, eroticized, and normalized.[431] The key is to address the underlying structures and relations of power that give rise to this landscape of both gun violence and the everyday violence experienced in the inner cities, through mass incarceration, abuse and neglect of people of color, the poor, undocumented workers, and others considered disposable.[432]

The threads running through these teacher and student-based movements share common ground in extending their current critiques of labor conditions and gun violence to a broader template that points to political and economic disenfranchisement, massive inequality, regressive tax policies, and a savage neoliberal economy rooted in the economizing and financialization of just about everything. The attack on public education and the rights and working conditions of teachers is one side of the neoliberal ledger. The other side is the explosion of the punishing state with its accelerated apparatuses of containment, militarized police, borders, walls, mass incarceration, the school-to-prison pipeline, and the creation of an armed society. These issues need to be connected as part of a wider refusal to equate rapacious, neoliberal capitalism with democracy.

The Parkland student movement and the teachers' walkouts have already advanced the possibilities of mass resistance by connecting the dots among a number of crises that each of these groups is experiencing. The "slow violence" of teacher disenfranchisement and pedagogies of repression need to be understood in relation to the fast violence of state and everyday violence that operates through a political and corporate culture that is engaged in a permanent war against democracy, while promoting in the militarization of everything. As Judith Levine points out, every public sphere has been transformed into a virtual war zone, "a zone of permanent vigilance, enforcement, and violence."[433] At issue here is the necessity for disruptive social movements that call for nothing less than the restructuring of American society. In the spirit of Martin Luther King, Jr., this means a revolution in values, a shift in public consciousness, and a change in power relations and public policies. The Parkland students and the brave teachers protesting across the nation are not only challenging the current attacks on public education, they also share an effort in constructing a new narrative about America — one that reclaims the public and ethical imagination and creates a broad based social movement capable of developing an equitable, just, and inclusive democracy.

No one movement or group rooted in an isolated problem can defeat the powerful and connected forces of neoliberal fascism. Protests against the gutting of teacher salaries, pensions, and health care benefits are not simply about school budgets, they are about a larger politics in which big corporations and the financial elite have waged a war on democracy and instituted policies that produce a massive redistribution of wealth upward into the hands of the ruling elite. Energized young people and teachers are creating a new optics for both change and the future. The Parkland students have embraced support for a grassroots movement and teachers are following their lead. Both groups are primed for action and are ready to challenge not only those eager to dismantle the public education system but also a systemic culture of symbolic and structural violence that has undermined, if not destroyed, the formative culture and commanding institutions crucial to a vibrant democracy. These groups recognize that education is a winning issue for the American public, and most people still view education as one of the few paths through which their children can gain access to decent jobs and a good life.[434] The usual neoliberal bromides advocating privatization, charter schools, vouchers, and teaching for the test have lost all legitimacy at a moment when the ruling elite act with impunity in destroying the promise of schools and a strong democracy. At the same time, liberal calls for gun reform, while making an appeal to moderation, fail to address the institutional violence that now shapes American society. A new society needs a new language, the energy of a democratic formative culture, and a movement guided by the kind of insight that Ursula K. Le Guin once captured: "We will not know our own injustice if we cannot image justice. We will not be free if we do not imagine freedom. We cannot demand that anyone try to attain justice and freedom who has not had a chance to imagine them as attainable."[435]

During the last two decades, elements of a new political formation and a movement can be seen in Moral Monday Movement, the New Poor People's Campaign, and the all-inclusive Movement for Black Lives. All of these movements share a criticism of the interconnecting forces of poverty, racism, sexism, the culture of policing, and the call for dismantling the institutions, ideologies, policies, and structures that support a punitive and cruel capitalist system. Tactically, they have been incessant in exposing the violence of the state and the need to create the conditions for the poor and others disenfranchised groups to gain a voice and greater sense of individual and collective agency in order to work together across racial, gender, sexual, and class lines to form a new political movement. At the center of all of these movements are efforts to raise consciousness, make education a vital part of their politics, and an attempt to reclaim historical memory, fit events together in a larger narrative, resist moralizing classifications, recognize shared values, and develop unwavering coalitions.

The more recent protests we have witnessed by teachers and students across the nation in 2018 point to another possibility of fashioning a new public imagination, one that moves beyond the narrow realm of specific interest to a more comprehensive grasp of politics that is rooted in a practice of open defiance willing to disrupt corporate tyranny and state violence. This is a politics that refuses liberal centrism, the extremism of the right, and a deeply unequal society modeled on the iniquitous precarity and toxic structures of savage capitalism.[436] On the contrary, this new political horizon foreshadows the need to organize new political formations, massive social movements, and a third political party that can make itself present in a variety of institutional, educational, social, and cultural spheres.[437] No one has expressed this more clearly and with greater political urgency than Stanley Aronowitz in his prescient 2006 book *Left Turn: Forging a New Political Future*. He writes:

> Before us is the urgent necessity of launching the anti-capitalist project in the United States and, with great specificity, making plain what we may mean by an alternative to the authoritarian present. We are faced with the urgent need to reignite the radical imagination. We simply have no vehicle to undertake this work — a party that can express the standpoint of the exploited and oppressed that, in the current historical conjuncture, must extend far beyond the poor

and the workers, since capital and the state have launched a major assault on the middle classes. In short, we need a political formation capable of articulating the content of the 'not-yet' — that which is immanent in the present but remains unrealized.[438]

What the teacher and student protests have made clear is that change and coalition building are possible and that real change through new political formations can be made through mass collective movements inspired by hope in the service of a radical democracy, one that believes "we can make a better world."[439] This is a movement that must make education vital to its politics and be willing to develop educational spheres which listen to and speak to the concrete problems that educators, students, minorities of color and class, and others face in a world moving into the abyss of tyranny. Theirs is a politics of direct action, as we have seen in the teacher and student protests. School reform in all of its manifestations will succeed if teacher, students, and others connect it to wider struggles for minority rights, economic justice, and social equality. Under such circumstances, ethical horizons can be invoked and broadened, shared responsibilities embraced, new and inclusive narratives invented, and new modes of political intervention and collective struggle adopted. What we have learned from the student and teacher demonstrations is that politics depend "on the possibility of making the public exist in the first place" and that what we share in common is more important than what separates us.[440] At a time when tyranny is on the rise and the world seems deprived of imaginative struggles, such courageous acts of mass resistance are a welcome relief and hopeful indicator of an ongoing struggle that refuses to cancel out the future as a radical democratic project. Crucial to such a movement is the ability to transform a major protest movement(s) into a political formation that is capable of demonstrating that there is a real and long term strategy and alternative to neoliberal capitalism. In part, this means addressing what it means pedagogically to change public consciousness by providing a narrative, language, and set of expectations in which people recognize themselves and the conditions that shape their lives for better or worse. In part, this means talking about principles, values, visions, and what kind of future people want for themselves, their children, neighbors, and others.

Chapter 8

Beyond Neoliberal Fascism

*If there is no struggle, there is no progress. ..... Power
concedes nothing without a demand. It never did
and it never will."
— Frederick Douglass*

THE THREADS of a general political and ideological crisis run deep
in American history, and with each tweet and policy decision, Trump
pushes the United States closer to a full-fledged fascist state. His
words sting, but his policies can kill people. Trump's endless racist
taunts, dehumanizing expressions of misogyny, relentless attacks on
all provisions of the social state, and his ongoing contempt for the
rules of law serve to normalize a creeping fascist politics. Moreover, his
criminogenic disdain for any viable sense of civic and moral responsibility gives new meaning to an ethos of selfishness and a culture of
cruelty, if not terror, that have run amok. Yet, it is becoming more difficult for the mainstream media and pundits to talk about fascism as a
looming threat in the United States in spite of the fact that, as Michelle
Goldberg observes, for some groups "such as undocumented immigrants, it is already here."[441]

The smell of death is everywhere under this administration. The erosion of public values and the rule of law is now accompanied by a

developing state of emergency with regards to a looming global environmental catastrophe.[442] An ecological disaster due to human caused climate change has accelerated under the Trump administration and appears imminent.[443] Trump's ongoing attempt to pollute the ecosystem through his rollback of environmental protections will result in the deaths of thousands of children who suffer from asthma and other lung problems. Moreover, his privatized and punitive approach to health care will shorten the lives of millions of poor people, uninsured youth, undocumented immigrants, the unemployed, and the elderly. His get tough law and order policies will result in more police violence against blacks while his support for the arms industry, military budget, and gun laws will accelerate the death of the marginalized both at home and abroad. As I write this, the national debt is soaring — soon topping $1 trillion — because of runaway military spending and a $1.5 trillion tax giveaway to the ultra-rich and major corporations. The response on the part of Mitch McConnell and other leading Republicans is to cut entitlements such as Medicare, Medicaid, and social security.[444] Such policies are about more than the human suffering produced by austerity policies, they also point to the presence of a war culture in which civic life under capitalism is modeled after a form of perpetual warfare with its capacity and willingness to produce immense violence against the poor, working class, youth, women, and those populations marginalized by race, religion, and sexual orientation. We are at a critical juncture in United States history. All of our democratic institutions are under siege, matched only by a disastrous slide from the promise of democratic aspirations into something much darker. Under the Trump regime, all bets are off regarding the sustainability of democracy, if not life itself.

The appointment of Brett M. Kavanaugh, a right-wing ideologue, to the United States Supreme Court, in spite of allegations against him of sexually assaulting two women, further reveals both the dangerous politicization of the judicial nomination process and the authoritarian politics that now dominate American society. The control of the court by ideological fundamentalists has been a long sought goal of Republican Party extremists. Now the American people, especially women, the poor, and people of color will pay a terrible price for Kavanaugh's appointment. Many commentators have focused on the danger the Court's right-wing ideological leaning poses to Roe vs. Wade, but other vital programs are also at risk such as Social Security, Medicare, child labor laws, the minimum wage, and laws protecting unions and worker safety. Given the Republican Party's efforts to expand voter suppression practices against vulnerable populations of color, it would not be surprising if they prompted the court to take away America's voting rights. The Kavanaugh affair is a symptom of the deeper roots of a fascist politics at work in American society. Kavanaugh is not only a blatant symbol of a toxic masculinity; he is also emblematic of a boisterous and unchecked expression of ruling class white privilege. This is especially true given the racist double standard that characterizes America's justice system. As Amanda Klonsky put it in *The Chicago Sun-Times*:

> Why does Judge Brett Kavanaugh, accused of sexual assault, feel entitled to a lifetime appointment to the Supreme Court of the United States, while my formerly incarcerated students — often jailed for crimes like battery from fistfights — are left unemployed, sometimes for life, banned from even the most entry-level work? That Kavanaugh is under consideration for appointment to the Supreme Court at all throws the racist double standard in our justice system into sharp relief. There is one standard of behavior for African-American and Latinx young people, who are harshly punished for crimes in adolescence, and quite another for wealthy white boys, who can be accused of sexual assault and still go on to be nominated to serve on the most important court in the world.[445]

Kavanaugh perfectly aligns with Trump's racism and his decisions on matters of civil rights and racial justice will more than likely further reproduce a long legacy of white racism and state violence in the United States. This is especially tragic and ominous given that Trump's contempt for people of color appears boundless and legitimates the notion of whiteness as a site of terror. He slanders and humiliates black athletes, black women, and any other person of color who calls him on his racism and white supremacist views. Moreover, his thuggery in support of police brutality and mass incarceration further accelerates the growth of a racialized carceral state. In addition, Trump's pardons sanction a new kind of legal illegality by using the rule of law to exonerate those who break it and legitimate acts of lawlessness as examples of the rule of law. This is evident in his pardon of former Arizona sheriff Joe Arpaio, who was a convicted criminal before being exonerated by Trump.

In a brutish and deeply troubling display of misogyny, Trump vi-
ciously mocked the testimony of Christine Blasey Ford who accused
Kavanaugh of a sexual assault. Drawing laughter and shouts from a
crowd in Southaven, Mississippi, Trump went further, following up his
vile remarks by stating that men were the real victims of the #MeToo
movement because they were being unfairly accused of sexual harass-
ment, and that many males would lose their jobs.[446] It is hard to miss
the irony of this statement coming from a man who has been accused
of sexual misconduct by at least twenty-two women and has been
caught on tape bragging about grabbing women by the crotch and is
now the US President. What is worth noting here is not only his indifference to shocking levels violence waged against women but also the
degree to which misogyny has always been endemic to fascist politics.

It is easy for the mainstream press to go after those politicians who
remain silent in the face of Trump's sexism and racism. Yet, there is
little interest in situating his misogyny and white supremacy within a
neoliberal fascist politics. This silence is especially scandalous given
Trump's alignment with neo-Nazis, white nationalists, and other militant groups who argue for racial cleansing and increasingly commit
violent acts against people of color who oppose their views.[447] The
mainstream media endlessly whitewashes Trump's politics, which too
often view policy decisions more as the infantilized outbursts of an impetuous tweeting teenage bully rather than as a full-fledged threat to
the laws and values that constitute a democracy currently in peril.[448]
The mainstream press argues that Trump's rhetoric is divisive, humiliating, and hateful, but rarely is it associated with the rhetoric of fascist
politics or, for that matter, with the power and moneyed interests of
the financial elite.

One example stands out. For weeks, the media focused on the controversial confirmation process of US Supreme Court nominee Brett
Kavanaugh and the women who accused him of sexual violence and
later spent an inordinate amount of time reporting on Trump's calling adult film actor and director, Stormy Daniels, "Horseface." Yet, it
had almost nothing to say about the Trump administration's dangerous rollback of vehicle emissions rules or the horrific news that over
1600 detained, unaccompanied migrant children had been roused
from their shelters and foster homes in the middle of the night and
sent to what Bill McKibben termed "as a concentration camp near the

Mexican border."⁴⁴⁹ This evasion is even more frightening since Trump, not to mention most of his critics, seem unaware of the incremental and accumulated terror unleashed by past fascists. Trump appears reckless when implementing policies that echo faintly the genocidal practices used by Nazis in their concentration camps. While Trump has not gassed tens of thousands of children as Hitler did, putting children in tents in the middle of the desert in Tornillo, Texas suggests crossing a moral and political line that opens the door to even more extreme forms of barbarism. Underlying Trump's zero tolerance agenda is the cruel belief that "making life as horrible for immigrants — either those trying to cross the border, or those living undocumented here — will reduce the flow of immigration and the size of the undocumented presence."⁴⁵⁰ Such cruelty is a central ideological element of Trump's racist notion that the presence of undocumented workers means more crime, a positon largely supported by Trump's lies rather than a plethora of research.⁴⁵¹ It also is crucial to his consistent false claim that Mexico is purposely sending criminals across the border.

At the same time, his anti-democratic proclivities are on display almost every day. For instance, Trump's open infatuation with demagogues such as Vladimir Putin, Jair Bolsonaro and Kim Jong-un is matched only by his consistent vilification of America's democratic allies. One clear-cut example is his ludicrous claim that trade wars with Canada are justified because Canada represents a threat to America's national security. The latter is uttered at the same time that Trump calls Kim Jong-un terrific. Trump has not only normalized racism in the United States and given new legitimacy to the hate filled rants and ideologies of neo-Nazis and white nationalists, he has deepened the crisis of democracy by elevating emotion over reason and turning civic illiteracy into a virtue. When embraced by the powerful and removed from any notion of the material consequences, ignorance turns deadly for those who have to suffer from practices of social abandonment, terminal exclusion, and state violence.

State sanctioned ignorance is more than fodder for late night comedy shows, it also provides the psychological conditions for certain individuals and groups to associate "pollution" and disposability with what Professor Richard A. Etlin calls "a biologically racialist worldview, which divides the human race according to the dichotomy of the pure and impure, the life-enhancing and the life-polluting."⁴⁵² This is a language mobilized by the energies of the ethically dead and echoes strongly with the anti-Semitism that was at the center of the genocidal policies of the Third Reich. This poisonous anti-Semitic discourse has returned vigorously in Hungary, Poland, and a number of other countries now moving towards fascism. It is also surfacing among alt right and other neo-Nazi groups in the United States. Unsurprisingly, there are also coded hints of it in Trump's language. Trump is more careful with his displays of anti-Semitism, especially given the uproar that followed his many comments that mimic the language and values of right-wing extremists.

One of the most revealingly ideological comments made by Trump during the Kavanaugh affair was contained in a tweet aimed at the women who had confronted Senator Flake and other Republican senators over their support for Kavanaugh. Trump stated, "The very rude elevator screamers are paid professionals only looking to make Senators look bad. Do not fall for it. Also, look at all the professional made identical signs. Paid for by Soros and others. These are not signs made in the basement from love."[453] Trump exposed more than the level of political corruption and hatred of women that now defines American politics, he also appropriated an anti-Semitic discourse to discredit both the women to whom he is referring and dissent in general. Many conservative pundits and commentators have also followed Trump's lead and claimed that Soros paid protesters. This vile display of anti-Semitism directed at Soros is not new for Trump. As Greg Sargent pointed out in *The Washington Post*, anti-Semitism directed at Soros played a "starring role in Trump's 2016 closing ad, which was the perfect expression of this type of exclusionary populist demagoguery."[454] Not only do Trump's comments and the earlier ad mirror anti-Semitic propaganda from the 1930s, they also legitimate the vicious attacks on George Soros in a number of Eastern European countries including Poland, Romania, and Serbia. However, President Viktor Orban of Hungary is leading the pack in his attack on Soros as part of a larger attack on Jews.

Trump's coded endorsement of Orban's attack on Jews, whom he appears to blame for all of Hungary's problems, is particularly repellent given its viciousness and the horrors of the past it echoes. For instance, recalling the genocidal rhetoric aimed at Jews in the past by the Nazis, Orban commemorated the 170th anniversary of the Hungarian Revolution of 1848 by stating the following (without mentioning Jews directly):

They do not fight directly, but by stealth; they are not hon-
ourable, but unprincipled; they are not national, but international; they do not believe in work, but speculate with
money; they have no homeland, but feel the whole world is
theirs. They are not generous but vengeful and always attack
the heart — especially if it is red, white and green [the colors
of the Hungarian flag].[455]

Prior to the recent election in Hungary, Orban plastered images of
George Soros throughout the country. Soros is both Hungarian and a
Jew and was a perfect symbol for Orban to vilify in his efforts to take
over the country. Soros is dangerous to Orban because of his pro-
motion of the open society, open borders, cosmopolitanism, human
rights, and democracy. That he is Jewish made it easier for Orban to
attack him personally without having to express openly his hatred of
democracy. That Trump would use a reference taken out of the poisonous playbook of the fascist Viktor Orban is both revealing and
dangerous. Not only is it dangerous because such rhetoric indexes a
fascist politics and the potential perils that follow, but also because
of the silence that surrounded Trump's reference to Soros with all of
its toxic implications. Even if Trump is not consciously anti-Semitic, he
should know better since, as journalist Ron Kampeas points out, his
comments traffic "in conspiracies of control and destruction identified
with classical anti-Semitism."[456] Trump's consistently coded support
for an ideology embraced by neo-Nazis and other white nationalists
is not new. The discourse of blood and soil propelled an emotionally
charged language of hate, reification, dehumanization, and eventually
mass murder. Acting as if one forgets this history is less a sign of historical ignorance than a complicitous practice of reviving the conditions
that give birth to the horrors of the past.

Trump's defenders might argue that Trump is not an anti-Semite because two of his former lawyers were Jewish — Roy Cohn and Michael
Cohen. Moreover, his daughter converted to Judaism. This may be
true, and Trump may just be so stupid to know and not to care when
he is rehearsing an anti-Semitic stereotype, and so ignorant of history that he can't put together the threat of rising anti-Semitism in
Europe and the history of genocide that it produced. Writers such as
Michael Wolf and Bob Woodward who have chronicled the post-2016
chaos in the White House have indicated that Trump has overt white
supremacists such as Stephen Miller making decisions for him.[457] In

this case, the Kavanaugh hearings may signal a danger that far exceeds the misogyny and Vichy-type silence revealed by the spineless Republican Party and the Trump administration. Mitch McConnell and the other gravediggers of democracy in the Congress could care less about Trump's crude language, governing style, character, or potential revelations of criminal acts. They have no qualms or reservations about supporting a fascist politics as long as they get what they want with their alliance with the racists, xenophobic ultra-nationalists, and white nationalists. According to the renowned historian Christopher R. Browning, the Republican Party, in particular has received a big pay off in selling their souls to Trump's worldview. He writes:

> Huge tax cuts for the wealthy, financial and environmental deregulation, the nominations of two conservative Supreme Court justices (so far) and a host of other conservative judicial appointments, and a significant reduction in government-sponsored health care (though not yet the total abolition of Obamacare they hope for). Like Hitler's conservative allies, McConnell and the Republicans have prided themselves on the early returns on their investment in Trump.[458]

The Kavanaugh appointment exposes what politicians such as Robert Reich and historians such as Timothy Snyder view as alarming and frightening parallels between the United States and the Hitler's regime, or what the Yale historian Jason Stanley calls an accelerating fascist politics.[459] Their analyses seem overly cautious. There is little doubt that Kavanaugh's appointment to the Supreme Court is an abomination because of not only his alleged sexual assaults, but also his equally revealing and right-wing ideological rant against the left, Hillary Clinton, and the Democratic Party during his Senate hearing. More ominous, when comprehended within the context of an emerging fascist politics, is the recognition that his appointment is part of a broader effort on the part of the Trump administration to modify radically the rule of law and individual rights, further depriving them of any meaning and cutting them off from any viable humanitarian standards.

We are in the midst of an American version of fascism, which is not to suggest a fascism modeled exclusively after Nazi Germany. In the United States, fascist rhetoric has become normalized, white terror is no longer coded, and ultra-nationalism has merged into a love affair between the US and a host of ruthless dictators. Of course, the US has a long tradition of civil liberties, but it also has a long tradition of lawlessness, and the latter is now winning out. It thrives under the guise of a neoliberalism that has fueled for the past 40 years vast inequalities in wealth and power, producing a level of political and economic corruption that signals not just a hatred of democracy, but also a unique style of American fascism. Its policies are cruel and its language is barbaric. As author Nancy MacLean reminds us in *Democracy in Chains*, the financial elite and intellectual spokespersons for the radical right refer to the social state as a "parasite economy," welfare recipients as "moochers," and as Mitt Romney once infamously noted "addressing an audience of $50,000 per plate donors, '47 percent' of voters were, in effect, leeches on 'productive' Americans."[460]

The Kavanaugh hearings should serve to remind us once again that we live in increasingly dangerous times. It is important to remember that fascism begins not with violence, police assaults, or mass killings, but with language. Not only have we learned this from the rise of fascism in the 1930s in Europe but also in the current historical moment — a moment in which lawlessness, misogyny, white nationalism, and racism are resurgent all over the globe. If fascism begins with language, so does a strong resistance willing to challenge it. This is even more reason for individuals, institutions, labor unions, educators, young people, and others not to be silent in the face of the current fascist turn in the United States and elsewhere. In the face of the hatred, racism, misogyny, and deceit that have become part of a state sanctioned public dialogue, no one can afford to look away, fail to speak out, and risk silence. This is especially true at a time when history is used to hide rather than illuminate the past, when it becomes difficult to translate private issues into larger systemic considerations, and people willingly allow themselves to be both seduced and trapped into spectacles of violence, cruelty, and authoritarian impulses. Under such circumstances, the terror of the unforeseen becomes all the more ominous.

Any viable notion of change will have to reject the notion that capitalism and democracy are identical and that participatory democracy begins and ends with elections. Capitalism, in its currently extreme form produces massive forms of exploitation, misery, and suffering. Rejecting the fundamental principles of capitalism is crucial to undoing the myth that political power is separate from economic power and that capitalism has nothing to do with corrupt modes of governance. This is precisely the myth that upholds the false assumption that whatever problems currently exist under the Trump administration are endemic to Trump's alleged mental health, ignorance, and other character flaws. In actuality, the fascist politics now shaping the United States have been in the making for decades and are systemic to neoliberal capitalism and are deeply entwined with iniquitous relations of power. Rob Urie illuminates the issue, particularly in relation to class divisions. He writes:

> The class relations of American political economy are antithetical to the notion of a unified public interest. The point isn't to suggest that this or that authoritarian leader isn't authoritarian, but rather to sketch in the political backdrop to argue that the lived experience of social, economic and political repression is lived experience, not academic theories or bourgeois fantasies. The circumstances of investment bankers stripping assets, industrialists relocating factories built by workers to low-wage locations and tech 'pioneers' using licenses and patents to extract economic rents is systemically 'authoritarian' in the sense that democratic consent to do so was neither sought nor given.[461]

It is time to build community led broad based social movements from the bottom up. This means starting in local communities and expanding to the state and national levels. As William J. Barber II has pointed out, such movements must be "deeply moral, deeply constitutional, anti-racist, anti-poverty, pro-justice, [and] pro-labor."[462] They must also reject finance capitalism and embrace education as central to a politics willing to fight to persuade people to reclaim their sense of agency and power and push at the frontiers of the ethical imagination. Education has to be a central component of such a strategy because it is vital for comprehending how culture deploys power and produces those desires, values, and modes of identity that support a neoliberal and market-driven view of the world. Moreover, ignorance thins politics, depoliticizes people, and prepares the groundwork for a toxic politics. Not only does democracy in our complex era of globalization require people who are educated, informed, thoughtful, well read, and attentive to the interrelated domains of power, culture, politics, and everyday life, it requires recognizing that the crisis of agency is at the center of the current turn to illiberal democracies across the globe. This is a profoundly political issue for unpacking how power works and how it can be used to align the current crisis of capitalism and politics with a crisis of ideas.

Marx was certainly right in arguing that the point is not to understand the world but to change it; what he underemphasized was that the world could not be changed if one does not understand what is to be changed. As Terry Eagleton rightly notes "Nobody can change a world they didn't understand."[463] Moreover, the lack of resistance to oppression signals more than apathy or indifference, it also suggests that, as Brad Evans puts it, we don't have an alternative vision of the world.[464] Political struggle is dependent on political will to change, which is central to any notion of informed agency willing to address the radical and pragmatic issues of our time. In addition to understanding the world in which we now live, an informed public must connect what it knows and learns to the central task of bringing their ideas to bear on society as a whole. This means that a critical consciousness must be informed by a vision — a broad notion of sustaining both human life, other life forms, and the planet — and matched by fervent willingness to take risks and challenge the destructive narratives that are seeping into the public realm and becoming normalized. Any dissatisfaction with injustice necessitates combining the demands of moral witnessing with the pedagogical power of persuasion and the call to address the tasks of emancipation. We need individuals and social movements willing to disturb the normalization of a fascist politics and oppose racist, sexist, and neoliberal orthodoxy. As Robin D. G. Kelley observes, we cannot confuse catharsis and momentary outrage for revolution.[465] In a time of increasing tyranny, resistance appears to have lost its usefulness as a call to action.

For instance, the novelist Teju Cole has argued, "'resistance' is back in vogue, and it describes something rather different now. The holy word has become unexceptional. Faced with a vulgar, manic, and cruel regime, birds of many different feathers are eager to proclaim themselves members of the Resistance. It is the most popular game in town."[466] Cole's critique appears to be born out by the fact that the most unscrupulous of liberal and conservative politicians such as Madeline Albright, Hillary Clinton, and even James Clapper, the former director of national intelligence, are now claiming that they have joined the resistance against Trump's fascist politics. Even Michael Hayden, the former NSA chief and CIA director under George W. Bush, has joined the ranks of Albright and Clinton in condemning Trump as a protofascist. Writing in the *New York Times*, Hayden ironically chastised Trump as a serial liar and in doing so quoted the renowned historian Timothy Snyder, who stated in reference to the Trump regime that "Post-Truth is pre-fascism."[467] The irony here is hard to miss. Not only did Hayden head Bush's illegal National Security Agency warrantless wiretapping program while the head of the NSA, he also lied repeatedly about his role in Bush's sanctioning and implementation of state torture in Afghanistan and Iraq.

This tsunami of banal resistance was on full display when an anonymous member of the Trump's inner circle published an op-ed in the *New York Times* claiming that he/she and other senior officials were part of "the resistance within the Trump administration."[468] The author was quick to qualify the statement by insisting such resistance had nothing to do with "the popular 'resistance' of the left." To prove the point, it the author notes that the members of this insider resistance liked some of Trump's policies such as "effective deregulation, historic tax reform, a more robust military and more."[469] Combining resistance with the endorsements of such reactionary policies reads like fodder for late-night comics. The Democratic Party now defines itself as the most powerful political force opposing Trump's fascist politics. What it has forgotten is the role it has played under the Clinton and Obama presidencies in creating the economic, political, and social conditions for Trump's election in 2016. Such historical and political amnesia allows them to make the specious claim that they are now the party of resistance. Resistance in these instances has little to do with civic courage, a defense of human dignity, and the willingness not to just bear witness to the current injustices but struggle to overcome them. Of course, the issue is not to disavow resistance as much as to redefine it as inseparable from fundamental change that calls for the overthrow of capitalism itself. In addition, any viable struggle for change has to differentiate between a short-lived and momentary protest and a movement, which "requires more discipline, forethought, and understanding of the problems and their place in history."[470] Momentary relief is no substitute, however well intentioned, for the long-term investment in time, planning, and organization that produces a movement.

While the call to resist neoliberal fascism is to be welcomed, it has to be interrogated and not aligned with individuals and ideological forces that helped put in place the racist, economic, religious, and educational forces that helped produce it. What all of these calls to resistance have in common is an opposition to Trump rather than to the conditions that created him. Trump's election and the Kavanaugh affair make clear that what is needed is not only a resistance to the established order of neoliberal capitalism but a radical restructuring of society itself. That is not about resisting oppression in its diverse forms but overcoming it — in short, changing it.[471]

While it is crucial to condemn the Kavanaugh hearings for their blatant disregard for the Constitution, expressed hatred of women, and symbolic expression and embrace of white privilege and power, it is necessary to enlarge our criticism to include the system that made the Kavanaugh appointment possible. Kavanaugh represents not only the deep-seated rot of misogyny but also as Grace Lee Boggs has stated "a government of, by, and for corporate power."[472] We need to see beyond the white nationalists and neo-Nazis demonstrating in the streets in order to recognize the terror of the unforeseen; the terror that is state sanctioned and hides in the shadows of power. Such a struggle means more than engaging material relations of power or the economic architecture of neoliberal fascism, it also means taking on the challenge producing the tools and tactics necessary to rethink and create the conditions for a new kind of subjectivity as the basis for a new kind of democratic socialist politics. We need a comprehensive politics that brings together various single interest movements so that the threads that connect them become equally as important as the particular forms of oppression that define their singularity.[473] In addition, we need intellectuals willing to combine intellectual complexity with clarity and accessibility, embrace the high stakes investment in persuasion, and cross disciplinary borders in order to theorize and speak with what Rob Nixon calls the "cunning of lightness" and a "methodological promiscuity" that keeps language attuned to the pressing the claims for justice.[474]

Trump has surfaced the dire anti-democratic threats that have been expanding under an economic system stripped of any political, social, and ethical responsibility. This is a form of neoliberal fascism that has redrawn and expanded the parameters of what was once thought, after the genocidal practices and hate filled politics of the 1930s and '40s in Europe, too horrific to ever become possible again. The impossible threat has returned and is now on our doorsteps, and it needs to be named, exposed, and overcome by those who believe that the stakes are much too high to look away and not engage in organized political and pedagogical struggles.

II

Hannah Arendt once wrote that terror was the essence of totalitarianism. She was right, and we are now witnessing the dystopian visions of the new authoritarians who trade in fear, hatred, demonization, violence, and racism. This will be Trump's legacy. It is easy to despair in times of tyranny, but it is much more productive to be politically and morally outraged and to draw upon such anger as a source of hope and action. Without hope even in the most dire of times, there is no possibility for resistance, dissent, and struggle. A critical consciousness is the prerequisite for informed agency and hope is the basis for individual and collective resistance. Moreover, when combined with collective action, hope translates into a dynamic sense of possibility, enabling one to join with others for the long haul of fighting systemic forms of domination. Courage in the face of tyranny is a necessity and not an option, and we can learn from both the past and the present about resistance movements and the power of civic courage and collective struggle and how such modes of resistance are emerging among a number of groups across a wide variety of landscapes.

What is crucial is recognition of the need not to face such struggles alone, not to allow ourselves to feel defeated in our isolation or to give in to the crippling neoliberal survival-of-the-fittest ethos that dominates everyday relations. Radical politics begins when one refuses to face one's fate alone, learns about the workings and mechanisms of power, and rejects the dominant mantra of social isolation. There is strength in numbers. One of the most important things we can do to sustain a sense of courage and dignity is to imagine a new social order and a new political formation that can bring it into fruition. That is, we must constantly work to revive a radical political imaginary by talking with others in order to rethink what a new politics and society would look like, one that is fundamentally anti-capitalist, and dedicated to creating the conditions for new democratic political and social formations. This suggests creating new public spheres that make such

a dialogue and act of solidarity possible while simultaneously struggling against the forces that gave rise to Trump, particularly those that
suggest that totalitarian forms are still with us.

As I have stressed throughout this book, rethinking politics anew
also suggests the possibility of building broad-based alliances in order to create a robust economic and political agenda that connects
democracy with a serious effort to interrogate the sources and structures of inequality, racism, and authoritarianism that now plague the
United States. There is an urgent political need to think through what it
would mean to create a robust and new powerful political formation.
In this case, one that would align a number of progressive activist bas-
es ranging from Moveon.org, the Green Party, the New Poor People's
Campaign Movement, the Working Families Party to the major labor unions, the Movement for Black Lives, the Socialist Alternative
Movement, Bernie Sanders's followers, and other groups in a united
front. This constitutes a major challenge for a fragmented left and
points to the necessity of opening up new lines of understanding,
dialogue, and modes of political thinking in the effort to develop an
expansive and unified social movement. The challenge is enormous
for developing what Seth Adler calls "a cross-partisan focused, for-
mation-cohering organization."[475] However, it is essential in a political
climate where both political parties are ruled by right-wing and liberal
moneyed interests.

An effective nonviolent movement for democratic socialism does not
need vanguards, political purity, or the seductions of ideological orthodoxy. On the contrary, it needs an informed and energized politics
without guarantees, one that is open to new ideas, self-reflection, and
thoughtfulness. Instead of ideologies of certainty, unchecked moral-
ism, and a politics of shaming, we need to understand the conditions
that makes it possible for people to internalize forms of domination
and that means interrogating forgotten histories and existing pedagogies of oppression. Recent polls indicate that two thirds of Americans
say this is the lowest point in American politics that they can recall.
Such despair offers the possibility of a pedagogical intervention, one
that provides a political opening to create a massive movement for
organized struggle in the United States.

Rebecca Solnit has rightly argued that while we live in an age of despair. She states that hope is a gift we that we cannot surrender be-

cause it amplifies the power of alternative visions, offers up stories in which we can imagine the unimaginable, enables people to "move from depression to outrage," and positions people to take seriously what they are for and what they are against. This suggests trying to understand how the very processes of learning constitute the political mechanisms through which identities — individual and collective — are shaped, desired, mobilized, and take on the worldly practices of autonomy, self-reflection, and self-determination as part of a larger struggle for economic and social justice.

First, it is crucial to develop a discourse of critique and possibility that rejects the ongoing normalizing of existing relations of domination and control while simultaneously repudiating the notion that capitalism and democracy are one and the same. It would be wise to heed the words of National Book Award winner, Ursula K. Le Guin, when she writes "We live in capitalism. Its power seems inescapable. So did the divine right of kings. Any human power can be resisted and changed by human beings."[476] This is a particularly urgent task given that as Fredric Jameson famously stated, "it is easier to imagine the end of the world than it is to imagine the end of capitalism."[477] What Mark Fisher called "capitalist realism" is hardwired into the public psyche and endlessly legitimated in the mainstream media, higher education, and other increasingly corporate controlled disimagination machines. In a world falling apart, capitalist realism argues that no alternative is possible and all action is pointless. As Fisher observes, capitalist realism reproduces "the widespread sense that not only is capitalism the only viable political and economic system, but also that it is now impossible even to *imagine* a coherent alternative to it."[478]

Second, it is crucial to develop a language in which it becomes possible to imagine a future much different from the present, one that refuses to privatize hope with a crude individualism. Such a language needs to radicalize the meaning of struggle, which as Samir Amin notes means that individuals need to become "aware of the obsolete character of capitalism [which] governs their capacity to produce positive alternatives. It is necessary and possible."[479] Radicalizing the meaning of struggle necessitates a vision that points to a proactive agenda that includes issues such as instituting free higher education, eliminating runaway inequality, creating universal health care, reforming the criminal justice system, ending the off-shoring of jobs, eliminating global warming, taking money out of politics, taxing Wall Street trading, cutting military spending, and developing extensive safety nets for the most vulnerable. Such struggles call for structural changes and go far beyond modes of resistance that focus exclusively on Trump.[480] Waiting for Trump to fail, collapse, or fall out of favor does not constitute either a viable vision for change or an acceptable political strategy. Radical rather than reformist change must be at the heart of any politics that wants to address the most vital needs and problems Americans face, especially if such change properly addresses what it means to sustain a viable participatory socialist democracy. In this way, the political does not dissolve into the Trump tweet fest or what might be called the scourge of Trumpism.[481]

To address this challenge there is a strong need for those struggling to invent a new understanding of politics to develop a language of militant possibility and a comprehensive politics that draws from history, rethinks the meaning of politics, and imagines a future that does not imitate the present. We need what Gregory Leffel calls a language of "imagined futures," one that "can snap us out of present-day sociopolitical malaise so that we can envision alternatives, build the institutions we need to get there and inspire heroic commitment."[482] Such a language has to create political formations capable of grasping neoliberal fascism as a totality, a single integrated system whose shared roots extend from class and racial injustices under financial capitalism to ecological problems and the increasing expansion of the carceral state and the military-industrial-academic complex.[483] Nancy Fraser is right in arguing that we need a subjective response capable of connecting diverse racial, social and economic crises and in doing so addressing the objective structural forces that underpin them.[484]

Third, it is imperative to reject the notion that all problems are individual issues and can only be solved as a matter of individual responsibility and action. This is one of neoliberalism's most powerful ideological tenets, working to make the personal the only politics that matters while detaching private troubles from the wider world. Challenging this individualization of the social opens the possibility to produce alternative vision of a just society. In addition, it makes central to its politics the urgent task of changing consciousness as a precondition for political action and the need to build autonomous spaces in which it becomes possible to connect issues of institutional change with social transformation.

Fourth, there is a need, I believe, for a discourse that is historical, relational, and comprehensive. As I have suggested throughout this book, memory matters both in terms of reclaiming lost narratives of struggle and for assessing visions, strategies and tactics that still hold enormous possibilities in the present. At the same time, developing a relational discourse also means connecting the dots around issues that are often viewed in isolated terms. For instance, it is urgent for progressives to make visible the threads that connect the denial of health care and the effects of climate change, voter suppression and systemic racism, poverty and housing cuts, and low wages and the rise of the carceral state. All of these issues are linked and connect, at the very least, with a neoliberal fascist political attack on democracy. When taken together these issues point to a politics of connection similar to what Martin Luther King, Jr. was fighting for in the last few years of his life. Moving beyond a single-issue orientation means also means developing a more comprehensive vision of politics and change.

A comprehensive politics is one that does at least two things. On the one hand, it tries to understand a plethora of problems from massive poverty to the despoiling of the ecosystem within a broader understanding of power. That is, it connects the dots among diverse forms of oppression. In this instance, the focus is on the totality of politics, one that focuses on the power-relations of global capitalism, the rise of illiberal democracy, the archives of authoritarianism, and the ascendancy of financial capital. A totalizing view of oppression allows the development of a language that is capable of making visible the ideological and structural forces of the new forms of domination at work in the United States and across the globe. On the other hand, as I have argued previously, such an understanding of politics makes it possible to bring together a range of crucial issues and movements so as to expand the range of oppressions while at the same time providing a common ground for these diverse groups to be able to work together in the interest of the common good and a broad struggle for democratic socialism. Any radical notion of democratization if it is to truly challenge the current stage of neoliberal fascism cannot afford to separate various struggles but to bring them together.

Finally, any viable language of emancipation needs to connect the dots between real possibilities for social action and change. It needs to develop a discourse of what Ron Aronson calls social hope. He writes:

Social hope, the disposition to act collectively to change a situation, entails that we act not blindly but with a sense of possibility. The cold stream demands that we prepare ourselves and assess the conditions under which we are operating. The hope of social movements calls for objective, clearheaded organization and action, and an appreciation of the circumstances in which we may be successful. This realistic stream of hope mingles with the visionary stream that motivates us; without both, there is no hope. Hope uniquely combines our longing, our own real intention, and our sense of potency with real possibility, the subjective and the objective.[485]

Aronson is right in arguing that naming what is wrong in a society is important but it is not enough, because such criticism can sometimes be overpowering and lead to an immobilizing despair or, even worse, a stagnating cynicism. Hope engages deeply with the present but still dares to imagine a life beyond capitalism. As Ariel Dorfman has argued, progressives need a language that is currently missing from our political vocabulary, one that insists that "alternative worlds are possible, that they are within reach if we're courageous enough, and smart enough, and daring enough to take control of our own lives."[486]

I am referring to a notion of informed social hope that does not overlook any forms of oppression at the same time as it focuses on realizing a future in which matters of justice, equality, freedom, and joy matter. Casino capitalism is a toxin that has massive ecologies of immiseration and has fueled the rise of a neoliberal fascism that in its many forms terrorizes entire populations, endlessly producing rootless refugees and massive poverty while at the same time threatening the life of the planet itself.[487]

The time has come for an international social movement that joins together fragmented and isolated points of resistance into a broad constellation that illuminates a future of democratic renewal. Modest gains can be fought for as part of a broader strategy of enabling oppressed groups "to regain confidence in their power" and assign to themselves "the goal of leaving capitalism behind."[488] Such a strategy would have to revive the radical imagination and the task of thinking about a future without capitalism and oppression. It would have to launch a comprehensive education program to provide alternative narratives, memories, and histories that enable the capacities for informed judgment, ethical responsibilities, and civic courage. And last but not least, it would need to build and support those alternative public spheres where a new conversation can be opened up about the creation of a new progressive and socialist political formation. As Marx said, there is nothing to lose but our chains.

Endnotes

1.   Paxton, Robert O. "The Five Stages of Fascism." *The Journal of Modern History,* Vol. 70, No. 1 (March 1998): 6-7. http://theleder.com/docs/Misc/Paxton_Five%20Stages%20of%20Fascism.pdf

2.   Madrigal, Alexis C. "What Facebook Did to American Democracy." *The Atlantic* (October 2017). https://www.theatlantic.com/technology/archive/2017/10/what-facebook-did/542502/

3.   See: Fuchs, Christian. *Digital Demagogue: Authoritarian Capitalism in the Age of Trump and Twitter*. London: Pluto Press, 2018.

4.   Allen, Mike. "Trump's historic gift to media." *Axios* (September 2018).   https://www.axios.com/donald-trump-news-media-ratings-profits-bce82032-f9f0-4d70-8e9d-ed4623461e6c.html

5.   Engelhardt, Tom. "UnFounding Father: Why We Need to Stare at You Know Who." *Truthdig,* (November 2017). http://www.truth-out.org/opinion/item/42768-unfounding-father-why-we-need-to-stare-at-you-know-who

6.   Graves, Lucia. "This is Sinclair, 'The Most Dangerous US Company You've Never Heard Of'." *The Guardian* (August 2017). https://www.theguardian.com/media/2017/aug/17/sinclair-news-media-fox-trump-white-house-circa-breitbart-news

7.   Lerer, Lisa. "On Politics: Fox's Friends." *The New York Times* (September 2018). https://www.nytimes.com/2018/09/25/us/politics/on-politics-jerry-brown-democrats.html?rref=collection%2Fsectioncollection%2Fpolitics&action=click&contentCollection=politics&region

=stream&module=stream_unit&version=latest&contentPlacement=4
&pgtype=sectionfront

8.   Bell, David A. "When the Farce Is Tragedy." *Dissent Magazine* (February 2018). https://www.dissentmagazine.org/online_articles/trump-year-one-tragedy-farce-right-wing-media

9.   Dale, Frank. "Trump Says Response to Hurricane Maria Was 'Unsung Success' Despite Nearly 3,000 Deaths," *ThinkProgress* (September 2018). https://thinkprogress.org/donald-trump-puerto-rico-hurricane-maria-response-ed242fdba8da/

10.   Cochrane, Emily and Glenn Thrush. "Disaster Relief Usually Sails Through Congress. The Sticking Point Now: Puerto Rico." *The New York Times* (April 2019). https://www.nytimes.com/2019/04/11/us/politics/disaster-relief-puerto-rico.html?emc=edit_cn_20190412&nl=politics&nlid=5156379320190412&te=1

11.   Cassidy, John. "Trump's Assault on American Governance Just Crossed a Threshold." *The New Yorker* (May 2018). Online: https://www.newyorker.com/news/our-columnists/trumps-assault-on-american-governance-just-crossed-a-threshold

12.   "I Am Part of the Resistance Inside the Trump Administration." *The New York Times* (September 2018). https://www.nytimes.com/2018/09/05/opinion/trump-white-house-anonymous-resistance.html

13.   "There Ought to Be a Law." *The New York Times* (September 2018). https://www.nytimes.com/2018/09/06/opinion/trump-illegal-protests-justice.html

14.   Dawsey, Josh. "'Two easy wins now in doubt': Trump renews attack on Sessions." *The Washington Post* (September 2018). https://www.washingtonpost.com/politics/two-easy-wins-now-in-doubt-trump-renews-attack-on-sessions-citing-indictments-of-two-gop-congressmen-ahead-of-midterms/2018/09/03/e6f1356a-afac-11e8-9a6a-565d92a3585d_story.html?utm_term=.a493d00155d2

15.   DiMaggio, Anthony. "Full-On Fascism: Trump Makes the Transition in his War on the Press." *CounterPunch* (September 2018). https://www.counterpunch.org/2018/09/11/full-on-fascism-trump-makes-the-transition-in-his-war-on-the-press

16.   Ibid. Chris Hayes.

17.   Martin, Will. "Ranked: The 29 Richest Countries in the World." *Business Insider* (May 2018). https://www.businessinsider.com/the-richest-countries-in-the-world-2018-5

18.   Statement on Visit to the USA, by Professor Philip Alston, United Nations Special Rapporteur on Extreme Poverty and Human Rights." *United Nations Human Rights* (December 2017). http://www.ohchr.org/EN/NewsEvents/Pages/DisplayNews.aspx?NewsID=22533

19.   Luhby, Tami. "9 million fewer Americans expected to have health insurance in 2019." *CNN Money* (February 2018). http://money.cnn.com/2018/02/26/news/economy/obamacare-trump-insurance/index.html

20.   Paxton, Robert O. *Vichy France: Old Guard and New Order, 1940-1944.* New York: Columbia University Press, 2001. See also: Pascal, Julia. "Vichy's shame." *The Guardian* (May 2002). https://www.theguardian.com/world/2002/may/11/france.weekend7

21.   Cole, Teju. "Resist, Refuse." *The New York Times* (September 2018).   https://www.nytimes.com/2018/09/08/magazine/teju-cole-resistance-op-ed-resist-refuse.html

22.   Sykes, Charles J. "Year One: The Mad King." *The New York Review of Books* (November 2017). https://www.nybooks.com/daily/2017/11/10/year-one-the-mad-king/

23.   Worth noting is that *The Washington Post* reported that after 365 days in office, Trump has told his 2,000[th] lie. See: Kessler, Glenn and Meg Kelly, "President Trump has made more than 2,000 false or misleading claims over 355 days," In *The Washington Post* (January 2018). https://www.washingtonpost.com/news/fact-checker/wp/2018/01/10/president-trump-has-made-more-than-2000-false-or-misleading-claims-over-355-days/?utm_term=.03d28c4520a7

24.   Evans. Richard J. *The Third Reich in Power*, 213-214. New York: Penguin, 2005.

25.   Levitsky, Steven and Daniel Ziblatt. *How Democracies Die.* New York: Crown, 2018.

26.   Hedges, Chris. *America: The Farewell Tour,* 19-20. New York: Simon & Schuster, 2018.

27.   Taylor, Jessica. "Trump: Democrats 'Un-American,' 'Treasonous' During State of The Union." *NPR (*February 2018). https://www.npr.org/2018/02/05/583447413/trump-democrats-un-american-treasonous-during-state-of-the-union

28.   Ibid.

29.   See: Stanley, Jason. *How Fascism Works: The Politics of Us and Them*. New York: Random House, 2018.

30.   Taibbi, Matt. "Trump's Absurd Similarities With Wrestler 'Ravishing' Rick Rude." *Rolling Stone* (March 2017). https://www.rollingstone.com/politics/videos/see-trumps-absurd-similarities-with-wrestler-ravishing-rick-rude-20160301

31.   Klein, Naomi. *No Is Not Enough,* 55. Toronto: Random House, 2017.

32.   Donnelly, Grace. "Top CEOs Make More in Two Days Than an Average Employee Does in One Year." *Fortune* (July 2017). http://fortune.com/2017/07/20/ceo-pay-ratio-2016/

33.   Higham, Scott and Lenny Bernstein. "The Drug Industry's Triumph over the DEA." *The Washington Post* (October 2017). https://www.washingtonpost.com/graphics/2017/investigations/dea-drug-industry-congress/?utm_term=.85ba69a19bf1

34.   Sleeper, Jim. "A Tyranny Years in the Making." *Democracy Journal* (March 2016). http://democracyjournal.org/arguments/a-tyranny-years-in-the-making/

35.   Cohen, Roger. "Trump's Corruption of the American Republic." *The New York Times* (February 2018). https://www.nytimes.com/2018/02/02/opinion/trump-corruption-republic.html

36.   Goddard, Taegan. "Trump Orders Pentagon to Plan a Military Parade." *Political Wire* (February 2018). https://politicalwire.com/2018/02/06/trump-orders-pentagon-plan-military-parade/

37.   Carter, Brandon. "Huckabee Sanders: Dems Need to Decide If They 'Hate' Trump' More than They Love This Country'." *The Hill* (February 2018).

http://thehill.com/homenews/administration/372615-huckabee-sanders-dems-need-to-decide-if-they-hate-trump-more-than

38.   Rodríguez, Nicole. "Trump Administration wants to arrest mayors of 'sanctuary cities'." *Newsweek* (January 2018). http://www.newsweek.com/trump-administration-wants-arrest-mayors-sanctuary-cities-783010

39.   Blum, Bill. "Is Devin Nunes an American Hero or Trump's New Coffee Boy?" *Truthdig* (February 2018). https://www.truthdig.com/articles/devin-nunes-american-hero-trumps-new-coffee-boy/

40.   Gessen, Masha. "How Democrats Fall Short in Challenging Trump's Anti-Immigrant Fervor." *The New Yorker* (February 2018). https://www.newyorker.com/news/our-columnists/how-democrats-fall-short-in-challenging-trumps-anti-immigrant-fervor

41.   St. Clair, Jeffrey. "Between the Null and the Void." *CounterPunch* (January 2018). https://www.counterpunch.org/2018/01/12/between-the-null-and-the-void/

42.   Trump's State of the Union address can be found at https://www.whitehouse.gov/briefings-statements/president-donald-j-trumps-state-union-address/

43.   Cole, Juan. "The Fascist Underpinnings of Trump's Speech." *Truthdig,* (January 2018). https://www.truthdig.com/articles/fascist-underpinnings-trumps-state-union/

44.   Ibid.

45.   Levy, Jacob T. "The Weight of Words." *Niskanen Center* (February 2018). https://niskanencenter.org/blog/the-weight-of-the-words/

46.   Tomasky, Michael. "The Worst of the Worst." *The New Yorker* (February 2018). http://www.nybooks.com/articles/2018/02/22/trump-wolff-worst-of-the-worst/

47.   Roger Cohen, "Trump's Corruption of the American Republic." *The New York Times* (February 2018). https://www.nytimes.com/2018/02/02/opinion/trump-corruption-republic.html

48.   See, for example, the conservative apologist for Trump, Rich Lowry: "The 'Trump is a despot' Crew is the real threat to democracy."

The New York Post (January 2018). https://nypost.com/2018/01/18/
the-trump-is-a-despot-crew-is-the-real-threat-to-democracy/.
See also: Wolff, Michael. *Fire and Fury: Inside the Trump White House.*
New York: Harper, 2018.

49.   Brown, Wendy. "Apocalyptic Populism." *Eurozine,* (Sept 2017).
http://www.eurozine.com/apocalyptic-populism/;   Fraser,   Nancy.
"From Progressive Neoliberalism to Trump — and Beyond," *American
Affairs* 1:4 (Winter 2017). https://americanaffairsjournal.org/2017/11/
progressive-neoliberalism-trump-beyond/

50.   Frum, David. "How to Build an Autocracy." *The Atlantic* (March,
2017). https://www.theatlantic.com/magazine/archive/2017/03/how-
to-build-an-autocracy/513872/. An extended version of this theme can
be found in: Frum, David. *Trumpocracy: The Corruption of the American
Republic*. New York: Harper, 2018.

51.   Levy, Jacob T. "The Weight of Words." *Niskanen Center* (February
2018). https://niskanencenter.org/blog/the-weight-of-the-words/

52.   See: Street, Paul. "Capitalism: The Nightmare." *Truthdig* (September
2017).   https://www.truthdig.com/articles/capitalism-the-nightmare/.
See also the now classic: Piketty, Thomas. *Capital in the Twenty-First
Century*. Cambridge: Belknap Press, 2017. and Aronowitz, Stanley and
Michael J. Roberts, eds. *Class: The Anthology*. New York: John Wiley &
Sons, 2018.

53.   Isaac, Jeffrey C. "Why Is Trump's Authoritarianism So Hard for
Some to Recognize?" *Public Seminar* (January 2018). http://www.pub-
licseminar.org/2018/01/why-is-trumps-authoritarianism-so-hard-for-
some-to-recognize/

54.   Evans, Richards J. "A Warning From History." *The Nation* (February
2017). https://www.thenation.com/article/the-ways-to-destroy-democracy/

55.   See: Hill, Samantha Rose. "American Politics and The Crystallization
of Totalitarian Practices." *Medium* (December 2016).   https://medi-
um.com/quote-of-the-week/american-politics-and-the-crystalliza-
tion-of-totalitarian-practices-464e1f02f514#.fyuncour9

56.   Gopnik, Adam. "A Year of Donald Trump in the White House," *The
New Yorker* (January 2018). https://www.newyorker.com/news/daily-
comment/a-year-of-donald-trump-in-the-white-house

57.   Thurman, Judith. "Philip Roth E-Mails on Trump." *The New Yorker* (January 2017). https://www.newyorker.com/magazine/2017/01/30/philip-roth-e-mails-on-trump

58.   Abramsky, Sasha. "How Trump Has Normalized the Unspeakable." *The Nation* (September 2017). https://www.thenation.com/article/how-trump-has-normalized-the-unspeakable/

59.   Leffel, Gregory. "Is Catastrophe the only cure for the weakness of radical politics?" *Open Democracy* (January 2018). https://www.open-democracy.net/transformation/gregory-leffel/is-catastrophe-only-cure-for-weakness-of-radical-politics

60.   Klein, Naomi. *No Is Not Enough*, 220. Canada: Random House, 2017.

61.   Phillips, Amber. "'They're rapists.' President Trump's campaign launch speech two years later." *The Washington Post* (June 2017). https://www.washingtonpost.com/news/the-fix/wp/2017/06/16/theyre-rapists-presidents-trump-campaign-launch-speech-two-years-later-annotated/?noredirect=on&utm_term=.b97e3474f477

62.   Baer, Drake. "Trump's 'Inner Cities' Fetish Is Nostalgic, Messy Racism." *The Cut* (October 2016). https://www.thecut.com/2016/10/why-trump-saying-inner-cities-is-racist-and-wrong.html

63.   Dawsey, Josh. "Trump derides protections for immigrants from 'shithole' countries." *The Washington Post* (January 2018). washingtonpost.com/politics/trump-attacks-protections-for-immigrants-from-shithole-countries-in-oval-office-meeting/2018/01/11/bfc0725c-f711-11e7-91af-31ac729add94_story.html

64.   Baker, Peter and Katie Rogers. "In Trump's America, the Conversation Turns Ugly and Angry, Starting at the Top." *The New York Times* (June 2018). https://www.nytimes.com/2018/06/20/us/politics/trump-language-immigration.html

65.   Austin-Hillary, Nicole. "Trump's Racist Language Serves Abusive Immigration Policies." *Human Rights Watch* (May 2018). https://www.hrw.org/news/2018/05/22/trumps-racist-language-serves-abusive-immigration-policies

66.   Obeidallah, Dean. "Trump's attacks on LeBron fit a disturbing

pattern." *CNN* (August 2018). https://www.cnn.com/2018/08/05/opinions/trump-lebron-pattern-opinion-obeidallah/index.html

67.   Fouhy, Beth. "Trump: Obama a 'Terrible Student' Not Good Enough for Harvard." *NBC News New York* (April 2011). https://www.nbcnewyork.com/news/local/Trump-Obama-Wasnt-Good-Enough-to-Get-into-Ivy-Schools-120657869.html

68.   For an excellent list of Trump's racist and bigoted remarks, see: López, German. "Donald Trump's long history of racism, from the 1970s to 2018." *Vox* (January 2018). https://www.vox.com/2016/7/25/12270880/donald-trump-racism-history. See also: Baker, Peter and Katie Rogers, "In Trump's America, the Conversation Turns Ugly and angry, starting at the Top." In *The New York Times,* (June 2018). https://www.nytimes.com/2018/06/20/us/politics/trump-language-immigration.html

69.   Ibid., Austin-Hillery, Nicole. "Trump's Racist Language Serves Abusive Immigration Policies."

70.   McKenzie, Scott. "Scientific information is the key to democracy." *The Conversation* (January 2018). https://theconversation.com/scientific-information-is-the-key-to-democracy-88620?utm_medium=email&utm_campaign=Latest%20from%20The%20Conversation%20for%20January%204%202018&utm_content=Latest%20from%20The%20Conversation%20for%20January%204%202018+CID_c92244b9da5fa91dfaa10c6cbd4fe095&utm_source=campaign_monitor_ca&utm_term=waging%20a%20war%20against%20scientific%20information

71.   White, Jeremy B. "A third of Americans think the media is the 'enemy of the people' following Trump's repeated 'fake news' attacks." *The Independent* (December 2017). http://www.independent.co.uk/news/world/americas/us-politics/americans-media-poll-trust-trump-fake-news-attacks-a8091991.html

72.   Baker, Peter. "For Trump, a Year of Reinventing the Presidency." *The New York Times* (December 2017). https://www.nytimes.com/2017/12/31/us/politics/trump-reinventing-presidency.html

73.   Ibid. Peter Baker.

74.   Ibid. Peter Baker.

75.   Paddock, Richard C. "Becoming Duterte: The Making of a Philippine Strongman." *The New York Times* (March 2017). https://www.nytimes.com/2017/03/21/world/asia/rodrigo-duterte-philippines-president-strongman.html

76.   Villamor, Felipe. "Rodrigo Duterte Says Donald Trump Endorses His Violent Antidrug Campaign." *The New York Times* (December 2016). http://www.nytimes.com/2016/12/03/world/asia/philippines-rodrigo-duterte-donald-trump.html

77.   Cohn, Marjorie. "Trump's Arpaio Pardon Signals to White Supremacists: 'I've Got Your Back'." *Truthdig* (August 2017). http://www.truth-out.org/news/item/41753-trump-s-arpaio-pardon-signals-to-white-supremacists-i-ve-got-your-back

78.   See: Zinn, Howard. *A People's History of the United States*. New York: Harper Perennial Modern Classics; Reissue edition, 2015.

79.   This theme is addressed, though problematically in: Bacevich, Andrew. "The President as Pimple." *Tom Dispatch,* (September 2018). www.tomdispatch.com/blog/176466/tomgram%3A_andrew_bacevich%2C_the_president_as_pimple/

80.   Gilroy, Paul. *Against Race*, 140. Cambridge: Harvard University Press, 2000.

81.   Steven, Levitsky and Daniel Ziblatt. "How a Democracy Dies." *The New Republic* (December 2017). https://newrepublic.com/article/145916/democracy-dies-donald-trump-contempt-for-american-political-institutions

82.   Ben-Ghiat, Ruth. "Beware of President Trump's Nefarious Language Games." *The Washington Post* (December 2017). https://www.washingtonpost.com/news/democracy-post/wp/2017/12/21/beware-of-president-trumps-nefarious-language-games/?utm_term=.dc9e11b2d2c9

83.   Klemperer, Victor. *The Language of the Third Reich*, 3, 167. New York: Bloomsbury, 2006.

84.   See: Leonhardt, David and Stuart A. Thompson, "Trump's Lies." *The New York Times.* (December 2017). https://www.nytimes.com/interactive/2017/06/23/opinion/trumps-lies.html?_r=0; Kessler, Glenn,

Megyn Kelly and Nicole Lewis, "President Trump has made 1,628 false or misleading claims over 298 days," In *The Washington Post* (November 2017). https://www.washingtonpost.com/news/fact-checker/wp/2017/11/14/president-trump-has-made-1628-false-or-misleading-claims-over-298-days/?utm_term=.ce2a734f0696

85.   Kessler, Glenn. "In a 30-minute Interview, President Trump Has Made 24 False or Misleading Claims." *The Washington Post* (December 2017). https://www.washingtonpost.com/news/fact-checker/wp/2017/12/29/in-a-30-minute-interview-president-trump-made-24-false-or-misleading-claims/?utm_term=.c83cf4f97f37

86.   Dale, Daniel. "Trump obliterates his dishonesty record: 132 false claims last week, 280 for July." *The Toronto Star* (August 2018). https://www.thestar.com/news/world/analysis/2018/08/09/trump-obliterates-his-dishonesty-record-132-false-claims-last-week-280-for-july.html

87.   I am drawing here from Cora Fisher's "An Artist's Bond with Her Imprisoned Father." *Hyperallergic* (November 2017). https://hyperallergic.com/410947/sable-elyse-smith-ordinary-violence-queens-museum-2017/

88.   Evans, Brad. "Remembering the 43." *BLARB:* the *Los Angeles Review of Books Blog* (September 2017). http://blog.lareviewofbooks.org/essays/remembering-43/

89.   Payne, Keith. *The Broken Ladder: How Inequality Affects the Way We Think, Live, and Die.* New York: Penguin Books, 2017.

90.   Gessen, Masha. "The Most Frightening Aspect of Trump's Tax Triumph." *The New Yorker* (December 2017). https://www.newyorker.com/news/our-columnists/the-most-frightening-aspect-of-trumps-tax-triumph

91.   Baker, Peter and Michael Tackett. "Trump Says His 'Nuclear Button' Is 'Much Bigger' Than North Korea's." *The New York Times* (January 2018). https://www.nytimes.com/2018/01/02/us/politics/trump-tweet-north-korea.html?_r=0

92.   Robinson, Cedric J. *Forgeries of Memory and Meaning: Blacks and the Regimes of Race in American Theater and Film before World War II*, 82. Chapel Hill, University of North Carolina Press; New edition, December 2007.

93.   Friedman, Lisa. "Trump Moves to Open Nearly All Offshore Waters to Drilling." *The New York Times* (January 2018). https://www.nytimes.com/2018/01/04/climate/trump-offshore-drilling.html?emc=edit_na_20180104&nl=breaking-news&nlid=51563793&ref=cta

94.   Jay Lifton, Robert. *Death in Life: Survivors of Hiroshima*, 479. Chapel Hill: University of North Carolina Press, 1987.

95.   Gray, John. "Forgetfulness: the dangers of a modern culture that wages war on its own past." *New Statesman* (October 12017). https://www.newstatesman.com/culture/books/2017/10/forgetfulness-dangers-modern-culture-wages-war-its-own-past

96.   Pruden, Wesley. "Trumpspeak, A Language Rich in Adjectives." *The Washington Times* (February 2017). https://www.washingtontimes.com/news/2017/feb/23/donald-trumps-speech-features-superlatives/

97.   Blake, Aaron. "19 things Donald Trump knows better than anyone else, according to Donald Trump." *The Washington Post* (October 2016). https://www.washingtonpost.com/news/the-fix/wp/2016/10/04/17-issues-that-donald-trump-knows-better-than-anyone-else-according-to-donald-trump/

98.   Evans, Richard J. *The Third Reich in Power*, 213. New York: Penguin, 2005.

99.   O'Gorman, Francis. *Forgetfulness: Making the Modern Culture of Amnesia,* 164. New York: Bloomsbury, 2017.

100.   Blakemore, Erin. "Donald Trump's War with the Past." *Longreads* (May 2017). https://longreads.com/2017/05/11/donald-trumps-war-with-the-past/

101.   Graham, David A. "Donald Trump's Narrative of the Life of Frederick Douglass." *The Atlantic* (February 2017). https://www.theatlantic.com/politics/archive/2017/02/frederick-douglass-trump/515292/

102.   Calamur, Krishnadev. "A Short History of 'America First'." *The Atlantic* (January 2017). https://www.theatlantic.com/politics/archive/2017/01/trump-america-first/514037/

103.   Allen, Chris. "What is Britain First – The Far-Right Group Retweeted by Donald Trump?" *The Conversation* (December 2017).

https://theconversation.com/what-is-britain-first-the-far-right-group-retweeted-by-donald-trump-88407

104.   Brinn, David. "Can 'Very Fine People' March with Neo-Nazis?" *Jerusalem Post (*August 2017). http://www.jpost.com/American-Politics/Commentary-The-very-fine-people-in-Charlottesville-502575

105.   President Obama's full speech can be found at https://www.nbcchicago.com/blogs/ward-room/obama-university-of-illinois-full-speech-492719531.html

106.   Blake, Aaron. "Trump's Embrace of a fraught term –'national-ist-could cement a dangerous racial divide." *The Washington Post* (October 2018). https://www.washingtonpost.com/politics/2018/10/23/trumps-embrace-fraught-term-nationalist-could-cement-dange-rous-racial-divide/?utm_term=.8623f760f614

107.   Ali,Wajahat."TheRootsoftheChristchurchMassacre."*TheNewYork Times* (March 2019). https://www.nytimes.com/2019/03/15/opinion/new-zealand-mosque-shooting.html

108.   Ben-Ghiat, Ruth. "Beware of President Trump's Nefarious Language Games." *The Washington Post* (December 2017). https://www.washingtonpost.com/news/democracy-post/wp/2017/12/21/beware-of-president-trumps-nefarious-language-games/?utm_term=.dc9e11b2d2c9

109.   Chauncey DeVega interviews Brian Klass: "Is Trump am 'Aspiring Despot' or a 'Bumbling Showman'?" *Salon* (December 2017). https://www.salon.com/2017/12/19/author-brian-klaas-is-trump-an-aspir-ing-despot-or-a-bumbling-showman-yes/

110.   Ibid.

111.   Dorfman, Ariel. "How to Read Donald Trump on Burning Books but not ideas." *TomDispatch,* (September 2017). http://www.tomdispatch.com/blog/176326/tomgram%3A_ariel_dorfman%2C_a_tale_of_two_donalds/

112.   Ibid.

113.   Abramsky, Sasha. "How Trump Has Normalized the Unspeak-able." *The Nation* (September 2017). https://www.thenation.com/article/how-trump-has-normalized-the-unspeakable/

114.   Ibid. Abramsky amplifies this line of thought in his book, *Jumping at Shadows: The Triumph of Fear and the End of the American Dream.* New York: Nation Books, 2017.

115.   See: Dreier, Peter. "American Fascist." *Common Dreams*, (January 2017). http://www.commondreams.org/views/2017/01/20/american-fascist

116.   Kaye, Harvey J. "Who Says It Can't Happen Here?" *Bill Moyers*, (Feb 2017). http://billmoyers.com/story/says-cant-happen/

117.   Kelley, Robin D. G. "Birth of a Nation." *Boston Review* (March 2017). http://bostonreview.net/race-politics/robin-d-g-kelley-births-nation

118.   Coetzee, J.M. "Lies." *The New York Review of Books* (December 2017). http://www.nybooks.com/articles/2017/12/21/lies/

119.   Hill, Samantha Rose. "American Politics and the Crystallization of Totalitarian Practices." *Medium* (December 2016). https://medium.com/quote-of-the-week/american-politics-and-the-crystalliza-tion-of-totalitarian-practices-464e1f02f514#.fyuncour9

120.   Stephenson, Wen. "Learning to Live in the Dark: Reading Arendt in the Time of Climate Change." The *Los Angeles Review of Books,* (September 2017). https://lareviewofbooks.org/article/learning-to-live-in-the-dark-reading-arendt-in-the-time-of-climate-change/

121.   Arendt, Hannah. "Personal Responsibility Under Dictatorship." in Jerome Kohn, ed., *Responsibility and Judgement.* New York: Schocken Books, 2003.

122.   Bertoldi, Nicola. "Are We Living Through a New 'Weimar era'?: Constructive Resolutions for Our Future." *OpenDemocracy* (January 2018). https://us1.campaign-archive.com/?e=d77f123300&u=9c663f-765f28cdb71116aa9ac&id=367a142d39

123.   Dorfman, Ariel. "Trump's War on Knowledge." *The New York Review of Books* (October 2017). http://www.nybooks.com/daily/2017/10/12/trumps-war-on-knowledge/

124.   Giridharadas, Anand. *Winners Take All: The Elite Charade of Changing the World.* New York: Knopf, 2018.

125. Monbiot, George. "Neoliberalism – The Ideology at the Root of All Our Problems." *The Guardian* (April 2016). http://www.the-guardian.com/books/2016/apr/15/neoliberalism-ideology-prob-lem-george-monbiot

126. See: Geiselberger, Heinrich. *The Great Regression*. London: Polity Press, 2017.; Fawcett, Edmund. "The Hard Right and Its Threats to Democratic Liberalism." *OpenDemocracy* (April 2018). https://www.opendemocracy.net/edmund-fawcett/hard-right-and-its-threats-to-democratic-liberalism;

127. Finchelstein, Federico. *From Fascism to Populism in History,* xi. Oakland: University of California Press, 2017.

128. Two excellent examples can be found in: Grossberg, Lawrence. *Under the Cover of Chaos: Trump and the Battle for the American Right*. London: Pluto Press, 2018.; and Boggs, Carl. *Fascism Old and New: American Politics at the Crossroads*. New York: Routledge, 2018

129. Ibid. p. xiv.

130. Isaac, Jeffrey C. "Is there illiberal democracy?" *Eurozine*. (August 2017). http://www.eurozine.com/is-there-illiberal-democracy/

131. For an analysis of the complex legacy of right-wing and fascist forces that have contributed to Trump's election and his popularity among fringe groups, see: Burley, Shane. *Fascism Today: What it is and How to End It.* Chicago: AR Press, 2017.

132. Mishra, Pankaj. "A Gandhian Stand Against the Culture of Cruelty." *The New York Review of Books,* (May 2018). http://www.nybooks.com/daily/2018/05/22/the-culture-of-cruelty/

133. Neoliberalism has a long and complex history and takes a variety of forms. I am using the more generic elements of neoliberalism when I use the term in this essay. See: Birch, Kean. "What Exactly is Neoliberalism?" *The Conversation.* (November 2017). https://theconversation.com/what-exactly-is-neoliberalism-84755. For an extensive analysis of neoliberalism in terms of its history and variations, see: Dardot, Pierre and Christian Laval. *Never Ending Nightmare: How Neoliberalism Dismantles Democracy.* New York: Verso, 2019.; Wolff, Richard D. *Capitalism's Crisis Deepens: Essays on the Global Economic Meltdown*. Chicago: Haymarket, 2016; Brown, Wendy. *Undoing the*

Demos: Neoliberalism's Stealth Revolution. New York: Zone Books, 2015.; Giroux, Henry A. *Against the Terror of Neoliberalism*. New York: Routledge, 2008.; and Harvey, David. *A Brief History of Neoliberalism*. Oxford University Press, 2005.

134.   Bellamy Foster, John. "Neofascism in the White House." *Monthly Review* (April 2017). https://monthlyreview.org/2017/04/01/neofascism-in-the-white-house/

135.   Brown, Wendy. *Undoing the Demos: Neoliberalism's Stealth Revolution*, 9. New York: Zone Books, 2015.

136.   One brilliant source here is: Geiselberger, Henrich. *The Great Regression*. Cambridge: Polity Press, 2017.

137.   Crain, Caleb. "Is Capitalism a Threat to Democracy?" *The New Yorker* (May 2018). https://www.newyorker.com/magazine/2018/05/14/is-capitalism-a-threat-to-democracy

138.   Goldberg, Michelle. "Anniversary of the Apocalypse." *The New York Times* (November 2017). https://www.nytimes.com2017/11/06/opinion/anniversary-trump-clinton-election.html

139.   Mishra, Pankaj. "A Gandhian Stand Against the Culture of Cruelty." *The New York Review of Books* (May 2018). http://www.nybooks.com/daily/2018/05/22/the-culture-of-cruelty/

140.   Ibid.

141.   Street, Paul. "Capitalism: the Nightmare." *Truthdig* (September 2017). https://www.truthdig.com/articles/capitalism-the-nightmare/

142.   Shivani, Anis. "This is our neoliberal nightmare: Hillary Clinton, Donald Trump. And why the market and the wealthy win every time." *Salon* (June 2016). https://www.salon.com/2016/06/06/this_is_our_neoliberal_nightmare_hillary_clinton_donald_trump_and_why_the_market_and_the_wealthy_win_every_time/

143.   Wright Edelman, Marian. "Why America may Go to Hell." *Huffington Post* (November 2017). https://www.huffingtonpost.com/entry/why-america-may-go-to-hell_us_5a0f4dd4e4b023121e0e9281

144.   Ibid.

145. Mishra, Pankaj. "What Is Great about Ourselves." *London Review of Books* (November 2017). https://www.lrb.co.uk/v39/n18/pankaj-mishra/what-is-great-about-ourselves

146. O'Toole, Fintan. "Trial Runs for Fascism are in full flow." *Irish Times* (June 2018). https://www.irishtimes.com/opinion/fintan-o-toole-trial-runs-for-fascism-are-in-full-flow-1.354

147. Brown, Wendy. Undoing *the Demos: Neoliberalism's Stealth Revolution*, 210. New York: Zone Books, 2015.

148. See, especially: Yates, Michael D. *The Great Inequality*. New York: Routledge, 2016.; Joseph E. Stiglitz, Joseph E. *The Price of Inequality*. New York: Norton, 2012.

149. Bauman, Zygmunt. *Liquid Fear*, 89. London: Polity Press, 2006.

150. Brown, Wendy. "Apocalyptic Populism." *Eurozine*. (September 2017). http://www.eurozine.com/apocalyptic-populism/

151. Snyder, Timothy. "The Study of the Impossible, not the Inevitable." *Eurozine* (July 2018). https://www.eurozine.com/mapping-road-unfreedom/

152. Giroux, Henry A. "Challenging Trump's Language of Fascism." *Truthout* (January 2018). https://truthout.org/articles/challenging-trumps-language-of-fascism/

153. Snyder, Timothy. *On Tyranny: Twenty Lesson From the Twentieth Century*, 65. London: Polity Press, 2017.

154. Berkowitz, Roger. "Why Arendt Matters: Revisiting 'The Origins of Totalitarianism.'" The *Los Angeles Review of Books* (March 2017). https://lareviewofbooks.org/article/arendt-matters-revisiting-origins-totalitarianism/

155. Stonebridge, Lindsey. "Why Hannah Arendt is the philosopher for now." *The New Statesman* (March 2019). https://www.newstatesman.com/culture/books/2019/03/hannah-arendt-resurgence-philosophy-relevance

156. Gilroy, Paul. *Against Race,* 141. Cambridge: Harvard University Press, 2000.

157.   Kaplan, Erin Aubry. "Presidents used to speak for all Americans. Trump speaks for his racist, resentful white base." The *Los Angeles Times* (November 2017). http://www.latimes.com/opinion/la-oe-election-anniversary-updates-presidents-used-to-speak-for-all-1509745879-htmlstory.html

158.   Adorno, Theodor W. "The Meaning of Working Through the Past." *Guild and Defense*, 214. Translated by Henry W. Pickford. Cambridge: Harvard University Press, 2010.

159.   Arendt, Hannah. *The Origins of Totalitarianism*. New York: Harcourt, Brace, Jovanovich, 1973.

160.   Knott, Marie Luise. *Unlearning With Hannah Arendt*, 17. Translated by David Dollenmayer. New York: Other Press, 2011.

161.   Fateman, Johanna. "Wise Guys: On the Art of Nicole Eisenman." *ArtForum* (April 2019). https://www.artforum.com/print/201904/johanna-fateman-on-the-art-of-nicole-eisenman-78964

162.   Gilroy, Paul. *Against Race*, 139. Cambridge: Harvard University Press, 2000.

163.   Paxton, Robert O. *The Anatomy of Fascism*, 202. New York: Alfred A. Knopf, 2004.

164.   Corbett, Jesse. "'That this Even Has to be Said is Grotesque': Judge Orders Trump Admin to Stop Drugging Migrant Children." *CommonDreams* (July 2018). https://www.commondreams.org/news/2018/07/31/even-has-be-said-grotesque-judge-orders-trump-admin-stop-drugging-migrant-children

165.   Grabell, Michael and Topher Sanders. "Immigrant Youth Shelters: If You're a Predator, It's a Gold Mine." *ProPublica* (July 2018). https://www.propublica.org/article/immigrant-youth-shelters-sexual-abuse-fights-missing-children

166.   Honarvar, Ari. "A 6-Year-Old Girl Was Sexually Abused in an Immigrant-Detention Center." *The Nation* (July 2018). https://www.thenation.com/article/six-year-old-girl-sexually-abused-immigrant-detention-center

167.   "The Trump Administrations Legacy of Orphans." *The Washington*

Post (August 2018). https://www.washingtonpost.com/opinions/the-trump-administrations-legacy-of-orphans/2018/08/26/820df666-a7e0-11e8-97ce-cc9042272f07_story.html?utm_term=.bea64c5f5073

168. Dickerson, Caitlin. "Hundreds of Migrant Children Quietly Move to a Tent Camp on the Texas Border." *The New York Times* (September 2018). https://www.nytimes.com/2018/09/30/us/migrant-children-tent-city-texas.html

169. Blake, Mike. "Migrant Children Describe Tent City as 'Punishment' Experts Say." *Huffington Post* (October 2018). https://www.huffington-post.ca/entry/migrant-children-say-being-in-texas-tent-city-is-punishment_us_5bb2a902e4b00fe9f4f9ab0f

170. Dale, Frank."Trump took $10 million from FEMA's budget to pay for ICE detention centers." *ThinkProgress* (September 2018). https://thinkprogress.org/donald-trump-jeff-merkley-fema-ice-detention-center-immigration-rachel-maddow-c1f554bb7b1e/

171. Paxton, Robert O. "The Five Stages of Fascism." *The Journal of Modern History,* Vol. 70, No. 1 (March 1998). http://theleder.com/docs/Misc/Paxton_Five%20Stages%20of%20Fascism.pdf

172. Ibid.

173. Gilroy, Paul. *Against Race*, 144. Cambridge: Harvard University Press, 2000.

174. Boggs, Carl. "Obama's Imperial Presidency." *CounterPunch* (September 2018). https://www.counterpunch.org/2018/09/14/obamas-imperial-presidency/

175. Brown, Wendy. "Apocalyptic Populism." *Eurozine* (September 2017). http://www.eurozine.com/apocalyptic-populism/

176. Hacker, Jacob S. and Paul Pierson. *Winner-Take-All Politics*. New York: Simon & Schuster, 2010.; Frank, Thomas. *Rendezvous with Oblivion: Reports from a Sinking Society*. New York: Metropolitan Books, 2018.

177. Graham, David. "The Resignation of Tom Price." *The Atlantic* (September 2017). https://www.theatlantic.com/politics/archive/2017/09/tom-price-resigned/541608/

178. See: McCrummen, Stephanie. "Judgment Days: God, Trump, and the Meaning of Morality." *The Washington Post* (July 2018). https://www.washingtonpost.com/news/national/wp/2018/07/21/feature/god-trump-and-the-meaning-of-morality/?utm_term=.717092543ff0&wpisrc=nl_headlines&wpmm=1

179. See: Sehgal, Parul. "Toxic History, Poisoned Water: The Story of Flint." *The New York Times* (July 2018). https://www.nytimes.com/2018/07/03/books/review-poisoned-city-anna-clark-what-eyes-dont-see-mona-hanna-attisha-flint-water-crisis.html?hp&action=click&pgtype=Homepage&clickSource=story-heading&module=mini-moth&region=top-stories-below&WT.nav=top-stories-b

180. Klein, Naomi. *The Battle For Paradise: Puerto Rico Takes on the Disaster Capitalists*. Chicago: Haymarket, 2018.

181. Koball, Heather and Yang Jiang. *Basic Facts about Low-Income Children under 9 Years, 2016. New* York: National Center for Children in Poverty, 2018.

182. Goodman, Amy. "Blistering U.N. Report: Trump Administration's Policies Designed to Worsen Poverty & Inequality." *Democracy Now!* (June 2018). https://www.opendemocracy.net/phil-burton-cartledge/democratic-politics-beyond-liberal-democracy

183. Yee, Vivian and Miriam Jordan. "Migrant Children in Search of Justice: A 2-Year-Old's Day in Immigration Court." *The New York Times* (October 2018). https://www.nytimes.com/2018/10/08/us/migrant-children-family-separation-court.html?nl=top-stories&nlid=51563793ries&ref=cta

184. See: Lafer, Gordon. *The One Percent Solution: How Corporations are Remaking America One State at a Time*. Ithaca: Cornell University Press, 2017.

185. I take up these issues at length in another book of mine: *American Nightmare: Facing the Challenge of Fascism*. San Francisco: City Lights Books, 2018.

186. Hinton, Elizabeth. *From the War on Poverty to the War on Crime: The Making of Mass Incarceration in America*. Cambridge: Harvard University Press, 2017.

187. Paschall, Katherine, Tamara Halle, and Jessica Dym Bartlett, "Poverty rate rising among America's youngest children, particularly infants of color." *Childtrends.org* (September 2018). https://www.child-trends.org/poverty-rate-rising-among-americas-youngest-children-particularly-infants-of-color

188. Stern, Mark Joseph. "Brian Kemp's Bid for Governor Depends on Erasing the Black Vote in Georgia." *Slate* (August 2018). https://slate.com/news-and-politics/2018/08/georgia-voter-suppression-brian-kemps-bid-for-governor-depends-on-erasing-the-black-vote-its-working.html

189. Shivani, Anis. "This is Our Neoliberal Nightmare: Hillary Clinton, Donald Trump. And Why the Market and the Wealthy Win Every Time." *Salon* (June 2016). https://www.salon.com/2016/06/06/this_is_our_neoliberal_nightmare_hillary_clinton_donald_trump_and_why_the_market_and_the_wealthy_win_every_time/

190. Harvey, David. "Organizing for the Anti-Capitalist Transition." *Monthly Review* (December 2009). http://davidharvey.org/2009/12/organizing-for-the-anti-capitalist-transition/

191. Monbiot, George. *Out of the Wreckage: A New Politics for an Age of Crisis*, 132-133. New York: Verso, 2017.

192. On the domination of policy by the rich, see: Gilens, Martin and Benjamin I. Page. "Testing Theories of American Politics: Elites, Interest Groups, and Average Citizens." *Perspectives on Politics.* New York: American Political Science Association, 2014. https://scholar.princeton.edu/sites/default/files/mgilens/files/gilens_and_page_2014_-testing_theories_of_american_politics.doc.pdf;   White, Jeremy B. "Los Angeles sues drug companies for 'driving opioid epidemic' Lawsuit accuses companies of 'borrowing from the tobacco industry's playbook'." *The Independent* (May 2018). https://www.in-dependent.co.uk/news/world/americas/los-angeles-opioid-lawsuit-pharmaceuticals-mike-feuer-a8335516.html

193. Birch, Kean and Vlad Mykhnenko. "Introduction: A World Turned Right Way Up," *The Rise and The Fall of Neoliberalism: The Collapse of an Economic Order*, 7-8. New York: Zed Books, 2010.

194. Wieseltier, Leon. "How Voters' Personal Suffering Overtook Reason – and Brought us Donald Trump." *The Washington Post* (June 2016).   https://www.washingtonpost.com/posteverything/wp/2016/

06/22/how-voters-personal-suffering-overtook-reason-and-brought-us-donald-trump/

195. O'Toole, Fintan. "Trial Runs for Fascism are in full flow." *Irish Times* (June 2018). https://www.irishtimes.com/opinion/fintan-o-toole-trial-runs-for-fascism-are-in-full-flow-1.354

196. Norwood, Candace. "I Want 'My People' to 'Sit Up at Attention' Like in North Korea." *Politico* (June 2018). https://www.politico.com/story/2018/06/15/trump-north-korea-sit-up-attention-648969

197. See: Neiwert, David. *Alt-America: The Rise of the Radical Right in The Age of Trump.* New York: Verso, 2017.

198. See: Street, Paul. "Capitalism: The Nightmare." *Truthdig* (September 2017). https://www.truthdig.com/articles/capitalism-the-nightmare/ ; Buchheit, Paul. *Disposable Americans: Extreme Capitalism and the Case for a Guaranteed Income.* New York: Routledge, 2017.

199. Shivani, Anis. "This is our neoliberal nightmare: Hillary Clinton, Donald Trump. And Why the Market and the Wealthy Win Every Time." *Salon* (June 2016). https://www.salon.com/2016/06/06/this_is_our_neoliberal_nightmare_hillary_clinton_donald_trump_and_why_the_market_and_the_wealthy_win_every_time/

200. Coates, Ta-Nehisi. "The First White President." *The Atlantic,* (October 2017). https://www.theatlantic.com/magazine/archive/2017/10/the-first-white-president-ta-nehisi-coates/537909/

201. Feffer, John. "Donald Trump's Flight 93 Doctrine." *The Nation* (July 2017). https://www.thenation.com/article/donald-trumps-flight-93-doctrine/

202. Miroff, Nick, Amy Goldstein and Maria Sacchetti. "Deleted families: What Went Wrong with Trump's Family-Separation Effort." *The Washington Post* (July 2018). https://www.washingtonpost.com/local/social-issues/deleted-families-what-went-wrong-with-trumps-family-separation-effort/2018/07/28/54bcdcc6-90cb-11e8-8322-b5482bf5e0f5_story.html?utm_term=.d95992b65e7e&wpisrc=nl_evening&wpmm=1

203. Ben-Ghiat, Ruth. "Beware of President Trump's Nefarious Language Games." *The Washington Post* (December 2017). https://www.washingtonpost.com/news/democracy-post/wp/2017/12/21/

beware-of-president-trumps-nefarious-language-games/?utm_
term=.dc9e11b2d2c9

204. Sydney Parfitt Rose, Cihan Aksan, and Jon Bailes, eds. "One
Question Fascism (Part One)." Is Fascism making a comeback?" *State
of Nature Blog,* (December 2017). http://stateofnatureblog.com/one-
question-fascism-part-one/

205. Tharoor, Ishaan. "Trump's Racist Coda to a Terrible Week." *The
Washington Post* (August 2018). www.washingtonpost.com/world/2018/
08/24/trumps-racist-coda-terrible-week/?utm_term=.f39b47b85ae5

206. Burke, Jason. "Murders of Farmers in South Africa at 20-year Low,
Research Shows," *The Guardian* (June 2018). https://www.theguardian.
com/world/2018/jun/27/murders-of-farmers-in-south-africa-at-
20-year-low-research-shows

207. Burke, Jason and David Smith. "Donald Trump's land seizures
tweet sparks anger in South Africa." *The Guardian* (August 2018). https://
www.theguardian.com/us-news/2018/aug/23/trump-orders-close-
study-of-south-africa-farmer-killings

208. Kushner, Aviya. "'INFEST' – The Ugly Nazi History of Trump's
Chosen Verb About Immigrants," *Forward* (June 2016). https://forward.
com/culture/403526/infest-the-ugly-nazi-history-of-trumps-chosen-
verb-about-immigrants/

209. Cole, Juan. "What Have We Become? What We Have Always
Been." *Common Dreams* (May 2018). https://www.juancole.com/2018/05/
latinos-animals-undermen.html

210. Ibid.

211. Mindock, Clark. "Number of hate crimes surges in year of Trump's
election." *The Independent* (November 2017). https://www.independent.
co.uk/news/world/americas/hate-crimes-us-trump-election-surge-
rise-latest-figures-police-a8055026.html

212. Ibid. Ben-Ghiat, Ruth. "Beware of President Trump's Nefarious
Language Games."

213. Douglas-Gabriel, Danielle and Tracy Jan, "DeVos called HBCUs
'pioneers' of 'school choice.' It didn't go over well." *The Washington*

Post (February 2017). https://www.washingtonpost.com/news/grade-point/wp/2017/02/28/devos-called-hbcus-pioneers-of-school-choice-it-didnt-go-over-well/?noredirect=on&utm_term=.d530e2559251

214.   Dorfman, Ariel. "How to Read Donald Trump on Burning Books but not ideas." *TomDispatch,* (September 2017). http://www.tomdispatch.com/blog/176326/tomgram%3A_ariel_dorfman%2C_a_tale_of_two_donalds/

215.   Schmidt, Michael S. and Maggie Haberman Mueller. "Examining Trump's Tweets in Wide-Ranging Obstruction Inquiry." *The Washington Post* (July 2018). https://www.nytimes.com/2018/07/26/us/politics/trump-tweets-mueller-obstruction.html?nl=top-stories&nlid=15581699ries&ref=cta

216.   Lipsyte, Robert. "Donald Trump's War on Black Athletes." *The Nation* (July 2018). https://www.thenation.com/article/donald-trumps-war-sports/

217.   Freedland, Jonathan. "Inspired by Trump, the World Could be Heading Back to the 1930s." *The Guardian* (June 2018). Https://www.theguardian.com/commentisfree/2018/jun/22/trump-world-1930s-children-parents-europe-migrants

218.   Arendt, Hannah. "The Image of Hell." *Commentary* (September 1946).   https://www.commentarymagazine.com/articles/the-black-book-the-nazi-crime-against-the-jewish-people-and-hitlers-professors-by-max-weinreich/

219.   Dorfman, Ariel. "How to Read Donald Trump on Burning Books but not ideas." *TomDispatch* (September 2017). Http://www.tomdispatch.com/blog/176326/tomgram%3A_ariel_dorfman%2C_a_tale_of_two_donalds/

220.   Sunstein, Cass R. "It Can Happen Here." *The New York Review of Books* (June 2018). http://www.nybooks.com/articles/2018/06/28/hitlers-rise-it-can-happen-here/

221.   Francis Wilde interviews Pankaj Mishra. "'The Liberal Order Is the Incubator for Authoritarianism": A Conversation with Pankaj Mishra," The *Los Angeles Review of Books* (November 2018). https://lareviewofbooks.org/article/the-liberal-order-is-the-incubator-for-authoritarianism-a-conversation-with-pankaj-mishra/#!

222.   Han, Byung-Chul. *In the Swarm: Digital Prospects*, 13. Translated by Erik Butler. Cambridge, MA: MIT Press, 2017.

223.   Marcuse, Herbert. *An Essay on Liberation*, 14. Boston: Beacon Press, 1969.

224.   Cassegard, Carl. "Individualized Solidarity." *Eurozine* (July 2018). https://www.eurozine.com/individualized-solidarity/

225.   Bernstein, Richard J. "The Illuminations of Hannah Arendt." *The New York Times* (June 2016). https://www.nytimes.com/2018/06/20/opinion/why-read-hannah-arendt-now.html

226.   Nichols, John. "Donald Trump Is Putting Every Journalist in Every Country at Risk." *The Nation* (October 2018). https://www.thenation.com/article/donald-trump-is-putting-every-journalist-in-every-country-at-risk

227.   Bray, Mark. "Deporting US Citizens: Trump's New Fascistic Use of Law." *Truthout* (August 2018). https://truthout.org/articles/deporting-us-citizens-trumps-new-fascistic-use-of-law/

228.   Graham, David A. "Trump's Assault on the Rule of Law." *The Atlantic* (April 2018). https://www.theatlantic.com/politics/archive/2018/04/trumps-assault-on-rule-of-law/557600/

229.   Sontag, Susan. "The Imagination of Disaster." *Commentary* (October 1965): 42-48. http://americanfuturesiup.files.wordpress.com/2013/01/sontag-the-imagination-of-disaster.pdf

230.   Rubaii, Nadia and Max Pensky. "Preventing crimes against humanity in the US." *The Conversation* (June 2018). Online: https://theconversation.com/preventing-crimes-against-humanity-in-the-us-98679

231.   Kushner, Aviya. "'INFEST' – The Ugly Nazi History of Trump's Chosen Verb About Immigrants." *Forward* (June 2016). https://forward.com/culture/403526/infest-the-ugly-nazi-history-of-trumps-chosen-verb-about-immigrants/

232.   Giroux, Henry A. "Trump's Act of State Terrorism Against Children." *The Conversation* (June 2018). https://theconversation.com/trumps-act-of-state-terrorism-against-children-98612

233. Chávez, Aída. "'No one will believe baboon complaints' — racist abuse in immigration detention on the rise in trump era, report says." *The Intercept* (June 2018). Online: https://theintercept. com/2018/06/26/immigration-detention-center-abuse-ice

234. Sykes, Michael. "Detainee complaints reveal patters of abuse from ICE agents." *Axios* (April 2018). https://www.axios.com/complaints-reveal-pattern-of-sexual-assault-from-ice-agents-68ade4ed-bdea-4247-8652-5597ae9b5500.html

235. Miller, Ryan W. "New York's Kirsten Gillibrand, Bill de Blasio echo progressive calls to ,abolish ICE'." *USA Today* (June 2018). https://www. usatoday.com/story/news/politics/2018/06/29/kristen-gillibrand-bill-de-blasio-echo-progresive-calls-abolish-ice/746694002/

236. Qujinn, David. "Cynthia Nixon Calls ICE a 'Terrorist Organization' as She Calls for Its Abolishment." *People* (June 2018). https://people. com/politics/cynthia-nixon-ice-terrorist-organization-abolishment/

237. Kramer, Sasha. "Trump's Heartless Honduras Policy, in 15 Numbers." *In These Times* (September 2018). http://inthesetimes.com/ article/21427/honduras-temporary-protected-status-immigration-trump

238. Ibid.

239. Jordan, Miriam. "Trump Administration Says That Nearly 200,000 Salvadorans Must Leave." *The New York Times* (January 2018). https:// www.nytimes.com/2018/01/08/us/salvadorans-tps-end.html

240. Rucker, Philip and David Weigel. "Trump advocates depriving undocumented immigrants of due-process rights." *The Washington Post* (June 2018). https://www.washingtonpost.com/powerpost/ trump-advocates-depriving-undocumented-immigrants-of-due-process-rights/2018/06/24/dfa45d36-77bd-11e8-93cc-6d3beccdd7a3_story.html?utm_term=.1cd555feefa7

241. Shear, Michael D. and Ron Nixon. "Plan to Punish Immigrants for Using Welfare Could Boost G.O.P. Candidates." *The New York Times* (August 2018). https://www.nytimes.com/2018/08/07/us/politics/ legal-immigrants-welfare-republicans-trump.html

242. Novick, Ilana. "Stephen Miller's New Sinister Immigration Proposal." In *Truthdig*. (August 2018). https://www.truthdig.com/

articles/stephen-millers-new-sinister-immigration-proposal/

243. Regencia, Ted. "Senator: Rodrigo Duterte's drug war has killed 20,000." *Al Jazeera* (February 2018). https://www.aljazeera.com/news/2018/02/senator-rodrigo-duterte-drug-war-killed-20000-180221134139202.html

244. Greshko, Michael, Laura Parker, Brian Clark Howard, and Daniel Stone. "A Running List of How President Trump Is Changing Environmental Policy." *National Geographic* (August 2018). https://news.nationalgeographic.com/2017/03/how-trump-is-changing-science-environment/

245. Jacobs, Andrew. "Opposition to Breast-Feeding Resolution by U.S. Stuns World Health Officials." *The New York Times* (August 2018). https://www.nytimes.com/2018/07/08/health/world-health-breast-feeding-ecuador-trump.html

246. Ibid.

247. I authored an in-depth analysis of neoliberal fascism: "Neoliberal Fascism and the Echoes of History." *Truthdig* (August 2018). https://www.truthdig.com/articles/neoliberal-fascism-and-the-echoes-of-history/

248. Ibid. Jacobs., p. 2.

249. Mills, Wright. *The Politics of Truth: Selected Writings of C. Wright Mills*, 18. New York: Oxford University Press, 2008.

250. Goodman, Amy. "Books, Not Magazines: Outcry Grows over DeVos Plan to Divert Federal Funds For Guns in Schools." *Democracy Now.* (August2018).https://www.democracynow.org/2018/8/29/books_not_magazines_outcry_grows_over?utm_source=Democracy+Now%21&utm_campaign=8d6dcdce70-Daily_Digest_COPY_01&utm_medium=email&utm_term=0_fa2346a853-8d6dcdce70-190213053

251. Krugman, Paul. "Why it Can Happen Here." *The New York Times.* (August 2018). https://www.nytimes.com/2018/08/27/opinion/trump-republican-party-authoritarianism.html

252. Davis, Mike. "Who Will Build the Ark." *New Left Review* (January-February 2010). https://newleftreview.org/II/61/mike-davis-who-will-build-the-ark

253. Simon, Jonathan. *Governing Through Crime: How the War on Crime Transformed American Democracy and Created a Culture of Fear*. New York: Oxford University Press, 2007.

254. "Rick Gates, Wilbur Ross and the lure of Trump corruption." *The Washington Post* (August 2018). https://www.washingtonpost.com/blogs/plum-line/wp/2018/08/07/rick-gates-wilbur-ross-and-the-lure-of-trump-corruption/?utm_term=.1fef608cf2e3

255. Honneth, Axel. *Pathologies of* Reason, 188. New York: Columbia University Press, 2009.

256. Benjamin, Walter. *The Writer of Modern Life: Essays on Charles Baudelaire*, 160. Cambridge, MA: Harvard University Press, 2006.

257. Adorno, Theodor W. "The Meaning of Working Through the Past." *Guild and Defense*, 213-214. Translated by Henry W. Pickford. Cambridge: Harvard University Press, 2010.

258. Crain, Caleb. "Is Capitalism a Threat to Democracy?" *The New Yorker* (May 2018). https://www.newyorker.com/magazine/2018/05/14/is-capitalism-a-threat-to-democracy

259. Bellamy Foster, John. "Neofascism in the White House." *Monthly Review* (April 2017). https://monthlyreview.org/2017/04/01/neofascism-in-the-white-house/

260. Rogers, Melvin. "Democracy Is a Habit: Practice It." *Boston Review* (July 2018). http://bostonreview.net/politics/melvin-rogers-democracy-habit-practice-it

261. Silva, Jennifer M. *Coming Up Short: Working-Class Adulthood In An Age of Uncertainty*. New York: Oxford University Press, 2013.

262. Brown, Wendy. *"Undoing the Demos: Neoliberalism's Stealth Revolution*. New York: Zone Books, 2015.

263. See: Abramsky, Sasha. *Jumping at Shadows: The Triumph of Fear and the End of the American Dream*. New York: Nation Books, 2017.

264. Shivani, Anis. "This is our neoliberal nightmare: Hillary Clinton, Donald Trump. And why the market and the wealthy win everytime." *Salon* (June 2016) https://www.salon.com/2016/06/06/this_is_our_neoliber-

al_nightmare_hillary_clinton_donald_trump_and_why_the_market_
and_the_wealthy_win_every_time/

265.   Bauman, Zygmunt. "Does 'Democracy' Still Mean Anything? (And
in Case It Does, What Is It?)" *Truthout* (January 2011). https://truthout.
org/articles/does-democracy-still-mean-anything-and-in-case-it-
does-what-is-it/

266.   Brown, Wendy. "Apocalyptic Populism," *Eurozine* (September
2017). http://www.eurozine.com/apocalyptic-populism/

267.   Aksan, Cihan and Jon Bailes, eds., "One Question Fascism-
Is Fascism making a comeback?" (Part Two)," *State of Nature Blog*
(December 2017). http://stateofnatureblog.com/one-question-fascism-
part-two/

268.   Marx, Karl and Friedrich Engels *The Communist* Manifesto, 5. New
York: International Publishers, New Edition, 2014.

269.   Fox, Maggie. "Opioid overdose deaths may be undercounted by
70,000." *NBC News* (June 2018).https://www.nbcnews.com/storyline/
americas-heroin-epidemic/opioid-overdose-deaths-may-be-under-
counted-70-000-n887021. Also see: Macy, Beth. *Dopesick: Dealers,
Doctors, and the Drug Company that Addicted America*. New York: Little,
Brown and Company, 2018.

270.   Case, Anne and Angus Deaton. "Mortality and Morbidity in the
21st Century." *Brookings Papers on Economic Activity* (August 2017).
https://www.brookings.edu/wp-content/uploads/2017/08/case-
textsp17bpea.pdf

271.   Edgecliffe-Johnson, Andrew and Shannon Bond. "Trust in US
institutions slumps during Trump's first year." *Financial Times* (January
2018).   https://www.ft.com/content/28f719ae-fe67-11e7-9650-9c0ad-
2d7c5b5

272.   Goodman, Amy. "Blistering U.N. Report: Trump Administration's
Policies Designed to Worsen Poverty & Inequality." *Democracy Now!*
(June 2018). https://www.opendemocracy.net/phil-burton-cartledge/
democratic-politics-beyond-liberal-democracy

273.   Ben-Meir, Alon. "Child Poverty In America Is Indefensible."
The Huffington Post (October 2017). https://www.huffingtonpost.

com/entry/child-poverty-in-america-is-indefensible_us_59f21fabe
4b06acda25f485c

274. Lowenthal, Leo. "Atomization of Man." *False Prophets: Studies in Authoritarianism*, 182. New Brunswick, NJ: Transaction Books, 1987.

275. Personal correspondence. September 14, 2018.

276. Fisher, Mark. *Ghosts of My Life: Writings on Depression, Hauntology and Lost Futures*, 2 London: Zero Books, 2014.

277. Pramuk, Jacob. "Trump jokes he wants his 'people' to 'sit up at attention' when he speaks, like North Koreans do with Kim Jong-un" *CNBC* (June 2018). https://www.cnbc.com/2018/06/15/trump-wants-people-to-listen-to-him-like-north-koreans-do-to-kim-jong-un.html

278. Op. cit., Lowenthal, p. 185.

279. Harward, Donald W. "Risking Silence." *Inside Higher Ed* (August 2018). https://www.insidehighered.com/views/2018/08/28/higher-education-has-responsibility-speak-out-against-current-administrati-ons-false

280. Brown, Wendy. *Edgework: Critical Essays on Knowledge and Politics*, 59. Princeton: Princeton University Press, 2005.

281. Brenkman, John. "Raymond Williams and Marxism." In *Cultural Materialism: On Raymond Williams*, 261. Minneapolis: University of Minnesota Press, 1995.

282. George Monbiot provides an informative account of a number of attempts at developing a democratic sense of lived community informed by democratic values. See: Monbiot, George. *Out of the Wreckage: A New Politics for an Age of Crisis*. New York: Verso, 2017. For a theoretical frame work on theories of participatory democracy, see Wainwright, Hillary. *A New Politics from the Left*. London: Polity, 2018,; and Wolf, Richard. *Democracy at Work: A Cure for Capitalism*. Chicago: Haymarket Books, 2012.

283. Bourdieu, Pierre. *Acts of Resistance*, 11. New York: Free Press, 1998.

284. Wright Mills, C. "On Politics." *The Sociological Imagination*, 193. New York: Oxford University Press, 2000.

285.   Judt, Tony. "Transformations of the Public Sphere." *Social Science Research Council* (December 2011) http://publicsphere.ssrc.org/judt-the-disintegration-of-the-public-sector/

286.   Riotta, Chris. "Majority of Republicans say Colleges Are Bad for America (yes, really)." *Newsweek* (July 2017). http://www.newsweek.com/republicans-believe-college-education-bad-america-donald-trump-media-fake-news-634474

287.   See: Di Leo, Jeffrey R., Henry A. Giroux, Sophia A. McClennen, and Kenneth Saltman, *Neoliberalism, Education, and Terrorism*. New York: Routledge, 2014.

288.   I want to thank my student, Morgan Jaques, for alerting me to the following reference: Connley, Courtney. "Google, Apple and 13 other companies that no longer require employees to have a college degree." *CNBC* (August 2018). https://www.cnbc.com/2018/08/16/15-companies-that-no-longer-require-employees-to-have-a-college-degree.html

289.   Hardy, Ed. "Apple HR couldn't care less if you have a college degree." *Cult of Mac* (August 2018). https://www.cultofmac.com/571719/hired-apple-college-degree-required/

290.   Eagleton, Terry. "The ambition of advanced capitalism is not simply to combat radical ideas-it is to abolish the very notion that there could be a serious alternative to the present" *Red Pepper* (October 2013). https://www.redpepper.org.uk/death-of-the-intellectual/

291.   Brown, Wendy. *Undoing the Demos: Neoliberalism's Stealth Revolution*, 26-27. New York: Zone Books, 2015.

292.   Han, Byung-Chul. *The Burnout Society*, 1. Stanford: Stanford University Press, 2015.

293.   Gopnik, Adam. "Orwell's '1984' and Trump's America." *The New Yorker* (January 2017). http://www.newyorker.com/news/daily-comment/orwells-1984-and-trumps-america

294.   Ellingboe, Kristen and Ryan Koronowski. "Most Americans Disagree With Their Congressional Representative On Climate Change." *Thinkprogress* (March 2016). http://thinkprogress.org/climate/2016/03/08/3757435/climate-denier-caucus-114th-new-research/

295. Evans, Brad and Henry A. Giroux. *Disposable Futures: The Seduction of violence in the Age of the Spectacle*. San Francisco: City Lights, 2016.

296. Beck, Ulrich. *Twenty Observations on a World in Turmoil*, 53-59. London: Polity Press, 2010.

297. Chomsky, Noam. "The Death of American Universities." *Reader Supported News* (March 2015). http://readersupportednews.org/opinion2/277-75/29348-the-death-of-american-universities

298. Hedges, Chris. "The War on Language." *Truthdig* (September 2009). http://www.truthdig.com/report/item/20090928_the_war_on_language/

299. Aschoff, Nicole. "The Smartphone Society." *Jacobin Magazine*, Issue 17, (Spring 2015). https://www.jacobinmag.com/2015/03/smartphone-usage-technology-aschoff/

300. Stuart, Tessa. "Watch Trump Brag About Uneducated Voters, 'The Hispanics'." *Rolling Stone* (February 2016). http://www.rollingstone.com/politics/news/watch-trump-brag-about-uneducated-voters-the-hispanics-20160224

301. Furedi, Frank. *Culture of Fear Revisited*. New York: Bloomsbury, 2006.

302. McChesney, Robert W. *Rich Media, Poor Democracy: Communication Politics in Dubious Times.* New York: Free Press, 2015.; de Zengotita, Thomas. *Mediated: How the Media Shapes Our World and the Way We Live in It.* New York: Bloomsbury, 2006.

303. Honneth, Axel. *Pathologies of Reason*, 188. New York: Columbia University Press, 2009.

304. Saltman, Kenneth J. *Scripted Bodies: Corporate Power, Smart Technologies, and the Undoing of Public Education.* New York: Routledge, 2016.; Ravitch, Diane. *Reign of Error*. New York: Knopf, 2014.; Giroux, Henry A. *Education and the Crisis of Public Values.* New York: Peter Lange, 2015.

305. Olson, Gary and Lynn Worsham. "Staging the Politics of Difference: Homi Bhabha's Critical Literacy." *Journal of Advanced*

Composition (1999): 3-35.

306. Ness, Immanuel. *Southern Insurgency: The Coming of the Global Working Class*. London: Pluto Press, 2015.

307. Singer, Natasha. "The Silicon Valley Billionaires Remaking America's Schools." *The New York Times* (June 2017). https://www.nytimes.com/2017/06/06/technology/tech-billionaires-education-zuckerberg-facebook-hastings.html?_r=0

308. Caplan, Bryan. *The Case against Education: Why the Education System Is a Waste of Time and Money*. Princeton, Princeton University Press, 2018.

309. Coetzee, JM. "JM Coetzee: Universities head for extinction." *Mail & Guardian* (November 2013). http://mg.co.za/article/2013-11-01-universities-head-for-extinction

310. Bauman, Zygmunt and Leonidas Donskis. *Moral Blindness: The Loss of Sensitivity in Liquid* Modernity, 196. London: Polity, 2013.

311. Bauman, Zygmunt. *Liquid Modernity*, 215. London: Polity Press, 2001.

312. Brenkman, John. "Raymond Williams and Marxism." In Prendergast, Christopher. *Cultural Materialism: On Raymond Williams*, 239. Minneapolis: University of Minnesota Press.

313. Mohanty, Chandra. "On Race and Voice: Challenges for Liberal Education in the 1990s." In *Cultural Critique*, 192: 14 (1898-1990).

314. Eagleton, Terry. *The Idea of Culture*, 22. Malden, MA: Basil Blackwell, 2000.

315. Falk, Barbara. "Between past and future." *Eurozine* (May 2011) http://www.eurozine.com/between-past-and-future/

316. See: Newfield, Christopher. *The Great Mistake: How We Wrecked Public Universities and How We Can Fix Them*. Baltimore: John Hopkins University Press, 2016.; Donoghue, Frank. *The Last Professors: The Corporate University and the Fate of the Humanities*. New York: The Fordham University Press, 2018.; Giroux, Henry A. *The University in Chains*. New York: Routledge, 2007.

317. Hill, Richard. "Against the Neoliberal University." *Arena Magazine*, No. 140 (February 2016):

318. 13.

319. Nixon, Jon. "Hannah Arendt: Thinking Versus Evil." *Times Higher Education* (February 2015). https://www.timeshighereducation.co.uk/features/hannah-arendt-thinking-versus-evil/2018664.article?page=0%2C0

320. Butler, Judith. "The Criminalization of Knowledge." *The Chronicle of Higher Education* (May 2018). https://www.chronicle.com/article/The-Criminalization-of/243501

321. Aronowitz, Stanley. "What Kind of Left Does America Need?" *Tikkun* (April 2014). http://www.tikkun.org/nextgen/what-kind-of-left-does-america-need.

322. Nichol, Gene R. "Public Universities at Risk Abandoning Their Mission" *The Chronicle of Higher Education* (October 2008). http://chronicle.com/weekly/v54/i30/30a02302.htm

323. Case, Kristen. "The Other Public Humanities" *The Chronicle of Higher Education* (January 2014). http://m.chronicle.com/article/Ahas-Ahead/143867/

324. Britzman, Deborah. "Thoughts On the Fragility of Peace" *Lecture at McMaster University* (January 27, 2016).

325. Aronowitz, Stanley. *Against Schooling*, 50. Boulder: Paradigm Publishers, 2008.

326. Robbins, Bruce. "A Starting Point for Politics" *The Nation* (October 2016). https://www.thenation.com/article/the-radical-life-of-stuart-hall/

327. Aronowitz, Stanley. *Against Schooling*, 50. Boulder: Paradigm Publishers, 2008.

328. Forrester, Katrina. "Libidinal Politics." *Harper's Magazine* (February 2017). https://harpers.org/archive/2017/02/trump-a-resisters-guide/5/

329. Benjamin, Andrew. *Present Hope: Philosophy, Architecture, Judaism*, 10. New York: Routledge, 1997.

330. Shear, Michael D. "Trump Stuns Lawmakers With Seeming Embrace of Comprehensive Gun Control." *The New York Times* (February 2018). https://www.nytimes.com/2018/02/28/us/politics/trump-gun-control.html?hp&action=click&pgtype=Homepage&clickSource=story-heading&module=first-column-region&region=top-news&WT.nav=top-news

331. Cited in Christopher Ingraham. "For many mass shooters, armed guards aren't a deterrent, they're part of the fantasy." *The Washington Post* (March 2918). https://www.washingtonpost.com/news/wonk/wp/2018/03/01/for-many-mass-shooters-armed-guards-arent-a-deterrent-theyre-part-of-the-fantasy/?utm_term=.4d8d415c6287

332. Cited in Todd Spangler. "DeVos: Education Department won't stand in way of schools buying guns." *Detroit Free Press* (September 2018). https://www.freep.com/story/news/local/michigan/2018/09/01/betsy-devos-wont-stop-school-districts-buying-guns/1172180002/

333. Balingit, Moria hand Nick Anderson. "'No way I would do that': Educators decry Trump proposal to arm teachers." *The Washington Post* (February 2018). https://www.washingtonpost.com/local/education/no-way-i-would-do-that-educators-decry-trump-proposal-to-arm-teachers/2018/02/22/f85e9cdc-17e2-11e8-92c9-376b4fe57ff7_story.html?utm_term=.247b85020645

334. Popken, Ben. "America's Gun Business, By the Numbers." *NBC News* (October 2015). https://www.nbcnews.com/storyline/san-bernardino-shooting/americas-gun-business-numbers-n437566

335. Shear, Michael D., Sheryl Gay Stolberg and Thomas Kaplan. "N.R.A. Suggests Trump May Retreat From Gun Control." *The New York Times* (March 2018). https://www.nytimes.com/2018/03/01/us/politics/trump-republicans-gun-control.html

336. Rosen, David. "Killing by the Numbers: How Much More to Follow." *CounterPunch* (February 2018). https://www.counterpunch.org/2018/03/01/killing-by-the-numbers-how-much-more-to-follow/

337. Kloc, Joe. "Trump's America." *Harper's Weekly Review* (February 2018). https://harpers.org/blog/2018/02/weekly-review-47/

338. Bader, Eleanor J. "Corporal Punishment Lives On: Students Nationwide are being Paddled, Restrained." *Truthout* (April 2018).

https://truthout.org/articles/corporal-punishment-lives-on-students-nationwide-are-being-paddled-restrained/

339. Whitehead, John W. "Children of the American Police State: Just Another Brick in the Wall." *The Huffington Post* (August 2016). https://www.huffingtonpost.com/entry/children-of-the-american-_b_11654954.html

340. Sinyangwe, Sam. "Militarizing Schools, Criminalizing Students." *The Real News Network* (February 2018). http://therealnews.com/t2/index.php?option=com_content&task=view&id=31&Itemid=74&jumival=21213

341. Balthaser, Benjamin. "Arming Teachers, Killing Education." *Truthout* (March 2018). http://www.truth-out.org/opinion/item/43707-arming-teachers-killing-education-why-trump-s-proposal-has-nothing-to-do-with-safety

342. Ibid.

343. Gopnik, Adam. "Four Truths About the Florida School Shooting." *The New Yorker* (February 2018). https://www.newyorker.com/news/daily-comment/four-truths-about-the-florida-school-shooting?mbid=nl_Sunday%20Longreads%20

344. Patel, Jugal K. "After Sandy Hook, More Than 400 People Have Been Shot in Over 200 School Shootings." *The New York Times* (February 2018). https://www.nytimes.com/interactive/2018/02/15/us/school-shootings-sandy-hook-parkland.html

345. See the *Gun Violence Archive 2018*. http://www.gunviolencearchive.org/

346. Hsu, Tiffany. "Threat of Shootings Turns School Security Into a Growth Industry." *The New York Times* (March 2018). https://www.nytimes.com/2018/03/04/business/school-security-industry-surges-after-shootings.html

347. Ibid.

348. Lieberman, Jennifer L. "Why Technology Will Not Solve Our Criminal Justice Problems." *CounterPunch* (August 2018). https://www.counterpunch.org/2017/08/02/why-technology-will-not-solve-our-criminal-justice-problems/

349. Schwartz, Heather L., Rajeev Ramchand, Dionne Barnes-Proby, Sean Grant, Brian A. Jackson, Kristin Leuschner, Mauri Matsuda, and Jessica Saunders. "Can Technology Make Schools Safer?" *RAND Corporation Research Briefs* (2016). https://www.rand.org/pubs/research_briefs/RB9922.html

350. Ibid. Tiffany Hsu.

351. Sanchez, Ray and Holly Yan."Florida Gov. Rick Scott signs gun bill." *CNN* (March 2018). https://www.cnn.com/2018/03/09/us/florida-gov-scott-gun-bill/index.html

352. Ibid.

353. See: Eubanks, Virginia. *Automating Inequality: How High-Tech Tools Profile, Police, and Punish the Poor.* New York: St. Martin's Press, 2018.

354. I address this issue in detail in: Giroux, Henry A. *America at War with Itself.* San Francisco: City Lights, 2017.

355. St. Clair, Jeffrey. "American Carnage" *CounterPunch* (February 2018). https://www.counterpunch.org/2018/02/16/american-carnage/

356. Hennelly, Bob. "The ignored war within: America's addiction to violence starts young." *Salon* (March 2018). https://www.salon.com/2018/03/03/the-ignored-war-within-americas-addiction-to-violence-starts-young/

357. Wright Edelman, Marian. "Violence Against Children." *Children's Defense Fund* (February 2018). http://www.childrensdefense.org/newsroom/child-watch-columns/child-watch-documents/ViolenceAgainstChildren.html

358. Ibid. St. Clair.

359. Baldwin, James, Raoul Peck. *I Am Not Your Negro*, 95. New York: Vintage International, 2017.

360. Wright Edelman, Marian. "Our Children's Cry: Do Something." *Children's Defense Fund* (March 2018). http://www.childrensdefense.org/newsroom/child-watch-columns/child-watch-documents/OurChildrensCryDoSomething.html

361. Ibid.

362. Comaroff, Jean and John Comaroff. "Reflections on Youth, from the Past to the Postcolony." In Fisher Melissa S. and Greg Downey. *Frontiers of Capital: Ethnographic Reflections on the New Economy*, 268. Durham: Duke University Press, 2006.

363. Evans, Brad and Henry A. Giroux, *Disposable Futures: The Seduction of Violence in the Age of the Spectacle* San Francisco: City Lights Books, 2015.

364. See: Mcintyre, Lee. *Post-Truth*. Cambridge: MIT Press, 2018.

365. Norman Herr, "Television and Health," cited in Bob Hennelly, "The ignored war within: America's addiction to violence starts young," *Salon* (March 3, 2018). Online: https://www.salon.com/2018/03/03/the-ignored-war-within-americas-addiction-to-violence-starts-young/

366. Krugman, Paul. "Nasty, Brutish and Trump." *The New York Times* (February 2018). https://www.nytimes.com/2018/02/22/opinion/guns-nasty-brutish-trump.html?rref=collection%2Fcolumn%2Fpaul-krugman&action=click&contentCollection=opinion%C2%AEion=stream&module=stream_unit&version=search&contentPlacement=2&pgtype=collection

367. Bump, Phillip. "The economics of arming schools." *The Washington Post* (February 2018). https://www.washingtonpost.com/news/politics/wp/2018/02/22/the-economics-of-arming-americas-schools/?utm_term=.f48d191f93e8

368. Ibid.

369. Lach, Eric. "Donald Trump Celebrates Violence Against Journalists." *The New Yorker* (October 2018). https://www.newyorker.com/news/current/donald-trump-celebrates-violence-against-journalists

370. Chen, Stephanie. "Girl's arrest for doodling raises concerns about zero tolerance." *CNN* (February 2010). http://www.cnn.com/2010/CRIME/02/18/new.york.doodle.arrest/index.html

371. Brown, Wendy. "Apocalyptic Populism." *Eurozine* (September 2017). http://www.eurozine.com/apocalyptic-populism/

372.   Mills, C. W. "The Powerless People: The role of the Intellectual in Society." In *The Politics of Truth*, 18. New York: Oxford University Press, 2008.

373.   Fisher, Max. "What Explains U.S. Mass Shootings? International Comparisons Suggest an Answer." *The New York Times* (November 2017). https://www.nytimes.com/2017/11/07/world/americas/mass-shootings-us-international.html

374.   Blow, Charles. "America is the Gun." *The New York Times* (February 2018). https://www.nytimes.com/2018/02/25/opinion/america-is-the-gun.html

375.   Taylor, Keeanga-Yamahtta. "The Struggle for Black Lives Is an Integral Part of the Struggle Against Gun Violence." *Truthout* (February 2018). http://www.truth-out.org/opinion/item/43683-the-struggle-for-black-lives-is-an-integral-part-of-the-struggle-against-gun-violence.

376.   Lennard, Natasha. "Gun Control Has always been Racist–That Doesn't Mean we Shouldn't Support the Parkland Students' Movement." *The Intercept* (March 2018). https://theintercept.com/2018/03/01/florida-shooting-gun-control-police/

377.   Shepard, Steven. "Gun control support surges in polls." *Politico* (February 2018). https://www.politico.com/story/2018/02/28/gun-control-polling-parkland-430099

378.   Ibid., Taylor, Keeanga-Yamahtta. "The Struggle for Black Lives Is an Integral Part of the Struggle Against Gun Violence."

379.   Kaldor, Mary. "What Happens When Violence Is an Everyday Occurrence?" *The Nation*, (July 2016). https://www.thenation.com/article/what-happens-when-violence-is-an-everyday-occurrence/

380.   Bump, Philip. "Why Parkland students have emerged as a powerful political voice." *The Washington Post* (February 2018). https://www.washingtonpost.com/news/politics/wp/2018/02/19/why-parkland-students-have-emerged-as-a-powerful-political-voice/?utm_term=.53ee3949a862

381.   Paxton, Robert O. "The Five Stages of Fascism." *The Journal of Modern History,* Vol. 70, No. 1 (March 1998): 1-23. http://theleder.com/docs/Misc/Paxton_Five%20Stages%20of%20Fascism.pdf

382. Fraser, Nancy. "From Progressive Neoliberalism to Trump — and Beyond." *American Affairs Journal* (November 2017).

383. See: Giroux, Henry A. *American Nightmare: Facing the Challenge of Fascism*. San Francisco: City Lights Books, 2018.; Stanley, Jason. *How Fascism Works: The Politics of Us and Them*. New York: Random House, 2018.; Boggs, Carl. *Fascism: Old and New*. New York: Routledge, 2018.; Snyder, Timothy. *On Tyranny: Twenty Lessons From the Twentieth Century*. New York: Tim Duggan Books, 2017.

384. Giridharadas, Anand. *Winners Take All: The Elite Charade of Changing the World*. New York: Knopf, 2018.

385. Monbiot, George. *Out of the Wreckage: A New Politics for an Age of Crisis*, 37. New York: Verso, 2017.

386. Brown, Wendy and Jo Littler,."Where the fires are An interview with Wendy Brown." *Eurozine* (April 2018. https://www.eurozine.com/where-the-fires-are/

387. Lerner, Michael. "Overcoming Trump-ism: A New Strategy for Progressives." *Tikkun Magazine*, Vol. 32, No. 1, (Winter 2017). http://www.tikkun.org/nextgen/overcoming-trump-ism-a-new-strategy-for-progressives

388. I take this up in detail in: Giroux, Henry A. *American Nightmare: Facing the Challenge of Fascism*. San Francisco: City Lights Books, 2018.

389. Mason, Paul. "Overcoming the fear of freedom." *The Great Regression*, 89-103. Editor Heinrich Geiselberger. Polity Press, 2017: Cambridge, UK.

390. Massey, Doreen. "Vocabularies of the economy," *Soundings* (2013) http://lwbooks.co.uk/journals/soundings/pdfs/Vocabularies%20of%20the%20economy.pdf

391. Monbiot, George. *Out of the Wreckage: A New Politics for an Age of Crisis*, 35. New York: Verso, 2017.

392. Hill, Samantha Rose. "American Politics and the Crystallization of Totalitarian Practices." *Medium* (December 2016). https://medium.com/quote-of-the-week/american-politics-and-the-crystallization-of-totalitarian-practices-464e1f02f514#.fyuncour9

393. I take this up in great detail in Giroux, Henry A. *American Nightmare: Facing the Challenge of Fascism* (San Francisco: City Lights Books, 2018. See also: Neiwert, David. Alt-America: The Rise of the Radical Right in the Age of Trump. London: Verso, 2017.; Grossberg, Lawrence. Under the Cover of Chaos: Trump and the Battle for the American Right. London: Pluto Press, 2018.

394. Moyers, Bill. "Discovering What Democracy Means," *CommonDreams (*February 2007). https://www.commondreams.org/views/2007/02/12/discovering-what-democracy-means.

395. Arendt, Hannah. *Between Past and Future: Eight Exercises in Political Thought*, 193. New York: Penguin Books, 2006.

396. Bernstein, Richard J. *The Abuse of Evil*, 25. London: Polity, 2005.

397. Nixon, Rob. *Slow Violence and the Environmentalism of the Poor*. Cambridge: Harvard University Press, 2011.

398. Ibid. p. 2.

399. Smith, David. "'My Classroom Has Asbestos and Bats': A Message for Betsy DeVos." *The Guardian* (October 2018). https://www.theguardian.com/us-news/2018/oct/05/guardian-us-teacher-takeover-betsy-de-vos

400. Ibid. David Smith.

401. Ibid. David Smith.

402. Ibid. Rob Nixon p. 2.

403. Smith, David. "It didn't start with Trump: how America came to undervalue teachers" *The Guardian* (October 2018). https://www.theguardian.com/education/2018/oct/05/reagan-nation-at-risk-education-policy-trump-bush

404. Pear, Robert. "Education Chief Calls Union 'Terrorist,'" Then Recants." *The New York Times* (February 2004). https://www.nytimes.com/2004/02/24/us/education-chief-calls-union-terrorist-then-recants.html

405. Sanchez, Claudio and Cory Turner. "Obama's Impact on America's Schools." *NPR Ed* (January 2017) https://www.npr.org/sections/ed/2017/01/13/500421608/obamas-impact-on-americas-

schools. See also: Saltman, Kenneth. *The Politics of Education*. New York: Routledge, 2018.; Berliner, David C. and Gene V Glass. *50 Myths and Lies That Threaten America's Public Schools: The Real Crisis in Education*. New York: Teachers College Press, 2014.; Ravitch, Dianne. *The Death and Life of the Great American School System: How Testing and Choice Are Undermining Education*. New York: Basic Books, 2016.

406.   Rozsa, Matthew. "Betsy DeVos complains about striking teachers during meeting with 2018 Teachers of the Year." *Salon* (May 2016). https://www.salon.com/2018/05/02/betsy-devos-complains-about-striking-teachers-during-meeting-with-2018-teachers-of-the-year/

407.   See: Fraser, Steve. "Class Dismissed: Class Conflict in Red State America." *Tom Dispatch* (April 2018). http://www.tomdispatch.com/blog/176412/

408.   Lafer, Gordon. *The One Percent Solution: How Corporations are Remaking America One State at a Time*. Ithaca: Cornell University Press, 2017.

409.   Ibid.

410.   Cited in Lynn Parramore. "The Corporate Plan to Groom U.S. Kids for Servitude by Wiping Out Public Schools," *Institute of New Economic Thinking* (April 2018). https://www.ineteconomics.org/perspectives/blog/the-corporate-plan-to-groom-u-s-kids-for-servitude-by-wiping-out-public-schools

411.   Nimri Aziz, Barbara. "Let Our Teachers Teach and Leaders Lead." *CounterPunch* (March 2018). https://www.counterpunch.org/2018/03/29/let-our-teachers-teach-and-leaders-lead/

412.   McClennen, Sophia A. "We Have Failed Our Kids: Is It Time For a Young People's Campaign?" *Salon* (March 2018). https://www.salon.com/2018/03/31/we-have-failed-our-kids-is-it-time-for-a-young-peoples-campaign/

413.   Klein, Naomi. *No Is Not Enough: Resisting The New Shock Politics and Winning the World We Need*, 79-88. (Chicago: Haymarket Books, 2017.

414.   Srnicek, Nick and Alex Williams. *Inventing the Future: Postcapitalism and a World Without Work*, 2. London: Verso, 2016.

415. Aronoff, Kate. "West Virginia Showed how Necessary – and Difficult – Striking is." *In These Times* (April 2018). http://inthesetimes.com/article/21037/west-virginia-strike-organizing-teachers-south-charleston

416. Eidelson, Josh. "Teacher Strikes are Spreading Across America with No End in Sight." *Bloomberg* (April 2018). https://www.bloomberg.com/news/articles/2018-04-02/teacher-strikes-are-spreading-across-america

417. Will, Madeline. "Teacher Strikes are Heating up in More States." *Education Week* (September 2018). https://www.edweek.org/ew/articles/2018/09/12/teacher-strikes-are-heating-up-in-more.html

418. Elk, Mike. "Wave of teachers' wildcat strikes spreads to Oklahoma and Kentucky." *The Guardian,* (April 2018). https://www.theguardian.com/us-news/2018/apr/02/teachers-wildcat-strikes-oklahoma-kentucky-west-virginia

419. Owliaei, Negin. "Teacher Strikes Continue to Spread - A Symptom of Public Education Underfunding." *Real News Network* (April 2018). http://therealnews.com/t2/index.php?option=com_content&task=view&id=31&Itemid=74&jumival=21620

420. Allegretto, Sylvia. "Teachers across the country have finally had enough for the teacher pay penalty." *Economic Policy Institute* (April 2018). https://www.epi.org/publication/teachers-across-the-country-have-finally-had-enough-of-the-teacher-pay-penalty/

421. Blanc, Eric. "It's Oklahoma's Turn to Strike." *Jacobin* (March 2018). https://jacobinmag.com/2018/03/oklahoma-teachers-strike-west-virginia

422. Ibid.

423. Elk, Mike. "Wave of teachers' wildcat strikes spreads to Oklahoma and Kentucky." *The Guardian,* (April 2018). https://www.theguardian.com/us-news/2018/apr/02/teachers-wildcat-strikes-oklahoma-kentucky-west-virginia

424. Danilova, Maria. "94% of Teachers Say They Spend Their Own Money on Classroom Supplies." *Time* (May 2018). http://time.com/5277745/teachers-spend-money-on-school-supplies/

425. Fraser, Steve. "Class Dismissed: Class Conflict in Red State America." *Tom Dispatch* (April 2018). http://www.tomdispatch.com/blog/176412/

426. Bernd, Candice. "Arizona Educators Stage First Statewide Walkout as Teacher Revolt Grows." *Truthout,* (April 2018). https://www.thenation.com/article/trump-is-discarding-laws-and-assembling-a-war-cabinet-what-could-go-wrong/

427. Weingarten, Debbie. "Tens of Thousands Mobilize to Support Arizona Teachers amid Backlash." *TalkPoverty.org* (April 2018). https://talkpoverty.org/2018/04/27/tens-thousands-mobilize-support-arizona-teachers-amid-backlash/

428. Balingit, Moriah. "Arizona teachers end walkout despite falling short of aims." *The Washington Post* (May 2018). https://www.washingtonpost.com/news/education/wp/2018/05/03/arizona-teachers-end-walkout-despite-falling-short-of-aims/?utm_term=.61376c1ba2ca&wpisrc=nl_daily202&wpmm=1

429. McAlevey, Jane. "Teachers Lead in the Revolt Against Austerity." *The Bullet* (May 2018). https://socialistproject.ca/2018/05/teachers-lead-the-revolt-against-austerity/#more-2306

430. Alter, Charlotte. "The School Shooting Generation Has Had Enough." *Time.com* (March 2108). http://time.com/longform/never-again-movement/

431. Evans, Brad and Henry A. Giroux. *Disposable Futures: The Seduction of Violence in the Age of Spectacle*. San Francisco: City Lights Books, 2015.

432. For a brilliant analysis of U.S. gun culture and the debate surrounding it, see: Dunbar-Ortiz, Roxanne. *Loaded: A Disarming History of the Second Amendment*. San Francisco: City Lights Books, 2018.

433. Levine, Judith. "The 'Active Shooter' is the State." *Boston Review.* (March 2018). http://bostonreview.net/law-justice/judith-levine-end-us-violence-guns-are-only-first-step

434. Fain, Paul. "Republicans Like Higher Ed." *Insider Higher Education* (May 2018). https://www.insidehighered.com/news/2018/05/21/republicans-are-generally-positive-about-higher-education-new-survey

435.   Cited in Marian Wood Kolish, "The Imaginative Reality of Ursula K. Le Guin," *VQR* (March 2018). https://www.vqronline.org/interviews-articles/2018/03/imaginative-reality-ursula-k-le-guin

436.   On this issue, see: Hedges, Chris. "Tariq Ali: The Time Is Right for a Palace Revolution." *Truthdig,* (March 2015). http://www.truthdig.com/report/item/tariq_ali_the_time_is_right_for_a_palace_revolution_20150301

437.   See: Aronowitz, Stanley. "What Kind of Left Does America Need?" *Tikkun* (April 2014). http://www.tikkun.org/nextgen/what-kind-of-left-does-america-need. Also see: Lerner, Michael. "Overcoming Trump-ism: A New Strategy for Progressives." *Tikkun* (Winter 2017): 4-9.; Lerner, Michael. "Yearning for a World of Love and Justice: An introduction to the Ideas of *Tikkun* and the Network of Spiritual Progressives (NSP)." *Tikkun* (April 2015). http://www.tikkun.org/nextgen/yearning-for-a-world-of-love-and-justice-the-worldview-of-tikkun-and-our-network-of-spiritual-progressives

438.   Aronowitz, Stanley. *Left Turn: Forging a New Political Future*, 160. Boulder: Paradigm, 2006.

439.   Aronson, Ronald. *We: Reviving Social Hope*, 13. Chicago: University Chicago Press, 2017.

440.   Bottici, Chiara. "Imaginal Politics in the Age of Trumpism." *Global-e* (November 2017) http://www.21global.ucsb.edu/global-e/november-2017/imaginal-politics-age-trumpism

441.   Goldberg, Michelle. "First They Came for the Migrants." *The New York Times* (June 2018). https://www.nytimes.com/2018/06/11/opinion/trump-border-migrants-separation.html

442.   Davenport, Carol. "Major Climate Report Describes a Strong Risk of Crisis as Early as 2040." *The New York Times* (October 2018). https://www.nytimes.com/2018/10/07/climate/ipcc-climate-report-2040.html?emc=edit_fb_20181010&nl=frank-bruni&nlid=5156379320181010&te=1. See the full report by U.N. Intergovernmental Panel on Climate Change (IPCC) at http://www.ipcc.ch/report/sr15/

443.   Mooney, Chris and Brady Dennis. "The world has just over a decade to get climate change under control, U.N. scientists say." *The Washington Post* (October 2018). https://www.washingtonpost.com/

energy-environment/2018/10/08/world-has-only-years-get-climate-change-under-control-un-scientists-say/?noredirect=on&utm_term=.9b9c017545e2&wpisrc=nl_most&wpmm=1

444. Digby Parton, Heather. "Now Mitch McConnell wants massive cuts to social programs after GOP blew up the deficit." *Salon* (October 2018). https://www.salon.com/2018/10/17/now-mitch-mcconnell-wants-massive-cuts-to-social-programs-after-gop-blew-up-the-deficit/

445. Klonsky, Amanda. "What Brett Kavanaugh Can Teach Us about Racism in America's Legal System." *Chicago Sun-Times* (October 2018). https://chicago.suntimes.com/opinion/brett-kavanaugh-racism-criminal-justice-senate/

446. Sonmez, Felicia. "Trump Mocks Kavanaugh Accuser Christine Blasey Ford" *The Washington Post* (October 2018). https://www.washingtonpost.com/politics/trump-mocks-kavanaugh-accuser-christine-blasey-ford/2018/10/02/25f6f8aa-c662-11e8-9b1c-a90f1daae309_story.html?utm_term=.f6b8b839f9e5

447. On this issue, see: Neiwert, David. *Alt-America: The Rise of the Radical Right in the Age of Trump.* New York: Verso, 2017.

448. For an excellent analysis of Trump and his use of twitter in the age of demagogues, see: Fuchs, Christian. *Digital Demagogue*. London: Pluto Press, 2018.

449. McKibben, Bill. "The Trump Administration Knows the Planet is Going to Boil. It Doesn't Care" *The Guardian* (October 2018). https://www.theguardian.com/commentisfree/2018/oct/02/trump-administration-planet-boil-refugee-camps?CMP=share_btn_tw

450. Sargent, Greg. "A Shouting Match inside White House Unmasks One of Trump's Biggest Lies." *The Washington Post* (October 2018). https://www.washingtonpost.com/blogs/plum-line/wp/2018/10/19/a-shouting-match-inside-white-house-unmasks-one-of-trumps-biggest-lies/?utm_term=.afec197443b8

451. Rizzo, Salvador. "Trump's Claim that Immigrants Bring 'Tremendous Crime' Is Still Wrong." *The Washington Post* (January 2018). https://www.washingtonpost.com/news/fact-checker/wp/2018/01/18/trumps-claim-that-immigrants-bring-tremendous-crime-is-still-wrong/?utm_term=.b0d4128f3ee7

452.   Etlin, Richard E. "Introduction," In *Art, Culture, and Media Under the Third Reich*, 22. Chicago: University of Chicago Press, 2002.

453.   Choi, Mathew. "Trump Calls Kavanaugh Protesters 'Rude Elevator Screamers'." *Politico* (October 2018). https://www.politico.com/story/2018/10/05/hatch-women-protesters-grow-up-873308

454.   Sargent, Greg. "Think Trump and GOP Minority Rule is Bad Now? Here's How It Could Get Much Worse." *The Washington Post* (October 2019). https://www.washingtonpost.com/blogs/plum-line/wp/2018/10/09/think-trump-and-gop-minority-rule-is-bad-now-heres-how-it-could-get-much-worse/?noredirect=on&utm_term=.74e8554fee90&wpisrc=nl_most&wpmm=1

455.   Paris, Erna. "Viktor Organ's War on George Soros and Hungary's Jews." *The Globe and Mail* (June 2018). https://www.theglobeandmail.com/opinion/article-viktor-orbans-war-on-george-soros-and-hungarys-jews

456.   "Trump Accuses George Soros of Paying for Signs at anti-Kavanaugh Protest." *JTA* (October 2018). Online: https://www.haaretz.com/us-news/trump-accuses-george-soros-of-paying-for-signs-at-anti-kavanaugh-protest-1.6531592

457.   Wolf, Michael. *Fire and Fury: Inside the Trump White House*. New York: Henry Holt, 2018.; Woodward, Bob. *Fear: Trump in the White House*. New York: Simon & Schuster, 2018.

458.   Browning, Christopher R. "The Suffocation of Democracy." *New York Review of Books* (October 2018). https://www.nybooks.com/articles/2018/10/25/suffocation-of-democracy/

459.   Reich, Robert. "The American Fascist." *RobertReich.org*, (March 2016) http://robertreich.org/post/140705539195.; Snyder, Robert. *On Tyranny: Twenty Lesson From the Twentieth Century*. London: Polity Press, 2017.; Stanley, Jason. *How Politics Works: The Politics of Us and Them*. New York: Random House, 2018.

460.   MacLean, Nancy. *Democracy in Chains: The Deep History of the Radical Right's Stealth Plan for America*, 211. New York: Viking, 2017.

461.   Urie, Rob. "American Fascism." *CounterPunch* (September 2018). https://www.counterpunch.org/2018/09/17/american-fascism/

462.   Barber II, William J. "We are witnessing the birth pangs of a Third Reconstruction." *ThinkProgress* (December 2016). https://thinkprogress.org/rev-barber-moral-change-1ad2776df7c#.4h0jv9rzt

463.   Eagleton, Terry. "The Ambition of Advanced Capitalism Is Not Simply to Combat Radical Ideas-It Is to Abolish the Very Notion that There Could Be a Serious Alternative to the Present." *Red Pepper* (October 2013). https://www.redpepper.org.uk/death-of-the-intellectual/

464.   Evans, Brad. "A World Without Books." *Atrocity Exhibition: Life in the Age of Total Violence*, 177. Los Angeles: LARB Books, 2019.

465.   Kelley, Robin DG. "Sorry, Not Sorry." *Boston Review* (September 2018) http://bostonreview.net/race-literature-culture/robin-d-g-kelley-sorry-not-sorry

466.   Cole, Teju. "Resist, Refuse." *The New York Times* (September 2018) https://www.nytimes.com/2018/09/08/magazine/teju-cole-resistance-op-ed-resist-refuse.html

467.   Hayden, Michael. "The End of Intelligence" *The New York Times* (April 2018). https://www.nytimes.com/2018/04/28/opinion/sunday/the-end-of-intelligence.html

468.   "I Am Part of the Resistance Inside the Trump Administration." *The New York Times* (September 2018). https://www.nytimes.com/2018/09/05/opinion/trump-white-house-anonymous-resistance.html?-module=inline

469.   Ibid. Anonymous.

470.   Personal correspondence from my dear friend, Oscar Zambrano. October 21, 2018.

471.   Alexander, Michelle. "We Are Not the Resistance." *The New York Times,* (September   2018). https://www.nytimes.com/2018/09/21/opinion/sunday/resistance-kavanaugh-trump-protest.html

472.   Boggs, Grace Lee with Scott Kurashige. The Next American Revolution: Sustainable Activism for the Twenty-First Century, 36. Oakland: University of California Press, 2012.

473.   Mouffe, Chantal. *For a Left Populism*. London: Verso, 2018.

474. Nixon, Rob. *Slow Violence and the Environmentalism of the Poor*, x. Cambridge: Harvard University Press, 2011.

475. Adler, Seth. "By Party or By Formation." *The Bullet-Socialist Project* (July 2018). https://socialistproject.ca/2018/06/by-party-or-by-formation/

476. Le Guin, Ursula K. "Ursula K Le Guin's speech at National Book Awards: 'Books aren't just commodities'." *The Guardian* (November 2014).   https://www.theguardian.com/books/2014/nov/20/ursula-k-le-guin-national-book-awards-speech

477. Jameson, Fredric. "Future City." *New Left Review* 21 (May-June 2003). https://newleftreview.org/II/21/fredric-jameson-future-city

478. Fisher, Mark. *Capitalist Realism: Is There No Alternative?*, 2. Winchester, UK: Zero Books, 2009.

479. Amin, Samir. "The defence of humanity requires the radicalisation of popular struggles." *Socialist Project* (October 2018). https://socialistproject.ca/2018/10/defence-of-humanity-requires-radicalisation-of-popular-struggles/

480. Some examples of this can be found in: Selwyn, Benjamin. "A Manifesto for Socialist Development in the 21st Century." *The Bullet-Socialist Project* (September 2018). https://socialistproject.ca/2018/09/manifesto-for-socialist-development-in-21st-century/. See also the Vision and Platform for the Movement for Black Lives at https://policy.m4bl.org/downloads/

481. Klein, Naomi. *No Is Not Enough: Resisting The New Shock Politics and Winning the World We Need*. Chicago: Haymarket Books, 2017.

482. Leffel, Gregory. "Is Catastrophe the Only Cure for the Weakness of Radical Politics?" *Open Democracy* (January 2018). https://www.opendemocracy.net/en/transformation/is-catastrophe-only-cure-for-weakness-of-radical-politics/

483. For an analysis of the origins of fascism in American capitalism, see: Roberto, Michael Joseph. *The Coming of the American Behemoth*. New York: Monthly Review Press, 2019.

484.   Fraser, Nancy. "From Progressive Neoliberalism to Trump – and Beyond." *American Affairs* (Winter 2017, Vol. I, No 4. https://americanaffairsjournal.org/2017/11/progressive-neoliberalism-trump-beyond/

485.   Aronson, Ronald. *We: Reviving Social Hope*, 33. Chicago: University of Chicago Press, 2017.

486.   Dorfman, Ariel. "How to Read Donald Trump on Burning Books but Not Ideas." *TomDispatch* (September 2017). http://www.tomdispatch.com/blog/176326/tomgram%3A_ariel_dorfman%2C_a_tale_of_two_donalds/

487.   See the Intergovernmental Panel on Climate Change report, *Global Warming of 1.5C* (2018). http://www.ipcc.ch/report/sr15/

488.   Amin, Samir. "The defence of humanity requires the radicalisation of popular struggles." *Socialist Project* (October 2018). https://socialistproject.ca/2018/10/defence-of-humanity-requires-radicalisation-of-popular-struggles/

Index

L

language ii, 10, 11, 19-22, 23-27, 29-35, 37-42, 44, 48, 51-54, 56, 59, 61, 68, 70-79, 80-83, 93, 98-99, 105-118, 125, 136, 139, 144, 158, 163, 165, 171-174, 178, 181-184
Wayne LaPierre 126
LBGTQ+ 144
Gregory Leffel 182
Steven Levitsky 12, 29
Ursula K. Le Guin 163, 181
Don Lemon 24, 75
Natasha Lennard 140
Primo Levi 43
Judith Levine 162
Taylor Levy 57
Jacob Levy 17, 19
Sinclair Lewis 21, 55
Libya 60
Huey Long 28
Leo Lowenthal 93

M

Nancy MacLean 174
Trayvon Martin 131
Karl Marx 92, 176, 185
Doreen Massey 147
Theresa May 36
Joseph McCarthy 28
Mitch McConnell 167, 173
Bill McKibben 169
Medicare 62, 146, 167
Mexico 23, 56, 170
militarism 9, 45, 46, 59, 60, 67, 83, 87, 92, 137–138
Stephen Miller 67, 82, 172
C. Wright Mills 84, 98
Pankaj Mishra 48, 209
George Monbiot 64, 145
Robert Mueller 8, 15, 61
Rupert Murdoch 6